Advanced corporate business transactions

Elizabeth A. Gillis, Editor
Miller Thomson LLP

2006
EMOND MONTGOMERY PUBLICATIONS
TORONTO, CANADA

Emond Montgomery Publications Limited
60 Shaftesbury Avenue
Toronto ON M4T 1A3
http://www.emond.ca/highered

Printed in Canada.
Reprinted October 2019.

We acknowledge the financial support of the Government of Canada.
Nous reconnaissons l'appui financier du gouvernement du Canada.

Canadä

Library and Archives Canada Cataloguing in Publication

Advanced corporate business transactions / Elizabeth A. Gillis, editor. Includes index.

ISBN 978-1-55239-186-0

1. Corporation law — Ontario — Textbooks.   2. Procedure (Law) — Ontario — Textbooks.   I. Gillis, Elizabeth A. (Elizabeth Anne), 1948–

KEO385.A33 2006   346.713'066   C2006-900454-4 KF1355.
A92 2006

Acquistions editor
Peggy Buchan

Marketing director
Dave Stokaluk

Copy editor
Christine Purden

Proofreader
Diane Gula

Production editor
Jim Lyons

Typesetter
Cindy Fujimoto

Indexer
Paula Pike

Cover designer
John Vegter, CBC Art Department

To all lawyers who support the use of law clerks and who contribute to the growth and development of corporate law clerks in their practices.

Contents

CHAPTER 4
Purchase and sale of a privately held business ... 237

Richard D. Leblanc, Miller Thomson LLP

CHAPTER 5
Financing the purchase of a privately held business 271

*Tom Tower and Elizabeth Hutchison,
    Miller Thomson LLP*

Author biographies

Catherine D'Aversa, Miller Thomson LLP, is a senior corporate law clerk who has extensive experience in the corporate/commercial, finance, and merger/acquisition practice areas. She specializes in assisting lawyers with tax-driven corporate reorganizations, motor vehicle dealer registration and licensing across Canada, and other complex corporate transactions and large projects.

Elizabeth A. Gillis, Miller Thomson LLP, is a law clerk and director of corporate services. She has extensive experience assisting lawyers in the corporate/commercial practice area. As a member of the firm's management team, she is responsible for the administration of corporate search services, corporate law clerks, and other paralegals. She is a Fellow member of and has served in various positions with the Institute of Law Clerks of Ontario, including president, secretary, and program committee member.

Elizabeth Hutchison, Miller Thomson LLP, is an associate in the area of corporate and commercial law, with a focus on corporate and commercial lending transactions. She has gained considerable experience representing both lenders and borrowers in various types of lending relationships, including asset/equipment finance and leasing transactions.

Sue Kavanagh, Perley-Robertson, Hill & McDougall LLP, is a law clerk and manager of corporate services with over 25 years' experience in corporate law. Her duties include the incorporation and maintenance of new businesses; due diligence reviews of corporate records; preparation of corporate documents for tax and corporate reorganizations, financings, and not-for-profit corporations; and various securities law matters. She is a founding member of the Ottawa Association of Law Clerks and an associate member and former director of the Institute of Law Clerks of Ontario.

Donna Kubota, President, Solutions Corporate Law Clerk Services Inc., has over 22 years' experience as a law clerk. She has extensive experience in many aspects of corporate/commercial law, ranging from due diligence searches and corporate reviews to tax-driven corporate reorganizations. She is an associate member of the Institute of Law Clerks of Ontario, the Paralegal Society of Ontario, and the Ontario Association of Professional Searchers of Records. Solutions Corporate Law Clerk Services Inc. is also an associate member of the Canadian Association of Paralegals.

Richard D. Leblanc, Miller Thomson LLP, practises in the areas of financial services, mergers and acquisitions, corporate and commercial law, franchise law, and intellectual property. He is a member of the Corporate Law Subcommittee of the Ontario Bar Association, and is a frequent writer and speaker on commercial and franchising matters.

Joyce McGuiney, Blake, Cassels & Graydon LLP, is a corporate law clerk with 25 years' experience and is currently the managing law clerk of transactions services. She has extensive experience in the area of due diligence and has assisted lawyers at the closing of corporate acquisitions, public offerings, takeovers, and reorganizations.

Tom Tower, Miller Thomson LLP, practises in the area of corporate and commercial law with an emphasis on commercial financings and insolvencies. He represents banks, trust companies, and other commercial lenders in various secured transactions, and represents both corporate and individual borrowers in their dealings with financial institutions. He has gained experience in different aspects of lending, including enforcement of security, commercial reorganizations, receiverships, and bankruptcy.

Acknowledgments

I wish to thank Judson Whiteside, Chair of Miller Thomson LLP, for believing in my abilities to complete the two volumes of this series on legal procedures for corporate law clerks.

I also wish to thank each of the writers in this volume, whose diligence and professional expertise have contributed to the growth and development of law clerks.

I wish to thank Miller Thomson LLP for providing the precedents used in chapters 1, 4, and 5, and Perley-Robertson, Hill & McDougall LLP for providing the precedents used in chapter 3.

I am grateful to Paul Emond and Dave Stokaluk of Emond Montgomery Publications for their enthusiasm and support for the project. I also thank Christine Purden for the thoroughness and care with which she copy-edited the manuscript, and Jim Lyons and Cindy Fujimoto of WordsWorth Communications for their patience and skill in overseeing production of the book.

Finally, I wish to thank my husband and my daughter for always believing in me and encouraging me to achieve my dreams.

Elizabeth A. Gillis
Toronto, January 2006

Introduction

Elizabeth A. Gillis, Miller Thomson LLP

This book is the second in a series of two on corporate legal procedures. In many years of working in a law firm as a law clerk, manager, and teacher, I have struggled to find a suitable text that would teach corporate law clerks the many different procedures and processes they are required to know. Failing to find such a text, I wrote up my own extensive notes on corporate procedures, which I shared with my students and which formed the basis of the first book in the series, *Advanced Corporate Legal Procedures*. That book studied the basic differences between various methods of carrying on business, the procedures and documents for incorporating and organizing corporations to do business, and the maintenance of federal and Ontario corporations, including how to carry out corporate structural changes. It also included a comprehensive chapter on incorporating and maintaining federal and Ontario not-for-profit corporations.

This second volume is a necessary complement to the first, and will, I hope, contribute to the growth and development of law clerks in the corporate practice. While the book is intended for law clerks taking community college courses or the Institute of Law Clerks of Ontario Associate Level Corporate Course, it will also benefit more experienced law clerks and lawyers. The authors are all experts in their fields, and they provide an in-depth examination of the legal procedures that law clerks need to know to assist lawyers in various types of transactions. The authors describe the law behind the procedures, as well as the documents and steps required to complete transactions, in a straightforward manner that new and experienced law clerks will find useful both in the classroom and in their work.

Chapter 1 describes various organizational tools used in a large law firm for successfully managing a large transaction. These suggestions can also be adapted for use in smaller situations. Chapter 2 discusses the types of due diligence that lawyers will carry out under different circumstances and describes in detail how to review a minute book and the types of corporate searches that are required. Chapter 3 examines the procedures to implement certain tax-driven transactions such as amalgamations, rollovers, and dissolutions. Chapter 4 describes the steps to follow, and the different points of law to be considered, when a corporation wishes to acquire either the shares or the assets of another business. Chapter 5 examines the process and requirements for financing the acquisition of a privately held corporation.

Finally, it is important to note that the material in this volume is accurate, subject to any errors and omissions, at the date of writing. Laws, regulations, policies, and procedures are constantly changing, and it is important to ensure that the procedures you follow are up to date at the time of their use.

CHAPTER 1

Managing a large transaction

Catherine D'Aversa, Miller Thomson LLP
Joyce McGuiney, Blake, Cassels & Graydon LLP

CHAPTER OVERVIEW

This chapter details the legal procedures and organizational systems used in managing a large transaction. Managing any transaction successfully, regardless of the size, requires: planning and replanning; collecting, organizing, and updating the information; keeping the information flowing; preparing documents in a standardized format; organizing the storage and circulation of completed documents; coordinating the closing of the transaction; dealing with any post-closing matters; and reporting on completion of the transaction. This chapter describes the law clerk's role and duties as a member of the team responsible for completing a large transaction. Examples of key planning techniques are provided, as well as a detailed guide to the closing of a complex transaction involving a corporate acquisition of another business.

CHAPTER OBJECTIVES

After completing this chapter, you should be able to:

1. Describe the responsibilities and duties of a law clerk as a team member in preparing for and completing a large transaction.
2. Identify techniques for working effectively within a team.
3. Describe procedures for processing, storing, and sharing information throughout the course of a large transaction.
4. Explain why a closing agenda is important and what it should include.
5. Describe an efficient approach to document signing in a transaction with many documents and several signing parties.
6. Describe a system for closing a transaction in an organized and efficient manner.
7. Explain the requirements for reporting on a transaction after closing.

PREPARING FOR A LARGE TRANSACTION

Setting the parameters

As the first step in managing a large transaction, the supervising lawyer (or responsible partner) calls a meeting to set the parameters of the assignment. The meeting is usually attended by the corporate law associates, clerks, and students who will work on the legal team responsible for completing the transaction. At this meeting, the supervising lawyer conveys preliminary information about the transaction, including the parties involved, the details of any letter of intent, and the nature of the transaction — for example, if it involves a planned corporate acquisition of another corporation (the "target"), whether the transaction is a purchase and sale of shares or a purchase and sale of assets of the target. Other matters discussed may include issues relating to any financing or funding of the purchase and the nature of the business being acquired. From this initial meeting, the participants know the size and scope of the transaction, how communication will be handled with the client and with outside counsel, and how responsibilities will be divided among the team members.

Establishing the legal team

The size of the team varies depending on the transaction. For example, if the transaction involves issues relating to intellectual property, real estate, tax, the environment, employees, the federal *Competition Act*, or the *Investment Canada Act*, the supervising lawyer may ask specialists within the firm to join the team. Their contribution will be to assist in the due diligence exercise and the drafting of certain provisions of the agreement of purchase and sale. If the target business is carried on in several jurisdictions, it may also be necessary to engage outside counsel in those jurisdictions. It is often the responsibility of the corporate law associate and the law clerk, the nucleus of the team, to coordinate the input from these internal and external specialists.

Once the team members are determined, it is important to ensure that they know their respective responsibilities, the time frame for completing critical tasks, and the reporting requirements. The emphasis here is on teamwork, and service to the client. If each team member knows his or her responsibilities and is mindful of the work being done by others on the team, there should be no duplication of effort and fewer complications at closing. The client will be impressed by: the team's efforts to contain costs and save time; well-organized, well-written, and concise reports incorporating the comments of all team members; and smooth closing of the deal on the date and in the manner anticipated. The client will not be impressed by: frequent calls or e-mails from various team members asking the same questions; volumes of disorganized, badly written, and poorly summarized paper; or time wasted sitting in a boardroom waiting for closing documents to be processed.

On a good team, information is shared with all team members, and followup ensures that reports and closing documents are ready on time. A good team works toward, and will be well prepared for, closing the deal.

Establishing the timetable

Although delays often arise as a result of business concerns or negotiating difficulties that are beyond the control of the legal team, it is important for the team to develop a timeline for completion of key stages of the transaction: conducting and reporting on due diligence, drafting documents, obtaining consents and approvals, and finalizing closing arrangements. A tentative date for closing is usually set in the letter of intent. It is important for the team to work with that deadline in mind, despite any setbacks and delays, to best serve the client.

Preparing a contact list

Once all the team members have been identified, it will be useful for them to consult the purchaser, the vendor, outside counsel, and any other interested parties, such as bankers or accountants, in compiling a comprehensive transaction contact list. This list should include the names, titles, business addresses, telephone and facsimile numbers, and e-mail addresses of:

- the firm's team members (along with their specialty areas of law);
- the team members of outside counsel;
- the principal contacts for the purchaser and the vendor; and
- any others who may need to be kept informed or contacted regularly in connection with the transaction.

Drafting a working checklist and closing agenda

One of the most important documents in successfully managing a large transaction is the working checklist. It is useful to start drafting this document at the first meeting of the team. Initially, the checklist is only used internally by the team, to identify pre-closing issues, closing documents, and post-closing items, the critical dates for each, and the party responsible for preparing or delivering each item. However, the checklist is a work in progress: with input from all team members, it evolves into the closing agenda for all parties to the transaction. At that point, outside parties also contribute to the checklist and should be kept informed when changes are made. The working checklist should still be used by the internal team members to keep track of the status of unresolved issues and the responsibilities associated with those issues.

The **closing agenda** is a step-by-step plan for closing. It begins with all the events that must occur before the parties meet to sign and deliver the closing documents. These "pre-closing matters" may include the entering into of the letter of intent and any confidentiality agreement, the successful completion of due diligence, the passing of the necessary corporate resolutions to approve the transaction, and the obtaining of requisite consents and approvals. The next steps in the closing agenda list all documents and deliveries required on the closing date ("closing matters"). The agreement of purchase and sale includes representations and warranties and conditions of closing. These provisions of the agreement dictate the documents to be delivered at closing. It is also important to list those documents to be prepared and delivered or actions to be taken after the closing date ("post-closing matters"), such as security discharges or registrations, changes in directors and

closing agenda
a step-by-step plan for closing, which outlines all of the necessary time lines, locations, parties, and signatories to the transaction, documentation requirements, and the escrow terms of the closing; it often functions as a checklist for completion of tasks and documentation relating to the transaction

officers, and the filing of requisite notices of change in all jurisdictions in which the target carries on business, *Investment Canada Act* notifications, and so on.

Figure 1.1, at the end of the chapter, shows a sample working checklist; figure 1.2 shows a sample closing agenda.

ROLE AND RESPONSIBILITIES OF THE LAW CLERK

The law clerk's role in a large transaction may vary from law firm to law firm and from transaction to transaction. In a large transaction, the law clerk is usually involved at every stage, up to and beyond closing. The law clerk's responsibilities may include:

- conducting and reporting on due diligence, including review of minute books, personal property security searches, and review of leases and contracts for change of control and assignment provisions;
- preparing and maintaining a reference binder and/or a due diligence binder (discussed in chapter 2);
- preparing the transaction contact list;
- preparing the working checklist and closing agenda;
- preparing or obtaining documents required on closing, such as resolutions, declarations, certificates, acknowledgments, resignations and releases, directions, receipts, and undertakings, for review by either the associate or the responsible partner;
- preparing colour-coded document files for each step of the transaction;
- cataloguing and filing documents and circulating copies for review and comment;
- organizing team meetings and updating the working checklist as necessary;
- arranging for the setup of the boardroom for pre-closing and closing meetings;
- obtaining certificates of status or compliance and updating searches in preparation for closing;
- assigning colour codes to signatories to expedite the signing of documents;
- setting up a pre-closing signing meeting;
- attending the pre-closing to assist as needed;
- attending the closing to assist as needed; and
- preparing the closing books and drafting the reporting letter.

MANAGING THE DUE DILIGENCE EXERCISE

Conducting and reporting on due diligence is discussed in greater detail in chapter 2. However, the importance of managing the due diligence exercise during the transaction cannot be overemphasized. The conduct of due diligence is an ongoing process throughout the transaction. The process begins almost immediately after the letter of intent is signed and continues up to the closing of the transaction. Ordinarily, the letter of intent specifies that the completion of the transaction is conditional on the results of the due diligence exercise. The corporate law clerk can be especially helpful in conducting and reporting on due diligence.

Each member of the team reviews the information supplied by the vendor that relates to his or her particular area of law and prepares a report summarizing the information reviewed and highlighting the areas of concern. It is often the responsibility of the law clerk to review minute books and identify deficiencies in them, to arrange for and summarize personal property security searches, and sometimes, with students and associates, to assist in the review and summary of leases and contracts to identify assignment or change-of-control provisions. The law clerk can also assist in compiling the reports of all team members in a comprehensive, indexed report for the client. In a large transaction with many diverse elements being handled by the transaction team, it is advantageous for the due diligence team to meet regularly and to provide initial, interim, and final reports to the supervising lawyer. Each report summarizes information received to date, identifies information still outstanding, and raises any questions on the scope of ongoing or additional due diligence, as applicable.

"MANAGING THE CLIENT"

"Managing the client" means understanding the client's objectives and setting up a clear line of communication between the law firm's team and the client's team so that information flows smoothly in both directions. The client must be kept informed about outstanding issues, problems with other counsel or with the target's employees and representatives, unforeseen costs, and unanticipated delays. The client must know what the legal team knows in order to make informed decisions about the purchase price and other conditions of closing.

Only one or two team members should communicate with the client during the transaction. The client should not be inundated with phone calls, e-mails, faxes, and correspondence from the entire team. The flow of information should be controlled, and the information provided should be clear, concise, and well presented.

MANAGING THE FLOW OF INFORMATION

Information management can make or break a transaction. It is for this reason that the responsibilities of team members must be clearly defined, deadlines must be set for the completion of specific tasks, and procedures must be established for disseminating the information gathered by each team member to the others on the team and to the client. Here are some tips for managing and imparting information:

- Arrange team meetings periodically throughout the transaction.
- Prepare initial, interim, and final written reports.
- Decide on a consistent reporting format and ask all team members to use this format.

- Use charts and diagrams where and when applicable.

- Share information with other team members that is related to their area of expertise by forwarding relevant documents to them or advising them of crucial information by memorandum or e-mail.

- "Cut to the chase": the other team members and the client want the major issues identified up front, not buried in the text along with less relevant issues.

- Report serious problems immediately to the supervising lawyer, in person or by telephone or e-mail — do not wait until written reports are finalized.

- If the transaction is particularly large, consider setting up a "data room" — a designated area of the law office or, as is becoming more prevalent, a virtual or electronic database where all information received and reviewed is organized and indexed, all reports are catalogued, and all closing documents are maintained up to the date of closing.

FILE AND DOCUMENT MANAGEMENT

In a large transaction, there may be several different departments within the firm and counsel in different jurisdictions outside the firm who will be conducting searches and preparing documentation. The team should determine:

- who is to receive copies of correspondence and drafts of documents for closing (both internally and externally);

- how documents will be circulated — that is, by e-mail, facsimile, or courier, or in Microsoft Word, Adobe Acrobat, or other formats;

- what format will be used for corporate resolutions and closing certificates, to ensure that deliveries are consistent;

- which hard-drive directory will be used to store documents relating to the transaction; and

- who will accumulate the closing documents as they are agreed to by the parties prior to closing, and how the documents will be organized for closing.

PREPARING FOR THE CLOSING

Once the closing date has been finalized, a number of procedures can be used to facilitate a quick and efficient closing. These include:

- Arranging for the other party's counsel to review and approve all closing documents in advance of the closing date.

- Ensuring, in advance, that certificates of status or compliance will be available on closing and obtaining the certificates just before the closing date.

- Preparing different colour-coded closing files for each aspect of the transaction and attaching colour-coded tabs for each signatory to the different documents.

- Reviewing the closing agenda well in advance to determine which closing deliveries are still outstanding.

- Reporting the outstanding documents and issues to the responsible lawyer prior to closing.

- Determining the staffing requirements required for the pre-closing and the closing, such as secretarial support, copy room support, food service support, and mail room support.

PRE-CLOSING

In a large transaction, there is often a **pre-closing** — a meeting at which counsel for both sides meet to resolve outstanding issues. Once the outstanding issues are resolved, the agreed-upon changes are made to the closing documents, and copies are executed. The parties themselves may also attend and commence signing the closing documents. This process can often take many hours to complete, extending into the evening and the next day. It will require the efforts of the supervising lawyer, the associate, the law clerk, and the student to keep the process moving, as the parties may tire and lose interest. While each team member will need breaks, to maintain the momentum, a team member should be present in the boardroom at all times with the parties and other counsel.

Once all the documentation has been reviewed and approved by counsel, signed by the client, and catalogued in the appropriate file, a review of the closing agenda with the team members is necessary to determine whether there are any outstanding issues that need to be dealt with before the closing date. The closing agenda should then be finalized and enough copies made for distribution to various parties on the closing date.

pre-closing
a meeting before the closing of a transaction at which counsel for both parties discuss and attempt to resolve outstanding issues, agreed-upon changes to documents are made, closing documents may be signed, and the closing date is confirmed

DOCUMENT SIGNING

Whether documents are signed at the pre-closing or the closing, it is helpful to set up a system to facilitate the signing procedure. In fact, a system is essential if there are several signatories and hundreds of documents to be signed. One effective method of controlling the documents and the signing is to seat the signing parties around the boardroom table and have the law clerk (or another team member) circulate the closing documents in the order shown in the closing agenda. Each signing party should refer to the closing agenda to identify and check off the document being circulated, and sign all documents flagged with the coloured tab assigned to that signatory. An index of signatories with the colour assigned to each should be prominently displayed. A second member of the team can then collect the signed documents from the last signatory, ensure that all parties have signed in the appropriate places, and then systematically return the documents to their folders and the folders to their boxes, in the order shown in the closing agenda. The team members circulating and collecting the closing documents can both supervise the signing and answer questions raised by the signing parties. The supervising lawyer or an associate should also be present to answer any questions about the content of the documents.

Although less formal arrangements may suffice for a smaller closing, it is the responsibility of the law clerk in a closing of any size to control the flow of documents and ensure that all documents are signed as appropriate.

THE CLOSING

If there is a successful pre-closing, the actual closing can be somewhat anti-climactic. At the closing, the final subsearches will have been completed and the certificates obtained and, provided that there are no problems with those searches or certificates, the closing will proceed. During the closing, signed documents are exchanged between counsel, any outstanding issues are resolved, any required undertakings are given, share certificates (on a share deal) are delivered, and the purchase price is paid.

It is a good idea to make notes on the closing agenda of any followup issues that arise during the exchange of documents.

ESCROW CLOSING

From time to time, although all documents have been signed and the parties are prepared to close, the closing may not be completed on the day and at the time scheduled. It could be that a mandatory consent has not yet been received, or there may be an unresolved issue in the agreement of purchase and sale, or an ancillary transaction that must occur before closing may not have been completed. Despite these delays, if the parties believe that the transaction will still close (but not on the date specified), they may agree to an **escrow closing**. In this case, the substance of the transaction — the assets and/or the share certificates and all closing documents — will be held by a third party, the escrow agent, until the outstanding issue has been resolved. In most transactions, counsel for one of the parties agrees to act as the escrow agent.

It is important that the closing agenda contain escrow provisions. In the event of an escrow closing, the mechanics of the closing will be handled in accordance with those provisions.

escrow closing
the delivery of the substance of the transaction on a particular date with the understanding that it is to be held by a third party, the escrow agent, until the unfulfilled condition of closing has been met

POST-CLOSING

Following the closing, there are usually a number of matters to be dealt with, including:

- notifications under various statutes,
- press releases,
- assignments of intellectual property or registrations of real property,
- registration or discharge of security interests,
- fulfillment of undertakings given in the purchase agreement or on closing, and
- updating the minute book.

These post-closing matters are usually the responsibility of the law clerk. It is important to complete them as soon as possible after closing.

REPORTING

The law clerk's responsibilities also may include completing the closing book and drafting a reporting letter to the client. Again, these matters should be dealt with as soon as possible after closing.

The closing agenda forms the basis of the index to the closing book. Original copies of signed documents delivered at closing are indexed and tabbed for identification in the closing book. Remember that the original resolutions, resignations, and share certificates, if applicable, should be inserted in the minute book and copies of these documents should be inserted in the closing book.

Depending on the nature of the transaction and the supervising lawyer, the firm may also provide a reporting letter to the client. The content of the reporting letter may also vary from lawyer to lawyer. The supervising lawyer may want to review each step of the transaction or may prefer to provide only an overview of the transaction.

CLOSING THE FILE

While the practice of archiving files once a transaction is completed may vary from firm to firm, all members of the team should ensure that all relevant materials from the transaction are forwarded to the supervising lawyer for the main file or can be easily retrieved from their own records.

KEY TERMS

closing agenda

escrow closing

pre-closing

FORMS AND PRECEDENTS

Figure 1.1: Sample checklist for managing a large transaction

Figure 1.2: Sample closing agenda

REVIEW QUESTIONS

1. List the various members of the legal team in a typical complex transaction.
2. Name the three stages in planning and completing a transaction.
3. List the steps involved in preparing the first draft of a closing agenda.
4. What is a contact list, and what information should be included on such a list?
5. What is a "data room"?
6. Why is it important to manage documents in a large transaction?
7. What are the typical responsibilities of a law clerk relating to pre-closing, closing, and post-closing matters?
8. List at least five ways to prepare for the closing date.
9. Why is it important to have a system in place when there are several signatories and a large volume of documents?
10. What is an escrow closing?
11. What is typically involved in reporting a large transaction?
12. List at least seven aspects of a law clerk's role in a typical large transaction.

FIGURE 1.1 SAMPLE CHECKLIST FOR MANAGING A LARGE TRANSACTION

Item	Task list	Comments
Team	Members of the project team are assigned specific responsibilities for completing the many different tasks involved in a large transaction; e.g.: • searches • due diligence • minute book reviews • purchase agreement • financing • ancillary agreements • corporate documents • ancillary documents • registrations • staffing • the closing	The responsible partner chooses the team, including, e.g.:: • tax/intellectual property/real estate/ litigation lawyers, • associates, • law clerks, • students, and/or • agents. At the initial meeting, the team drafts a preliminary timetable and working checklist; these are refined as the transaction progresses.
Information and Document Management	A contact list must be prepared, including all team members, parties to the transaction and their representatives, and any other interested individuals or organizations. Every team member must keep his or her files and documents organized; e.g.:: • All information related to the transaction should be kept in a hard-drive **central directory** (usually the responsible partner's directory) **with subdirectories for each** part of the transaction. • Hard copies of documents are kept in banker's boxes in labelled file folders by each team member, to be brought to team meetings, the pre-closing, and the closing. All documents should be prepared in accordance with a standardized format. File folders should be colour-coded and banker's boxes should be labelled for different parts of the transaction; e.g.:: • pre-closing documents • evidentiary matters • due diligence • regulatory matters • third-party matters • financing • agreements • payment • opinions • post-closing	Subdirectories could include: • project management (contact list, checklists, timetable, closing agenda) • due diligence • purchase agreement • ancillary agreements • corporate documents • financing • real estate/tax/litigation/intellectual property matters • post-closing matters Sub-subdirectories could include: • checklists • correspondence (letters, memos/faxes) • searches • reports • opinions • undertakings Keeping all documents in a central directory allows any team member to review documents relating to any aspect of the transaction.

FIGURE 1.1 CONTINUED

Item	Task list	Comments
Information and Document Management (cont.)	Documents should be assigned a number (recorded on a document index) before being filed in their respective folders (but note that numbers may change as the transaction proceeds toward closing).	Once the closing agenda is finalized, completed hard copies of documents can be numbered in the top right corner in small print in accordance with the agenda numbering.
Pre-closing	Prepare a draft **closing agenda** using the purchase agreement and checklist/timetable. Remove the checklist/timetable references in the closing agenda once the final agenda is ready for distribution outside the firm.	Organize the closing agenda with separate columns for the following information: 1. Action or documentation required 2. Responsible person 3. Signatories, including names of all parties and their representatives (entities and individuals); e.g.: • Corporate name * By:** • Name of law firm* By:** 4. Status/comments; e.g.: • Executed and delivered • To be delivered on closing • Facsimile signatures required • Undertaking to be provided • Settled
	Prepare an index of signatories, showing who is to sign which documents at which stage of the transaction, and assign colour codes to the various signatories/parties, to expedite the signing of documents.	
	Set up a **work station** (in the closing room or an adjoining room) consisting of: • computer and printer • photocopier and fax machines • transaction trolley with supplies; e.g.: paper, file folders, coloured tags, sign here tags, red seals, blue corners, hole punch, stapler, clips, etc.	Make sure the Systems Department loads all necessary programs; e.g.: • Adobe Acrobat • Word • Lotus Notes • Elite • PowerPoint The Systems Department must also test the station prior to closing to ensure that the programs and printer are working properly.

FIGURE 1.1 CONCLUDED

Item	Task list	Comments
Pre-closing (cont.)	**Timing**: to reduce the length of time it takes to close the transaction attempt to: • settle as many documents as possible prior to closing, • obtain facsimile signatures and any other possible signatures prior to closing, and • set up a schedule of signing times for groups of individuals (e.g., purchasers, vendors). Hold **status meetings** with team members in order to bring each other up to date on each aspect of the transaction and to redefine or reassign roles and responsibilities, if necessary. Prepare **pre-closing and closing plans**; i.e.: • who is attending (clients, team members, other firms, financing representatives, etc.) • who is signing, and when • staffing, drinks, food • physical facilities and hours of use	Inform building management if offices are to be used outside normal business hours; e.g., the lights and/or heat may be on timers that will automatically turn off lights or change temperature (heating/air conditioning). Arrange with building security for access to the building and offices outside normal business hours.
Closing	Co-ordinate the procedure for **signing of documents**; e.g.: • have one team member with the boxes of documents to be signed at one end of the table • seat the signatories around the table in order of their respective signatures • at the other end of the table, have a second team member check documents and folders (for signatures, dates, witnesses, etc.) and return each completed folder to the first team member, who inserts it back into the appropriate box. The responsible partner will supervise the **exchange of documents** and negotiate changes, undertakings, etc. • Start with #1 on the closing agenda. • Have one team member exchange documents in boxes with other side. • Have a second team member receive and check documents exchanged and insert them into appropriate boxes. • Have a third team member make notes of undertakings or changes to the agenda. • Have a fourth team member available to make copies and get additional signatures, etc.	This is important so that all aspects of the closing transaction are documented for reference at a later time. This is important so that the rhythm of movement of documents is never interrupted.

FIGURE 1.2   SAMPLE CLOSING AGENDA

Project Vacation — Closing Agenda
June 7, 200X

Purchase by

THE GREAT VACATION COMPANY OF CANADA INC.

of the shares in

SUN INC., FUN INC., and SURF INC.

<u>Closing Agenda</u>

Closing date and time:	June 12, 200X, 1:00 p.m.
Place:	Offices of Thorn & Associates LLP
	Suite 2500
	133 Queen Street
	West Forest, ON P5N 1P6

Capitalized Terms:

Capitalized terms used in this Closing Agenda shall have the meanings ascribed to them respectively in the Share Purchase Agreement dated June 7, 200X between The Great Vacation Company of Canada Inc., 100001 Ontario Limited, John Black, and Jane Black (the "Share Purchase Agreement").

I.   **Parties and Signatories**

Parties/representatives	Referred to as	Signatories
The Great Vacation Company of Canada Inc.	Vacation	William Red Earl Blue Craig Green
100001 Ontario Limited	Ontario	John Black
John Black	Principal	John Black
Jane Black	Principal's Spouse/Spouse	Jane Black
Ontario, Principal, and Principal's Spouse, collectively	Sellers	
Sun Inc.	Sun	John Black Jane Black
Fun Inc.	Fun	John Black Jane Black Joseph Black

FIGURE 1.2   CONTINUED

15

Parties/representatives	Referred to as	Signatories
Surf Inc.	Surf	John Black
		Joseph Black
Sun, Fun, and Surf, collectively	Target Group	
Rose & Mulberry LLP (counsel to Sellers, Ontario, and Target Group)	R&M	Paul Pettle
		Mark Leaves
		Jodi Stem
Thorn & Associates LLP (counsel to Vacation)	T&A	Paul Bush
		Lisa Dart

Escrow:

On the Closing Date, each document described in this Closing Agenda (other than those described under the heading "Matters To Be Completed Post-Closing") and delivered by or on behalf of the Party responsible for delivering such document (the "Responsible Party") shall be deemed to have been delivered in escrow by that Party (the "Closing Escrow") until:

1. every document described in this Closing Agenda has been delivered; and

2. all Parties have agreed that the Closing Escrow is terminated.

Legend

Standard delivery:	delivery of one executed original of each document or instrument to each of Vacation, the Sellers, R&M and T&A
OFR:	Out for review
OFS:	Out for signature
Settled:	Draft has been settled among parties
Y:	Signed and/or delivered
FAX:	Facsimile language required

FIGURE 1.2 CONTINUED

II.	Closing Requirements			
Action or documentation		Drafting responsibility	Executed by Delivery	Status/comments

A. Pre-closing Matters

1	Share Purchase Agreement	T&A	Vacation by: Ontario by: Principal Principal's spouse Sun by: Fun by: Surf by: Standard delivery	Y
2	Evidence of notice to Royal Bank of Canada of change of control of Target Group	R&M	Standard delivery	Y
3	Evidence of notice to Holiday Holdings Limited (Sun's landlord) of change of control of Sun	R&M	Standard delivery	Y
4	Rectification of minute books for Target Group in accordance with T&A memoranda of May 31, 200X	R&M	Sun by: Fun by: Surf by: Originals in respective minute books	To be signed prior to closing

B. Regulatory Matters

5	Short-form notification under the *Competition Act*	T&A	Original to Competition Bureau, copies to all others	Filed: May 24, 200X 7-day expiry: May 31, 200X
6	*Investment Canada Act* filing	T&A	Original to Investment Canada, copies to all others	To be filed before or within 30 days after closing

C. Evidentiary Matters

7	Certificate of Compliance for Vacation	T&A	Standard delivery	Ordered
8	Certificate of Status for Sun	R&M	Standard delivery	
9	Certificate of Status for Fun	R&M	Standard delivery	
10	Certificate of Status for Surf	R&M	Standard delivery	
11	Certificate of Status for Ontario	R&M	Standard delivery	

FIGURE 1.2   CONTINUED

Action or documentation	Drafting responsibility	Executed by Delivery	Status/comments

12   Vacation Officer's certificate certifying copies of:
• constating documents;
• bylaws; and
• directors' resolution authorizing:
   – the entering into and delivery of the Share Purchase Agreement and all documents contemplated thereby; and
   – the performance of its obligations thereunder
Certificate of Incumbency
	T&A	Vacation by:
		
		Standard delivery
			Settled

13 Vacation directors' resolution authorizing: • the entering into and delivery of the Share Purchase Agreement and all documents contemplated thereby; and • the performance of its obligations thereunder	T&A	Vacation directors by: Original to Vacation for filing in minute book	Settled

14   Ontario officer's certificate certifying copies of:
• constating documents;
• bylaws; and
• directors' resolution authorizing:
   – the entering into and delivery of the Share Purchase Agreement and all documents contemplated thereby; and
   – the performance of its obligations thereunder
Certificate of Incumbency
	T&A	Ontario by:
		
		Standard delivery
			Settled

15 Ontario directors' resolution authorizing: • the entering into and delivery of the Share Purchase Agreement and all documents contemplated thereby; and • the performance of its obligations thereunder	T&A	Ontario directors by: Original to Ontario for filing in minute book	Settled

FIGURE 1.2 CONTINUED

Action or documentation	Drafting responsibility	Executed by Delivery	Status/comments

16 Sun officer's certificate certifying copies of:
• constating documents;
• bylaws; and
• directors' resolution authorizing:
  – the entering into and delivery of the Share Purchase Agreement and all documents contemplated thereby; and
  – the performance of its obligations thereunder
and consenting to the sale of shares
Certificate of Incumbency
	T&A	Sun by:
		
		Standard delivery
			Settled

17 Sun director's resolution authorizing: • the entering into and delivery of the Share Purchase Agreement and all documents contemplated thereby; and • the performance of its obligations thereunder and consenting to the sale of shares	T&A	Sun directors by: Original to Sun for filing in minute book	Settled

18 Fun officer's certificate certifying copies of:
• constating documents;
• bylaws; and
• directors' resolution authorizing:
  – the entering into and delivery of the Share Purchase Agreement and all documents contemplated thereby; and
  – the performance of its obligations thereunder
and consenting to the sale of shares
Certificate of Incumbency
	T&A	Fun by:
		
		Standard delivery
			Settled

19 Fun directors' resolution authorizing: • the entering into and delivery of the Share Purchase Agreement and all documents contemplated thereby; and • the performance of its obligations thereunder and consenting to the sale of shares	T&A	Fun directors by: Original to Fun for filing in minute book	Settled

FIGURE 1.2 CONTINUED

Action or documentation	Drafting responsibility	Executed by Delivery	Status/comments
20 Surf officer's certificate certifying copies of: • constating documents; • bylaws; and • directors' resolution authorizing: – the entering into and delivery of the Share Purchase Agreement and all documents contemplated thereby; and – the performance of its obligations thereunder and consenting to the sale of shares Certificate of Incumbency	T&A	Surf by: Standard delivery	Settled
21 Surf directors' resolution authorizing: • the entering into and delivery of the Share Purchase Agreement and all documents contemplated thereby; and • the performance of its obligations thereunder and consenting to the sale of shares	T&A	Surf directors by: Original to Surf for filing in minute book	Settled
22 Vacation officer's certificate re: • truth and accuracy of representations, warranties; and • satisfaction of covenants and closing conditions	T&A	Vacation by: Standard delivery	Settled
23 Ontario officer's certificate re: • truth and accuracy of representations, warranties; • satisfaction of covenants and closing conditions; and • declaration of residency under *Income Tax Act*, s. 116	T&A	Ontario by: Standard delivery	Settled
24 Certificate of Principal re: • truth and accuracy of representations, warranties; • satisfaction of covenants and closing conditions; and • declaration of residency under *Income Tax Act*, s. 116	T&A	Principal Standard delivery	Settled

FIGURE 1.2   CONTINUED

Action or documentation	Drafting responsibility	Executed by Delivery	Status/comments
25 Certificate of Principal's Spouse re: • truth and accuracy of representations, warranties; • satisfaction of covenants and closing conditions; and • declaration of residency under *Income Tax Act*, s. 116	T&A	Principal's Spouse Standard delivery	Settled
D. Third-Party Matters			
26 Non-disturbance agreements from mortgagees in respect of each of the Surf's leased properties and registered on title, where applicable	T&A		Vacation/R&M
27 *Planning Act* consents for each of the leased properties of Surf, where applicable, or confirmation of compliance with *Planning Act*	T&A		Vacation/R&M
28 Phase I and II Environmental Reports and Asbestos Building Materials Surveys	T&A	Standard delivery	To be delivered by John Black on June 12, 200X
29 Notices of Lease to be registered on title for each of the leased properties of Surf	T&A		Prepared and delivered to R&M for execution
30 Delivery of mortgage discharge for mortgage Instrument No. ____	T&A/R&M	Standard delivery	Settled
31 Delivery of mortgage discharge for mortgage Instrument No. ____	T&A/R&M	Standard delivery	Settled
32 Delivery of financing change statement discharging *Personal Property Security Act* registration No. ____	T&A/R&M	Standard delivery	Settled
33 Delivery of financing change statement discharging *Personal Property Security Act* registration No. ____	T&A/R&M	Standard delivery	Settled
34 Delivery of financing change statement discharging *Personal Property Security Act* registration No. ____	T&A/R&M	Standard delivery	Settled
35 Delivery of financing change statement discharging *Personal Property Security Act* registration No. ____	T&A/R&M	Standard delivery	Settled
36 Release by Royal Bank of Canada of its interest in the Purchased Shares owned by Principal	R&M	Standard delivery	

FIGURE 1.2 CONTINUED

Action or documentation		Drafting responsibility	Executed by Delivery	Status/comments
E. Transfer of Shares				
37	Sun share certificate No. A1-3 for 98 class A special shares duly endorsed by Principal for transfer	Sellers (R&M)	Originals to Vacation, copies to others	To be endorsed on closing, then to be marked "Cancelled"
38	Sun share certificate No. A1-1 for 102 class A special shares duly endorsed by Principal's Spouse for transfer	Sellers (R&M)	Originals to Vacation, copies to others	To be endorsed on closing, then to be marked "Cancelled"
39	Fun share certificate No. A1 for 62,000 class A special shares duly endorsed by Principal for transfer	Sellers (R&M)	Originals to Vacation, copies to others	To be endorsed on closing, then to be marked "Cancelled"
40	Fun share certificate No. C1 for 9,200 common shares duly endorsed by Ontario for transfer	Sellers (R&M)	Originals to Vacation, copies to others	To be endorsed on closing, then to be marked "Cancelled"
41	Surf share certificate No. 1A for 130,267 class A special shares duly endorsed by Principal for transfer	Sellers (R&M)	Originals to Vacation, copies to others	To be endorsed on closing, then to be marked "Cancelled"
42	Surf share certificate No. C1 for 10 common shares duly endorsed by Ontario for transfer	Sellers (R&M)	Ontario by: Originals to Vacation, copies to others	To be endorsed on closing, then to be marked "Cancelled"
43	Receipt by Vacation re share certificates representing Purchased Shares	T&A	Vacation by: Standard delivery	Settled
F. Collateral Agreements and Other Matters				
44	Non-competition, non-solicitation, and non-disclosure agreement for 5-year period issued by Sellers in favour of Vacation	T&A	Sellers by: Standard delivery	Settled
45	Consulting Agreement between Vacation and Principal	T&A	Vacation by: Principal Standard delivery	Settled
46	Trade Mark Consent and Covenant for Further Assurances	T&A	Principal Standard delivery	Settled

FIGURE 1.2 CONTINUED

Action or documentation	Drafting responsibility	Executed by Delivery	Status/comments
G. Reorganization of Target Group			
47 Resignation by Principal and Principal's Spouse as directors and officers of Sun effective as of Closing Date	T&A	Principal and Principal's Spouse One original for each in Target Group, copies for all other parties	Settled
48 Resignation by Principal and Principal's Spouse as directors and officers of Fun effective as of Closing Date	T&A	Principal and Principal's Spouse One original for each in Target Group, copies for all other parties	Settled
49 Resignation by Principal and Principal's Spouse as directors and officers of Surf effective as of Closing Date	T&A	Principal and Principal's Spouse One original for each in Target Group, copies for all other parties	Settled
50 Sun shareholders' resolution electing directors for Sun	T&A	Vacation by: Originals to each in Target Group, copies for all other parties	
51 Fun shareholders' resolution electing directors for Fun	T&A	Vacation by: Originals to each in Target Group, copies for all other parties	
52 Surf shareholders' resolution electing directors for Surf	T&A	Vacation by: Originals to each in Target Group, copies for all other parties	
53 Consent of each new director to act as a director of Sun	T&A	Each new director Original for each minute book, copies for all other parties	
54 Consent of each new director to act as a director of Fun	T&A	Each new director Original for each minute book, copies for all other parties	
55 Consent of each new director to act as a director of Surf	T&A	Each new director Original for each minute book, copies for all other parties	

FIGURE 1.2   CONTINUED

23

Action or documentation	Drafting responsibility	Executed by Delivery	Status/comments
56 Sun directors' resolution appointing officers	T&A	Sun directors by: Originals to each in Target Group, copies for all other parties	
57 Fun directors' resolution appointing officers	T&A	Fun directors by: Originals to each in Target Group, copies for all other parties	
58 Surf directors' resolution appointing officers	T&A	Surf directors by: Originals to each in Target Group, copies for all other parties	
59 Ontario Form 1 for Sun	T&A	To be acknowledged by: Standard delivery	
60 Ontario Form 1 for Fun	T&A	To be acknowledged by: Standard delivery	
61 Ontario Form 1 for Surf	T&A	To be acknowledged by: Standard delivery	
62 Sun share certificate No. A1-4 in the name of Vacation for 300 class A common shares	T&A	Principal and Spouse Originals to Vacation, copies to T&A	Settled
63 Sun share certificate No. A1-5 in the name of Vacation for 300 class A special shares	T&A	Principal and Spouse Originals to Vacation, copies to T&A	Settled
64 Fun share certificate No. A-2 in the name of Vacation for 62,000 class A special shares	T&A	Principal and Spouse Originals to Vacation, copies to T&A	Settled
65 Sun share certificate No. C2 in the name of Vacation for 9,200 common shares	T&A	Principal and Spouse Originals to Vacation, copies to T&A	Settled
66 Surf share certificate No. 2A in the name of Vacation for 130,267 class A special shares	T&A	Principal and Spouse Originals to Vacation, copies to T&A	Settled
67 Surf share certificate No. C2 in the name of Vacation for 10 common shares	T&A	Principal and Spouse Originals to Vacation. copies to T&A	Settled

FIGURE 1.2   CONTINUED

Action or documentation	Drafting responsibility	Executed by Delivery	Status/comments
68 Release and Indemnity by Sellers in favour of Vacation and Target Group	T&A	Sellers by: Standard delivery	Settled
69 Release and Indemnity by Vacation in favour of Sellers	T&A	Vacation by: Standard delivery	Settled
70 Termination of shareholder agreement for Sun	T&A	Shareholders by:	Settled
71 Delivery by Sellers of minute books, share ledgers, and corporate seals for Target Group	R&M	Originals to Vacation	
72 Public announcement	Vacation/ Target Group	Standard delivery	Settled

H. Payment of Purchase Price and Repayment of Shareholder Loans

73 Certified cheques or bank drafts of Vacation payable in respect of the Purchase Price to: • Ontario in the aggregate amount of $8,565,191 • Principal in the aggregate amount of $3,870,774 • Principal's Spouse in the amount of $2,027,619	Vacation	Originals to Ontario, Principal, and Principal's Spouse, respectively; copies to all others	
74 Receipts for certified funds/bank drafts of: • Ontario in the amount of $8,565,191 • Principal in the amount of $3,870,774 • Principal's Spouse in the amount of $2,027,619	T&A	Ontario by: Principal Principal's Spouse Standard delivery	Settled
75 Direction of Sun to Vacation to pay the following in respect of the Shareholder Loans: • Principal in the amount of $1,123,697 • Principal's Spouse in the amount of $53,523 • Joseph Black in the amount of $47,924	T&A	Sun by: Standard delivery	Settled
76 Certified cheques or bank drafts of Vacation payable in respect of the Sun Shareholder Loans to: • Principal in the amount of $1,123,697 • Principal's Spouse in the amount of $53,523 • Joseph Black in the amount of $47,924	Vacation	Originals to Principal, Principal's Spouse, and Joseph Black, respectively; copies to all others	

FIGURE 1.2   CONTINUED

25

Action or documentation	Drafting responsibility	Executed by Delivery	Status/comments
77 Receipts for certified funds/bank drafts of: • Principal in the amount of $1,123,697 • Principal's Spouse in the amount of $53,523 • Joseph Black in the amount of $47,924	T&A	Principal Principal's Spouse Joseph Black Standard delivery	Settled
78 Direction of Fun to Vacation to pay $901,487 to Ontario to repay Shareholder Loans	T&A	Fun by: Standard delivery	Settled
79 $901,487 certified cheque or bank draft by Vacation payable to Ontario to repay Shareholder Loans	Vacation	Original to Ontario, copies to all others	
80 Receipt of Ontario for $901,487 certified funds/bank draft	T&A	Ontario by: Standard delivery	Settled
81 Direction of Surf to Vacation to pay Principal $1,772,393 to repay Shareholder Loans	T&A	Surf by: Standard delivery	Settled
82 $1,772,393 certified cheque or bank draft by Vacation payable to Principal to repay Shareholder Loans	Vacation	Original to Principal, copies to all others	
83 Receipt of Principal for $1,772,393 certified funds/bank draft	T&A	Principal Standard delivery	Settled
84 Calculation of cash shortfall	Sellers/ Vacation	Standard delivery	
85 Release from Closing Escrow	T&A	All parties by: Standard delivery	

I. Legal Opinions

86 Opinion letter of R&M	R&M	R&M by: Standard delivery	Settled
87 Opinion letter of T&A	T&A	T&A by: Standard delivery	Settled

FIGURE 1.2   CONCLUDED

Action or documentation	Drafting responsibility	Executed by Delivery	Status/comments
J. Matters To Be Completed Post-closing			
88 Register real estate discharges	T&A	Standard delivery	T&A to register
89 Transmit *Personal Property Security Act* discharges	T&A		T&A to transmit
90 Audited financial statements for the fiscal period ending as at the Closing Date for: • Sun • Fun • Surf	R&M/auditors of Target Group		Deloitte & Touche (Hamilton) to prepare
91 Income tax returns for the period ending as at the Closing Date for: • Sun • Fun • Surf	R&M/auditors of Target Group		Deloitte & Touche (Hamilton) to prepare
92 File Ontario Form 1 for Sun	T&A		Confirmation to R&M
93 File Ontario Form 1 for Fun	T&A		Confirmation to R&M
94 File Ontario Form 1 for Surf	T&A		Confirmation to R&M
95 Director's resolutions to: • fix year-end • appoint bankers • appoint signing officers for Sun	T&A	Sun directors by:	
96 Director's resolutions to: • fix year-end • appoint bankers • appoint signing officers for Fun	T&A	Fun directors by:	
97 Director's resolutions to: • fix year-end • appoint bankers • appoint signing officers for Surf	T&A	Surf directors by:	

CHAPTER 2

Due diligence and the commercial transaction

Donna Kubota, President, Solutions Corporate Law Clerk Services, Inc.

CHAPTER OVERVIEW

This chapter discusses the due diligence to be conducted as part of a commercial transaction, as well as the law clerk's role and responsibility in this process. The chapter focuses on legal due diligence with respect to transactions involving the purchase and sale of shares or assets of a target corporation, and secured financing transactions where a borrowing corporation secures a loan with its assets, real property, and/or personal property.

CHAPTER OBJECTIVES

After completing this chapter, you should be able to:

1. Understand the steps involved in the legal due diligence process and identify the law clerk's role in the process.

2. Identify and compile a detailed list of all the public corporate/commercial due diligence searches to be conducted against a corporation with the government authorities in each jurisdiction in which it carries on business.

3. Assemble and maintain a reference binder and a due diligence binder containing copies and lists of the corporate documents obtained and reviewed; copies of requests for information and/or documents sent to the corporations involved in a commercial transaction; results of public searches conducted against any corporation; copies of memos summarizing the review of the corporate records as well as any material contracts of the corporation; and copies of any other pertinent information that might be useful.

INTRODUCTION

due diligence
the comprehensive investigation into and review of the business, financial operations, and legal status of a corporation or business

Due diligence is the comprehensive investigation into and review of the business, financial operations, and legal status of a target corporation or business. The goal of the due diligence process is to provide a purchaser or lender with enough information to allow it to make a sound business decision and to limit its risk in a commercial transaction. The nature of the transaction will determine how extensive the due diligence process should be.

An important part of the due diligence process involves conducting public searches with appropriate government authorities to confirm a corporation's name, current corporate status, solvency, indebtedness, and current involvement in legal proceedings. These searches are typically conducted by a purchaser against a corporation whose shares or assets are to be acquired by the purchaser, or by a lender against a borrowing corporation in a secured financing transaction whereby the borrowing corporation secures a loan with its assets, real property, and/or personal property. In this chapter, wherever appropriate, a corporation against which a search is being conducted — whether a vendor, a lender, a purchaser, or a borrower — may be referred to as "Searchco" or "Targetco."

At the outset of any commercial transaction, you should discuss with the lawyer who is supervising the due diligence process the nature of the transaction and the legal due diligence to be conducted. This will assist you, the supervising lawyer, and the rest of the legal team in determining how extensive the legal due diligence should be, and will assist you in defining your role in this process.

Two types of due diligence

There are two types of due diligence: business due diligence and legal due diligence. In a transaction involving the purchase and sale of shares or assets of a target corporation ("Targetco"), the different due diligence responsibilities are often divided among the purchaser, the purchaser's accountants, and the purchaser's legal counsel.

BUSINESS DUE DILIGENCE

The business due diligence in an asset or share purchase transaction is often handled by the purchaser and the purchaser's accountants with a view to obtaining comprehensive financial information about Targetco's business operations. This information includes a complete description and listing of Targetco's assets, liabilities, financial status, employees, suppliers, and any other pertinent information. The business due diligence may involve a review of Targetco's financial statements; tax returns; listings of assets, fixtures, vehicles, machinery, and inventory; all accounts receivable; details about real property owned or leased; intellectual property such as trademarks and patents; insurance policies; pension benefit plans; and particulars of pending or threatened litigation matters.

The purpose of the business due diligence is to satisfy the purchaser that its contemplated purchase of shares or assets of Targetco is a sound business decision. The results obtained from the business due diligence will be very important in determining whether the purchaser decides to proceed with the transaction, and could also be important in the negotiation of the final purchase price.

LEGAL DUE DILIGENCE

The legal due diligence in a commercial transaction is generally conducted by legal counsel of the following parties:

1. in a share purchase or asset purchase transaction, by the purchaser of the shares or the purchaser of the assets; and

2. in a secured financing transaction, by the lender.

As well, to verify the accuracy of the representations and warranties being made in the share purchase agreement, asset purchase agreement, or loan agreement (including any supporting or ancillary agreements), it is prudent for similar due diligence to be conducted by legal counsel to the vendor (in a share purchase transaction), Targetco (in an asset purchase transaction), or the borrower (in a secured financing transaction).

Depending on the nature of the transaction, the legal due diligence may involve the following:

1. obtaining corporate information about the validity of the legal status of the vendor/borrower as disclosed by:

   a. corporate/commercial public searches conducted against the vendor/ borrower with government authorities in the jurisdiction in which it is formed ("the home jurisdiction") and in each jurisdiction where it carries on business, tracing its corporate history through name changes, amendments, continuances from other jurisdictions, and amalgamations; and

   b. a comprehensive corporate review, by the legal counsel of the purchaser/ lender, of the vendor/borrower's minute books and related corporate records;

2. reviewing all material contracts to which the vendor/borrower is a party (such as loan agreements, security agreements, leases, supplier agreements, and trademark licences) to determine the nature of each contract and whether the contracts:

   a. require third-party consents to be obtained prior to closing with respect to the sale of shares or assets or the borrowing of funds;

   b. contain triggering provisions regarding termination rights under the contract; or

   c. contain restrictions on the assignment of the contract or restrictions on a change of control of ownership of the vendor/borrower; and

3. conducting public searches against the purchaser/lender to confirm its status in the home jurisdiction and whether there are any encumbrances registered against it that may impair its ability to complete the transaction.

   The purpose of the legal due diligence is to enable legal counsel of each corporation involved in a commercial transaction to determine:

   • the accuracy and/or satisfaction of the representations and warranties contained in the draft agreement of purchase and sale, security agreement, and/or other agreement that is part of the transaction;

   • whether the legal counsel of each corporation will be able to render their respective legal opinions in support of the transaction; and

- if the legal counsel will be able to render legal opinions, the extent and nature of their opinions.

DETERMINING THE EXTENT OF PUBLIC SEARCHES

As a law clerk, you can play a significant role in coordinating and overseeing the requisite public due diligence searches to be conducted. Once the nature of the commercial transaction has been ascertained, your first step should be to consider the types of public corporate/commercial searches to be conducted. Different commercial transactions require different searches.

Share purchase transaction

In a simple share purchase transaction, the purchaser and the vendor enter into a share purchase agreement whereby the purchaser agrees to purchase from the vendor all or part of certain shares that the vendor legally and beneficially owns in a corporation (Targetco), on the terms and conditions and at the purchase price set out in the agreement. In this section, the corporation whose shares are being sold by the vendor to the purchaser will be referred to as "Targetco."

In a share purchase transaction, corporate/commercial searches should be conducted against both Targetco and the vendor of the shares to determine:

1. whether Targetco and the vendor are validly subsisting, are not involved in insolvency proceedings, and are not undischarged bankrupts;

2. whether there are any liens, encumbrances, or security interests registered by third parties against the assets or personal property of Targetco in its home jurisdiction and in each jurisdiction in which it carries on business; and

3. whether there are any liens, encumbrances, or security interests registered by third parties against the vendor in its home jurisdiction and in each jurisdiction in which it carries on business.

In a share purchase transaction, the purchaser will be purchasing not only the shares of Targetco but also its assets and liabilities. Therefore, it is important for the purchaser to know whether Targetco's assets are free and clear of any liens, encumbrances, or security interests of third parties. If the due diligence searches disclose any encumbrances registered against any of Targetco's assets, the purchaser should obtain from the vendor full details of the encumbrances and may require, as a condition of completing the transaction, that the encumbrances be discharged on or before closing.

Similarly, it is important to conduct searches against the vendor to determine whether, for example, it has pledged to a lender or otherwise encumbered any of the shares of Targetco registered in its name, and determine that the vendor is not insolvent, since insolvency would impair its ability to complete the transaction.

Asset purchase transaction

In a simple asset purchase transaction, the purchaser and the target corporation (Targetco) enter into an asset purchase agreement whereby the purchaser agrees to purchase from Targetco all or part of the assets of Targetco (which assets are typically described in the asset purchase agreement), on the terms and conditions and at the purchase price set out in the agreement. In this section, the corporation whose assets are being purchased by the purchaser will be referred to as "Targetco."

In an asset purchase transaction, corporate/commercial searches should be conducted against Targetco to determine:

1. whether Targetco is validly subsisting, is not involved in insolvency proceedings, and is not an undischarged bankrupt; and

2. whether there are any liens, encumbrances, or security interests registered by third parties against the assets or personal property of Targetco that are included in the transaction in its home jurisdiction and in each jurisdiction in which it carries on business.

It is also prudent to conduct an insolvency search against the purchaser to ensure that it is not involved in insolvency proceedings.

It is important for the purchaser to know whether it will be acquiring Targetco's assets free and clear of any liens, encumbrances, or security interests of third parties prior to closing. If the due diligence searches disclose any encumbrances registered against the assets being purchased, the purchaser may require, as a condition of completing the transaction, that the encumbrances be discharged on or before closing.

Secured financing transaction

In a simple secured financing transaction, a borrower borrows money from a lender (which may be an individual, another corporation, or a financial institution) pursuant to a loan agreement, and the repayment of the loan is secured by the borrower (as described below).

In a secured financing transaction, corporate/commercial searches should be conducted against the borrower to determine:

1. whether the borrower is validly subsisting, is not involved in insolvency proceedings, and is not an undischarged bankrupt; and

2. whether there are any liens, encumbrances, or security interests registered by third parties against the assets or personal property of the borrower in its home jurisdiction and in each jurisdiction in which it carries on business.

Furthermore, if the borrower is pledging its shares in a corporation as security for the loan, corporate/commercial searches should be conducted against that corporation to determine whether there are any liens, encumbrances, or security interests registered by third parties with respect to any of the issued shares of the corporation owned by the borrower, and whether the corporation is validly subsisting.

If the borrower is securing its assets in favour of the lender as part of a secured financing transaction, it is important for the lender to know whether it will be acquiring the borrower's assets free and clear of any liens, encumbrances, or security interests of third parties prior to closing.

COMMENCING DUE DILIGENCE PUBLIC SEARCHES

The first search that you should conduct is a complete and comprehensive corporate search against Searchco in its governing home jurisdiction. The procedures for searching vary depending on whether Searchco is a federal corporation, an Ontario corporation, a corporation formed by an amalgamation, or an extra-provincial corporation.

Federal corporations

If Searchco was formed under the *Canada Business Corporations Act* (CBCA) (or any predecessor statute), you should conduct a Strategis online database search against Searchco and obtain the federal corporations database online report for Searchco.

You should also request from Industry Canada copies of all articles of Searchco (including certificate and articles of incorporation, amalgamation, amendment, and continuance); Form 3 Notice of Registered Office; Form 6 Notice of Directors; Form 22 federal annual returns; and any other documents that have been filed on the public files with Industry Canada with respect to Searchco.

On the basis of the information obtained from the federal corporate search and the public documents, you should be able to determine the following information:

1. Searchco's current name (in English and/or French);

2. any recent former names of Searchco;

3. the registered office address of Searchco;

4. the mailing address of Searchco;

5. the status of Searchco's federal annual return filings;

6. the corporate status of Searchco;

7. the identity of any predecessor corporations of Searchco (if Searchco was formed by amalgamation); and

8. the names of the directors of Searchco.

Ontario corporations

If Searchco was formed under the *Business Corporations Act* (Ontario) (OBCA) (or any predecessor statute) or if it was registered to carry on business in Ontario under the *Corporations Information Act* (CIA), you should order an Ontario corporation profile report from the Companies and Personal Property Security Branch of the Ministry of Government Services (MGS) ("the Ontario Companies Branch"). You should also order and review the Ontario microfiche of Searchco (and make copies of all articles, corporate notices, expired business name registrations, and any other pertinent documents contained on the microfiche) to determine the following information:

1. Searchco's current name (in English and/or French);

2. any and all former names of Searchco;

3. Searchco's jurisdiction of incorporation;

4. any and all current or expired business names currently or formerly registered by Searchco in Ontario;

5. the municipalities in Ontario in which Searchco currently carries on business or has ever carried on business;

6. any predecessor corporations of Searchco;

7. confirmation that Searchco has not been dissolved; and

8. the names and addresses for searches of the directors and officers of Searchco.

The Ontario Companies Branch has published a very useful document on how to read a corporation profile report. This document can be obtained by contacting the Ontario Companies Branch.

If Searchco was formed in a jurisdiction outside Ontario but is registered to carry on business in Ontario, you should also conduct a search against Searchco in its home jurisdiction to obtain the same or similar corporate information obtained from a corporate search in Ontario.

Corporations formed by amalgamation

If the federal or Ontario corporate search results disclose that Searchco was formed by amalgamation, the supervising lawyer should discuss with the client whether or not corporate searches should be conducted against each predecessor corporation in its home jurisdiction, tracing the history back to the date of incorporation of each predecessor. If there is a lengthy corporate history, the lawyer should explain to the client the risks of not conducting such searches. Ultimately, the client will make the final decision whether to search or not. A sample corporate history chart illustrating the history of amalgamations of a corporation is shown in figure 2.1 at the end of the chapter.

Extra-provincial registrations

You should also determine whether Searchco is registered extra-provincially or carries on business in any other province or territory outside its home jurisdiction. If so, consideration should be given to conducting corporate searches in each such jurisdiction.

COMMERCIAL SEARCHES: WHO AND WHERE

The information obtained from the public corporate searches is fundamental and will help you determine which commercial searches need to be conducted. To begin, make a list of the following information:

1. all names under which Searchco currently carries on business or has ever carried on business, including:

   a. all current English and French forms of names and any combinations thereof ("current names"),

   b. any former English and French forms of names and combinations thereof,

   c. any predecessor names (including any former names of predecessor corporations), and

   d. any current and/or expired business names

   (items 1a to 1d above are collectively referred to as "current and former names"); and

2. all jurisdictions, municipalities, and business addresses where Searchco, under the current and former names, currently carries on business or has ever carried on business, including:

    a. the current registered office address ("current registered office address"),

    b. the current places of business ("current places of business"),

    c. any former registered office addresses, and

    d. any former places of business

    (items 2a to 2d above are collectively referred to as "current and former places of business").

With this information, commercial searches can be conducted against Searchco. Table 2.1 sets out the searches to be conducted against the various parties in different commercial transactions.

EXTRA-PROVINCIAL SEARCHES

Where corporate and/or commercial due diligence searches need to be conducted outside the jurisdiction where Searchco is located, the appropriate agents should be retained to conduct the relevant corporate/commercial searches against the current and former names of Searchco in each of the current and former places of business.

WHEN TO CONDUCT PUBLIC CORPORATE/COMMERCIAL SEARCHES

At the commencement of the commercial transaction

Ideally, you should start conducting the required corporate/commercial searches at the beginning of the commercial transaction so that all liens, encumbrances, and other charges against Searchco, as well as all corporate information, are disclosed and identified as soon as possible. This will allow sufficient time for Searchco to satisfactorily address any outstanding issues and encumbrances well before the closing date.

On closing

Immediately prior to the closing of the commercial transaction, you should update the initial public corporate/commercial searches conducted against Searchco to find out whether there have been any changes to the information disclosed in the original search results and whether any new registrations have been made against Searchco since the date of the original searches. Table 2.2 sets out the procedures for updating searches.

TABLE 2.1 SEARCHES TO BE CONDUCTED IN COMMERCIAL TRANSACTIONS

Type of transaction	Conducted against	Where?
Share purchase	The vendor under each of its current and former names	In each of the current and former places of business
	The purchaser under each of its current and former names	In each of the current and former places of business
Asset purchase	The corporation whose assets are being purchased by the purchaser, under each of its current and former names	In each of the current and former places of business
	The purchaser under each of its current and former names	In each of the current and former places of business
Secured financing	The borrower under each of its current and former names	In each of the current and former places of business
	If the borrower is pledging shares in a corporation as security for the loan, each of the corporation's current and former names	In each of the current and former places of business of the corporation whose shares are being pledged by the borrower

Note: The terms "current and former names" and "current and former places of business" are defined above under "Commercial Searches: Who and Where."

TABLE 2.2 SEARCHES TO BE UPDATED IN COMMERCIAL TRANSACTIONS

Type of transaction	Conducted against	Where?
Share purchase	The vendor under its current name (English and/or French and combination thereof)	In current registered office and current places of business
	The purchaser under its current name (English and/or French and combination thereof)	In current registered office and current places of business
Asset purchase	The vendor under its current name (English and/or French and combination thereof)	In current registered office and current places of business
Secured financing	The borrower under its current name (English and/or French and combination thereof)	In current registered office and current places of business
	If the borrower is pledging shares in a corporation as security for the loan, the current name (English and/or French and combination thereof) of the corporation	In current registered office and current places of business of the corporation whose shares are being pledged by the borrower

Note: The terms "current and former names" and "current and former places of business" are defined above under "Commercial Searches: Who and Where."

Certificate of status or compliance

On or immediately prior to the closing of the commercial transaction, you should obtain an Ontario certificate of status (if the governing jurisdiction is Ontario) or a federal certificate of compliance (if the governing jurisdiction is Canada) in respect of Searchco. Table 2.3 outlines the reasons for obtaining a certificate of status or compliance in different types of commercial transactions.

DESCRIPTION OF CORPORATE/COMMERCIAL SEARCHES

1. Table 2.4 contains a summary and a brief description of the types of corporate/commercial searches that you should consider conducting against Searchco. The searches summarized in items 1 to 8 are the standard corporate/commercial due diligence searches conducted in Ontario as part of a commercial transaction.

2. You should review the corporate/commercial search results and prepare a summary of the search results. A sample corporate/commercial search report to record the results of the standard due diligence searches is shown in figure 2.2 at the end of the chapter. The sample report may be customized to reflect any additional searches conducted.

3. Depending on the nature and extent of the commercial transaction, the searches summarized in items 9 to 26 may also need to be conducted. You should discuss with the supervising lawyer which of these additional searches should be conducted. Note that written consents from Searchco must be obtained and submitted to the government authorities in support of the request for some of these searches.

4. *Securities Act* searches: Unlike information about non-offering corporations, comprehensive corporate and financial information with respect to Canadian public companies is publicly accessible on an online system called **SEDAR**, which is the acronym for System for Electronic Document Analysis and Retrieval. SEDAR is the electronic filing system for the disclosure documents of public companies and mutual funds across Canada. Some of the documents available from SEDAR for public companies include annual reports, financial statements, press releases, prospectuses, and takeover bid materials. Through the SEDAR Website (http://www.sedar.com), you can access links to securities commissions in British Columbia, Alberta, Manitoba, Ontario, Nova Scotia, and Quebec, as well as links to the Montreal Exchange and the TSX Group (which includes the Toronto Stock Exchange and the TSX Venture Exchange).

SEDAR
System for Electronic Document Analysis and Retrieval; the electronic filing system for the disclosure documents of public companies and mutual funds across Canada

REFERENCE BINDER AND DUE DILIGENCE BINDER

One useful role of the law clerk in the legal due diligence process is to assist the legal team in establishing and maintaining a reference binder and a due diligence binder. The purpose of the reference binder is to ensure that there is one central place where all key reference materials are kept. Similarly, the purpose of the due diligence binder is to ensure that there is one central repository where all the legal

TABLE 2.3 CERTIFICATES OF STATUS OR COMPLIANCE TO BE OBTAINED IN COMMERCIAL TRANSACTIONS

Type of transaction	To be obtained by	Why
Share purchase	The purchaser's legal counsel in respect of the purchaser	To confirm the representations and warranties in the share purchase agreement and to support the legal opinion of the purchaser's legal counsel that the purchaser is validly subsisting in its home jurisdiction as at the date of the closing of the share purchase transaction
	The vendor's legal counsel in respect of the vendor	To confirm the representations and warranties in the share purchase agreement and to support the legal opinion of the vendor's legal counsel that the vendor is validly subsisting in its home jurisdiction as at the date of the closing of the share purchase transaction
	The vendor's legal counsel in respect of the target corporation	To confirm the representations and warranties in the share purchase agreement and to support the legal opinion of the vendor's legal counsel that the target corporation is validly subsisting in its home jurisdiction as at the date of the closing of the share purchase transaction
Asset purchase	The vendor's legal counsel in respect of the vendor	To confirm the representations and warranties in the asset purchase agreement and to support the legal opinion of the vendor's legal counsel that the vendor is validly subsisting in its home jurisdiction as at the date of the closing of the asset purchase transaction
Secured financing	The borrower's legal counsel in respect of the borrower	To confirm the representations and warranties in the loan agreement and to support the legal opinion of the borrower's legal counsel that the borrower is validly subsisting in its home jurisdiction as at the date of the closing of the secured financing transaction
	If the borrower is pledging its shares of a corporation as security for the loan, the borrower's legal counsel in respect of the target corporation	To confirm the representations and warranties in the loan agreement and to support the legal opinion of the borrower's legal counsel that the target corporation whose shares are being pledged by the borrower is validly subsisting in its home jurisdiction as at the date of the closing of the loan transaction

TABLE 2.4 CORPORATE/COMMERCIAL SEARCHES TO BE CONDUCTED AGAINST SEARCHCO

No.	Search	Why?	Who, where, how?
1	Corporate (Ontario)	To confirm the jurisdiction and corporate status of Searchco and to determine the corporate information on the public files at the Ontario Companies Branch, including Searchco's current corporate name, any French form of name, any former names, any predecessor names, any current registered business names, its registered office address, its directors, and its officers (all as reported to the Ontario Companies Branch).	Conducted online through Cyberbahn or Oncorp (by secure Web access) or in person at: Companies and Personal Property Security Branch, Ministry of Government Services, 375 University Avenue, 2nd Floor, Toronto, Ontario (or at any of the Land Registry offices in Ontario). Tel: 416-314-8880 Toll-free: 1-800-361-3223 http://www.cbs.gov.on.ca Ontario corporate documents available from the Ontario Companies Branch: • Corporation Profile Report, • Corporation Document List, • Business Names List (if applicable), • Business Names Report (with respect to business names registered by a corporation or in the case of sole proprietorships or general partnerships), • Point in Time Report (if applicable), • microfiche (and copies therefrom), • certificate of status, and • Limited Partnership Report (if applicable).
2	Corporate (Canada)	To confirm the jurisdiction and corporate status of Searchco and to determine the corporate information on the public files at Industry Canada, including Searchco's current corporate name, any French form of name, any former names, any predecessor names, its registered office address, and its directors (all as reported to Industry Canada).	Conducted online with Industry Canada using the Strategis database (http://www.strategis.ic.gc.ca/cgi-bin/sc_mrksv/corpdir/dataonline) or by mail or fax at: Corporations Canada, Industry Canada, Jean Edmonds Tower, 365 Laurier Avenue West, Ottawa, Ontario K1A 0C8. Tel: 613-941-9042 Fax: 613-941-5789 http://strategis.ic.gc.ca Federal corporate documents available from Industry Canada: • corporation data sheet, • copies of federal documents (articles, notices, and annual returns),

TABLE 2.4 CONTINUED

No.	Search	Why?	Who, where, how?
3	*Personal Property Security Act* (Ontario) (PPSA)	To determine whether there are any registrations made against Searchco under the former *Corporation Securities Registration Act* (Ontario) (such as debentures) and under the PPSA recorded in Ontario's Personal Property Security Registry System, which is the central computer-based registry system maintained by the Ministry of Government Services. This search will indicate whether the personal property of Searchco is encumbered and subject to the security interests of secured creditors. This search should be conducted in each jurisdiction in Canada (and the United States) in which Searchco owns property or assets.	In Ontario, conducted online directly with the Ontario Companies Branch (by account), Cyberbahn or Oncorp (also by secure Web access), or in person at: Companies and Personal Property Security Branch, Ministry of Government Services, 375 University Avenue, 2nd Floor, Toronto, Ontario. Tel: 416-325-8847 Toll-free: 1-800-267-8847 Fax: 416-325-0487 Available documents: • verbal (uncertified) PPSA printout, and • certified PPSA enquiry response.
4	*Bank Act* (Canada), s. 427	To determine whether any notices of intention to give security have been filed with the Bank of Canada in Ontario (or in any province or territory in Canada) against Searchco pursuant to s. 427 of the *Bank Act* (Canada). This search will indicate whether any banks have taken a security interest in the inventory and/or equipment of Searchco or the individual under s. 427 of the *Bank Act* (Canada).	Conducted online through the Canadian Securities Registration System (by secure Web access) or in person at: Canadian Securities Registration System, 425 University Avenue, 20th Floor, Toronto, Ontario. Tel: 416-204-3000 (Toronto) Toll-free: 1-800-561-1404 (British Columbia) https://bascsrs.et/bashome.nsf/pages/home (secure site)
5	*Bankruptcy and Insolvency Act* (Canada)	To determine whether there is a record of any bankruptcy or insolvency proceedings involving Searchco registered with the Office of the Superintendent of Bankruptcy in Ottawa (which encompasses information for all of Canada) pursuant to the *Bankruptcy and Insolvency Act* (Canada). This search will indicate whether Searchco is or has been bankrupt or whether an assignment, proposal to creditors, or receiving order has been made against it.	Conducted online (by secure Web access) with the Office of the Superintendent of Bankruptcy in Ottawa (by account). Tel: 613-941-2863 https://strategis.ic.gc.ca/sc_mrksv/bankruptcy/bankruptcysearch/engdoc (secure site)
6	*Bulk Sales Act* (Ontario)	To determine whether there are any bulk sales affidavits registered against Searchco in the Superior Court of Justice in each place or municipality where it carries on business pursuant to the *Bulk Sales Act* (Ontario). This search will indicate whether Searchco has made a sale of its stock in bulk out of the usual course of business.	Manually conducted in the Superior Court of Justice in each place or municipality where Searchco carries on business. In Toronto, the address is: 393 University Avenue, 10th Floor, Toronto, Ontario.
7	*Execution Act* (Ontario)	To determine whether there are any writs of execution, extent, or certificates of lien filed against Searchco in the Sheriff's Office in each place or municipality where it carries on business pursuant to the *Execution Act* (Ontario), which affects the real or personal property of Searchco. This search will indicate whether a judgment creditor has filed an execution or writ against Searchco for an unpaid judgment in the Sheriff's Office in the place or municipality where it carries on business	Conducted online (by secure Web access with Teranet) or in person in the Sheriff's Office in each place where the corporation carries on business. In Toronto, the address is: 3rd Floor, Suite 321, Atrium on Bay, 20 Dundas Street West, Toronto, Ontario. Teranet tel: 1-800-208-5263 http://www.teraview.ca

TABLE 2.4 CONTINUED

No.	Search	Why?	Who, where, how?
8	Provincial litigation (Ontario)	To determine whether there are any litigation actions filed in the Superior Court of Justice in Ontario involving Searchco.	Manually conducted at the Superior Court of Justice in the appropriate municipality/place in Ontario. In Toronto, the address is: 393 University Avenue, 10th Floor, Toronto, Ontario.
9	Federal Court	To determine whether there are any litigation actions involving Searchco under a federal statute.	Manually conducted at the Federal Court office in Ottawa and/or in the province where Searchco carries on business.
10	Real property	To determine the status and nature of Searchco's title to real property and whether there are any encumbrances, mortgages, or other charges registered against such real property.	Conducted online (by secure Web access) or manually conducted at the appropriate land registry office (or Land Titles Office) where the real property is located. Teranet tel: 1-800-208-5263 http://www.teraview.ca
11	Goods and services tax (GST)	Unremitted GST is a potential liability that may add to the purchaser's cost of the acquisition of the shares of Searchco.	Written inquiry should be made to the GST Office, Canada Revenue Agency (CRA), Sudbury, Ontario. Tel: 705-671-0541 Fax: 705-671-0405 *Note:* Written consent of Searchco required.
12	Provincial sales tax (PST) remittances	Unremitted PST is a potential liability that may add to the purchaser's cost of the acquisition of the shares of Searchco.	Written request can only be made by Searchco (not by Searchco's solicitor) for a retail sales tax clearance certificate indicating that no Ontario PST is owing. The request should be made to the local Retail Sales Tax Office. The request should include the name and registration number of the vendor, and the closing date of the transaction. In Toronto, the address is: Service Branch, Retail Sales Tax Branch, Ministry of Finance, 5 Park Home Avenue, Suite 200, Toronto, Ontario, M2N 6W8. Tel: 416-222-3226 Fax: 416-218-3738
13	Federal income tax *Income Tax Act* (Canada)	Unremitted income tax is a potential liability that may add to the purchaser's cost of the acquisition of the shares of Searchco.	The purchaser may submit a written request to attend at the local CRA office to confirm that federal tax returns have been filed (and possibly compare returns provided by the target corporation). Tel: 1-800-959-5525 *Note:* Written consent of Searchco is required. Alternatively, written request may be made under the *Access to Information and Privacy Act* (Canada).

TABLE 2.4 CONTINUED

No.	Search	Why?	Who, where, how?
14	Employment insurance, Canada Pension Plan, and income tax remittances (employer's source deductions)	Unremitted source deductions are a potential liability that may add to the purchaser's cost of the acquisition of the shares of Searchco.	The purchaser may submit a written request to visit the local CRA office to compare remittances received with payroll deductions listed in Searchco's accounting records. Tel: 1-800-959-5525 *Note:* Written consent of Searchco is required. Alternatively, written request may be made under the *Access to Information and Privacy Act* (Canada).
15	*Employer Health Tax Act* (Ontario)	Unremitted Ontario employer health tax is a potential liability that may add to the purchaser's cost of the acquisition of the shares of Searchco.	A written request for information may be made to the Regional Office where the business of Searchco is located. Information will be provided if the business account number accompanies the request. Tel: 1-800-263-7965 *Note:* Written consent of Searchco is required.
16	Provincial income tax *Corporations Tax Act* (Ontario)	Unpaid Ontario corporations tax is a liability that may add to the purchaser's cost of the acquisition of the shares of Searchco.	The purchaser may submit a written request for copies of Searchco's tax filings and communications. The address is: Corporations Tax Branch, Ministry of Finance, 33 King Street West, Box 620, Oshawa, Ontario L1H 8E9. Tel: 416-920-9048, ext. 6666 (Toronto) General: 1-800-263-7965 Fax: 905-436-4471 *Note:* Written consent of Searchco is required.
17	Employment and labour		
	Workplace Safety and Insurance Board (Ontario) (WSIB)	A search of the records of the WSIB may be conducted to ensure that Searchco has remitted to the WSIB all required payments.	The WSIB search must be requested by letter to the Assessment Department. The letter should detail exactly what information is required. The address is: 200 Front Street West, Toronto, Ontario M5V 3J1. Tel: 416-344-1007 Fax: 416-344-2707 http://www.wsib.on.ca *Note:* Written consent of Searchco is required.
	Employment Standards Act, 2000 (Ontario) (ESA)	A search of the Ontario Employment Standards Branch may be conducted to ensure that there are no outstanding claims against Searchco under the ESA.	Requests for a search under the ESA should be made under the *Freedom of Information and Protection of Privacy Act* (Ontario): 400 University Avenue, 7th Floor, Toronto, Ontario M7A 1T7. Tel: 416-326-7786 Fax: 416-314-8749 http://www.gov.on.ca/lab

TABLE 2.4 CONTINUED

No.	Search	Why?	Who, where, how?
18	Ontario Ministry of Labour *Occupational Health and Safety Act* (Ontario) (OHSA)	To determine whether all hazardous substances on the site are handled in accordance with the OHSA and to determine whether there are any outstanding orders against the property. The results of the search may be significant to a lender or a prospective purchaser because the cost of complying with any outstanding orders or implementing an appropriate labelling and handling system for hazardous materials could be expensive.	Requests for a search should be made under the *Freedom of Information and Protection of Privacy Act* (Ontario): 400 University Avenue, 7th Floor, Toronto, Ontario M7A 1T7. General inquiry: 416-326-7786 Fax: 416-314-8749 http://www.gov.on.ca/lab
19	Ministry of the Environment (Ontario) (MOE)	All present and previous owners and occupiers of a property are potentially liable for environmental contamination even if they have not caused it or did not know of it. Information available from the District and Regional Offices of the MOE includes: • certificates of approval and pending applications; • orders and/or pending orders; • waste generator registrations; • reports of spills, discharges; • occurrence, investigative, or other MOE reports; • correspondence; • complaints; • material safety data sheets; • PCB storage sites; • waste disposal sites; • waste generation and transportation registrations; • industrial sites producing or using coal tar; • *Ontario Water Resources Act* (OWRA) convictions and pending charges (discharge of waste into water, private sewage systems); and • *Pesticides Act* violations and orders.	Requests for a search should be made under the *Freedom of Information and Protection of Privacy Act* (Ontario): 135 St. Clair Avenue West, Toronto, Ontario M4V 1P5. General inquiry: 416-325-4000 Toll-free: 1-800-565-4923 Fax: 416-325-3159 http://www.ene.gov.on.ca

TABLE 2.4 CONTINUED

No.	Search	Why?	Who, where, how?
20	MOE index of orders and approvals	All present and previous owners and occupiers of a property are potentially liable for environmental contamination even if they have not caused it or did not know of it. Outstanding orders (or lack of certificate of approval) under the *Environmental Protection Act* (Ontario) or the OWRA are potential liabilities for a purchaser of assets or shares. Permits under the OWRA are required for: • withdrawal of water over 50,000 litres/day for purposes other than ordinary household use, and • waste discharge into water using well or sewage works that does not discharge into a sanitary sewer or drainage works.	Requests for a search should be made under the *Freedom of Information and Protection of Privacy Act* (Ontario): 135 St. Clair Avenue West, Toronto, Ontario M4V 1P5. http://www.ene.gov.on.ca
21	MOE investigation reports	To determine whether there are any existing investigations of Searchco by MOE under way.	Requests for a search should be made under the *Freedom of Information and Protection of Privacy Act* (Ontario): 135 St. Clair Avenue West, Toronto, Ontario M4V 1P5. http://www.ene.gov.on.ca
22	Environmental Office, Toronto	The Environmental Office contains a database of historical use of land in Toronto from 1860 to 1991. It is appropriate to determine whether there is possibility of environmental contamination on property located in Toronto.	Requests for information should be directed to City of Toronto, Public Health Environmental Office. Tel: 416-392-6788
23	Municipal health authorities *Health Protection and Promotion Act* (Ontario)	To determine whether any orders have been issued by a municipal health official. A health officer has the authority to order the elimination or decrease in effect of a health hazard. The order can include directions to: • vacate or close a premise, • carry out specified works, or • remove and clean up a health hazard. An order may be made to an owner, occupier, or administrator of a premises. The costs to bring a premises into compliance with an order may be significant.	Requests for information should be directed to Toronto and Mississauga Public Health Units. Toronto: 416-392-7401 Mississauga: 905-791-9400 The search is done according to municipal address, and the request must be in writing with the consent of the party to whom the order pertains. *Note:* Written consent of Searchco is required.
24	Environment Canada *Canadian Environmental Protection Act* (CEPA)	To determine whether there are any prosecutions, proceedings, or outstanding cleanup orders against Searchco. CEPA governs the import and export of toxic substances and hazardous waste materials, specific industries under federal jurisdiction, ocean dumping, and the release of toxic substances set out in the regulations.	Queries should be directed to Environment Canada, Environmental Protection. Tel: 416-973-1055

TABLE 2.4 CONCLUDED

No.	Search	Why?	Who, where, how?
25	Transport Canada Aircraft searches	To obtain particulars of aircraft registered with Transport Canada.	Requests for information should be directed to Transport Canada. *Note:* The Canadian registration number must be provided. Tel: 416-224-3237
26	Canada Shipping Shipping searches	To obtain particulars of ships registered with Canada Shipping.	Requests for information should be directed to: Canada Shipping, 4900 Yonge Street, Suite 300, Toronto, Ontario M2N 6A5, Attention: Donald Powers. Tel: 416-973-8142

due diligence materials, search results, and related corporate information are maintained and stored.

In a typical commercial transaction, an overwhelming volume of paper is generated by the vendor, the purchaser, and the purchaser's legal team of lawyers and law clerks. It is important for the legal team to stay organized; to keep track of what documents they possess, which documents they have or have not examined, and where the documents are stored; and to determine who will be responsible for following up on the outstanding matters.

You should start assembling both the reference binder and the due diligence binder at the onset of the commercial transaction and continue to maintain both binders and file the appropriate documents into each in a systematic and organized manner so that they can be easily accessed by the legal team.

Reference binder

The reference binder could contain the following documents:

1. the corporate information sheet with a brief summary of the corporate information regarding Searchco's directors, officers, issued shareholding, general signing authority, etc.;

2. a copy of all charter documents of Searchco;

3. a copy of all bylaws of Searchco;

4. a copy of any shareholder agreement, unanimous shareholder agreement, or similar agreements;

5. a copy of all extra-provincial licences or permits;

6. a copy of Searchco's financial statements for the last few years;

7. a copy of Searchco's most recent annual report (if any); and

8. a copy of any other pertinent corporate information that may be useful for the legal team to have readily available.

Due diligence binder

Depending on the nature and size of the commercial transaction, the due diligence binder could contain the following documents.

PUBLIC DUE DILIGENCE SEARCHES

Documentation of public corporate/commercial due diligence searches usually includes:

1. an overall summary of the analysis and results of the searches, together with the backup supporting search results; and

2. an overall summary of the analysis and results of any outstanding litigation proceedings.

DUE DILIGENCE REQUEST LIST

The due diligence binder should also include:

1. a list summarizing all documents and other relevant information that the vendor must provide to the purchaser to assist in the legal due diligence

process by the purchaser's legal counsel, as well as background information with respect to the business operations of the vendor; and

2. copies of any relevant correspondence to and from the vendor and/or the vendor's legal counsel with respect to the due diligence request list.

A sample due diligence request list is set out in figure 2.3 at the end of the chapter. Note that the sample list is not intended to be exhaustive. It should only be used as a reference tool and should be customized for each commercial transaction.

CORPORATE REVIEW: CORPORATE RECORDS AND CONTRACTS

In addition, the due diligence binder should contain key documents relating to the corporate review, including:

1. a copy of the memorandum summarizing the law clerk's corporate review of the corporate records of Searchco, together with copies of any backup supporting notes or worksheets ("corporate review memo");

2. copies of any relevant correspondence to and from the vendor and/or the vendor's legal counsel with respect to the corporate review memo;

3. a summary of all material contracts with information about the parties to the contract, the nature of the contract, and any other key provisions; and

4. copies of any internal firm memos prepared by members of the legal team regarding their legal due diligence review of any documents, material contracts, and/or other instruments.

A sample corporate review memo and the backup supporting worksheets are set out in figures 2.4 and 2.5, respectively, at the end of the chapter.

You should ensure that the reference binder and the due diligence binder are kept updated with additional documents and information as they become available and as the commercial transaction progresses up to closing.

CORPORATE REVIEW OF CORPORATE RECORDS

One very important aspect of legal due diligence involves the corporate review of the minute books and related corporate records of Searchco. The nature of the commercial transaction, the form of legal opinion that legal counsel will be required to give, and the covenants, representations, and warranties contained in the commercial agreement will often dictate how extensive or comprehensive the corporate review should be.

Before commencing with a corporate review, you should discuss with the supervising lawyer the details of the corporate review required for the purposes of the commercial transaction. For example, if the corporation has been formed by a series of different amalgamations, it should be determined beforehand whether you should request and review the corporate records of all or any of the predecessor corporations of Searchco.

A corporate review may involve a detailed review and analysis of some or all of the following information:

1. the applicable corporate statutes and regulations that formerly governed and that currently govern Searchco from the date of its formation to the current date (see figure 2.6 at the end of the chapter);

2. all articles of incorporation, amendment, or amalgamation, restated articles of incorporation, articles of arrangement, articles of continuance, articles of reorganization, articles of revival, letters patent, supplementary letters patent, special Acts, and any other instrument by which a corporation is incorporated (collectively, "the charter documents");

3. the minute books of Searchco (which include, without limitation, all bylaws, directors' and shareholders' resolutions and minutes, directors' registers, shareholders' registers, share transfer registers and shareholders' ledgers, share warrants, and share certificate books); and

4. all shareholder agreements (which include unanimous shareholder agreements), voting trust agreements, pledge agreements, stock option agreements, and any other agreements to which Searchco may be a party or bound.

(Items 2, 3, and 4 above are collectively referred to as "the corporate records.")

Scope of the corporate review in a share purchase transaction

Generally, in a share purchase transaction, it is critical to conduct a comprehensive and thorough corporate review of the corporate records in order to confirm, among other things, the validity of the share issuances and transfers and the election of directors. This form of corporate review is similar to conducting a chain of title search when searching title to real property. It is necessary to carefully trace through the share ownership of Searchco, back to the date of its incorporation, to ensure that all of its issued shares have validly flowed through to the current shareholders. As a result, if Searchco was formed by amalgamation, the corporate review should involve not only a detailed review of the corporate records of Searchco, but also a detailed review of the corporate records of the predecessor corporations, right back to their original formation.

In addition to the corporate review of Searchco's corporate records, it is also advisable to request and obtain the corporate records of every subsidiary corporation of Searchco, if any, and to conduct a similar corporate review of each subsidiary's corporate records.

Scope of the corporate review in an asset purchase transaction

The corporate review of the corporate records of Searchco in an asset purchase transaction may not need to be as comprehensive or extensive as the corporate review in a share purchase transaction. A careful corporate review should be conducted of Searchco's corporate records to confirm the incumbency of the directors and officers. However, subject to the nature of the legal opinion being given and the covenants, representations, and warranties being given by Searchco, it may not be necessary to conduct the corporate review of corporate records behind any amalgamation of Searchco. The corporate review should also disclose whether there are any restrictions in the articles, bylaws, or agreements to which Searchco is a party or by which it is bound that may restrict its powers to sell its assets or to perform its obligations under the asset purchase agreement.

Scope of the corporate review in a secured financing transaction

The corporate review of the corporate records of a borrower in a secured financing transaction is similar to the corporate review necessary in an asset purchase transaction to confirm the incumbency of the directors and officers. In addition, however, the corporate review in a secured financing transaction should disclose whether there are any restrictions on the borrowing authority of the borrower in the articles, bylaws, or agreements to which the borrower is a party or by which it is bound that may conflict with or restrict it from entering into the loan agreement with the lender and completing the financing contemplated by the agreement. You should note whether there are any loan agreements, security agreements, promissory notes, or other evidence of indebtedness disclosed as part of the corporate review that may affect the borrower's ability to fulfill its obligations to the lender under the loan agreement.

Purpose of the corporate review

Generally, the purpose of a corporate review is to confirm the validity of key matters regarding incorporation and powers, directors, and authorized and issued share capital of Searchco, including those detailed below.

INCORPORATION AND POWERS

The corporate review should:

1. verify the incorporation, organization, and existence of Searchco under the laws of the home jurisdiction of incorporation and under its charter documents;

2. determine whether there are any restrictions on the power, authority, or capacity of Searchco to own its assets and property and to carry on its business;

3. confirm that Searchco is authorized to enter into the commercial agreement and fulfill its obligations under the agreement; and

4. confirm that Searchco's bylaws have been validly enacted.

DIRECTORS

The corporate review should verify that:

1. Searchco's board of directors has been duly constituted; and

2. the provisions regarding the election, resignation, removal, and qualification of directors of Searchco are valid.

AUTHORIZED AND ISSUED SHARE CAPITAL

The corporate review should confirm:

1. the authorized share capital of Searchco;

2. that all issuances, transfers, redemptions, dispositions, conversions, subdivisions, and/or consolidations of the issued share capital of Searchco are in compliance with the applicable provisions or restrictions contained in Searchco's charter documents, any shareholder agreement, the governing statute at the particular time, and any other agreement that may affect the ability of the directors or the shareholders of Searchco to approve share transactions; and

3. that the share certificate books, minute book registers, and ledgers are accurate and complete up to the date of the corporate review.

A detailed summary of the information that you should consider and look for when conducting a corporate review of the corporate records is set out in figure 2.7 at the end of the chapter.

Preparing for the corporate review

Once the scope of the corporate review has been determined, you should obtain and assemble all the necessary documents and materials before commencing with the corporate review. Table 2.5 lists the documents and materials you will need to conduct the corporate review.

TABLE 2.5 CORPORATE REVIEW DOCUMENTS AND MATERIALS

No.	Document/material
1	All applicable relevant corporate statutes and regulations affecting Searchco that were in force during the period of existence of Searchco from the date of incorporation to the present (see figure 2.6)
2	All charter documents (obtained from the minute book and compared against copies obtained from and on the public files with the appropriate government authority)
3	All minute books
4	All bylaws
5	All share certificate books and share certificates (including issued and cancelled share certificates)
6	Any shareholder agreements or voting trust agreements
7	Any share pledge agreements or security agreements
8	Any share option agreements, share warrants, rights of first refusal, purchase plans, or other agreements granting a right with respect to the purchase or other acquisition of shares of Searchco
9	All extra-provincial licences, registrations, and permits from all jurisdictions in which Searchco is registered or licensed to carry on business (or, if Searchco is not so registered, a list of all such jurisdictions in which it carries on business)
10	All government notice filings and any other publicly filed documents including profile report, document list, microfiche, business names list, etc.

Special requirements for public corporations

There are special requirements for reviewing the corporate records of public corporations. In addition to documents and materials needed for the corporate review of corporate records of a non-offering corporation, you should request and review the materials shown in table 2.6 when reviewing the corporate records of a public or distributing corporation.

RECORDING THE CORPORATE REVIEW

After you have conducted a comprehensive corporate review of the corporate records of Searchco (and of any subsidiary corporation, as applicable), you should summarize the results of the corporate review in a memorandum to the supervising lawyer.

Corporate review memo

The corporate review memo should include the following items:

1. the purpose and scope of the corporate review;
2. the materials reviewed as part of the corporate review;
3. the results of the corporate review and the identification of corporate deficiencies and outstanding corporate matters; and
4. suggestions for rectification or curative actions to be taken.

Guidelines

It is critical that you make detailed written notes in the course of the corporate review and in tracing the corporate history of the corporation. Generally, the corporate review in a commercial transaction should focus on the validity of the issuance and transfer of shares of the corporation and the election of directors; whether they are all in compliance with the applicable governing statutes in force as of the material dates; and the bylaws and any shareholder agreements in force as of those dates.

You should identify any corporate deficiencies that are discovered in the course of the review and make suggestions for corrective or remedial action to be taken. You should also note all material transactions or contracts that are contained in or referred to in the corporate records, as well as any other significant or extraordinary matters. The corporate review may disclose information or contracts not previously known to legal counsel, and it may be appropriate to add that information to the due diligence request list.

The sample corporate review memo (figure 2.4) and backup supporting worksheets (figure 2.5) at the end of the chapter may be useful in recording the results of the review. Note that the information set out in the sample memo is not exhaustive or comprehensive. You should use discretion in determining what other matters should be raised or identified in the corporate review memo as part of the corporate review.

TABLE 2.6   ADDITIONAL CORPORATE REVIEW DOCUMENTS AND MATERIALS — PUBLIC CORPORATION

No.	Document	Comments
1	Stock option plans for senior executives and for employees	Each stock option plan and all amendments should be approved by board resolution and the appropriate number of shares reserved and set aside for option grants.
		Record the following information when reviewing stock option plans:
		• date option granted,
		• number of optioned shares,
		• exercise price per share, and
		• date of expiry of stock option.
		Note: If the option holder has not exercised the stock option by the expiry date, the allotted shares are returned to treasury.
2	Employee share ownership plan (ESOP)	The ESOP should be approved by board resolution.
		Record the following information when reviewing the ESOP:
		• date of establishment of the ESOP,
		• rights under the ESOP, and
		• all shares issued under the ESOP.
3	Listing on exchange(s)	Confirm that the listing agreement has been approved by board resolution and indicate where and when Searchco has been listed.
4	Transfer agent	Identify the transfer agent and note the transfer agent's particulars. Confirm that the appointment of the transfer agent has been properly documented by board resolution.
5	Prospectuses	
	• Preliminary prospectus	The preliminary prospectus should be approved by board resolution.
	• Final prospectus	The final prospectus should be approved by board resolution.
	• Underwriting agreement	The underwriting agreement should be approved by board resolution, together with the issuance to the underwriter of the shares for distribution to the public pursuant to the prospectus.
6	Share warrants	The form of share warrant should be approved by board resolution together with the issuance of the share warrants.
		Record the number of share warrants issued and the particulars thereof.
7	Private placements	Confirm that any private placement of shares has been approved by board resolution and note the number of shares issued as part of the private placement.
8	Takeover bids	Record the particulars of any takeover bid.
9	Committees	Record particulars of all committees established and approved by the board, and review the minutes of each committee.
	• Executive	
	• Audit	*Note:* Public corporations are required to have an audit committee.
	• Compensation	
10	Senior management remuneration	Record the remuneration of senior management and confirm whether there is liability insurance coverage. Also record any authorized executive compensation plans such as annual salary, bonus, and/or long-term stock options.

TABLE 2.6 CONCLUDED

No.	Document	Comments
11	Annual meeting materials	Review the following supporting documents in connection with an annual meeting of shareholders: • notice calling the annual meeting, • form of proxy, • information circular, • confirmation of mailing, • minutes of board and annual shareholder meetings and particulars of resolutions passed, and • scrutineer's report confirming quorum.
12	Material contracts	Record the particulars of all material contracts disclosed in minute books, including date, parties, and a brief description of each contract. Also record whether any directors have disclosed an interest in any contract.
13	Escrowed shares pursuant to escrow agreement	Record the particulars of any escrow agreement, including date of agreement, name of escrow agent, number of shares deposited with escrow agent, and terms of release of escrowed shares.
14	Shareholder rights plan	Record the particulars of any shareholder rights plan, including date of issuance, components of "rights offering," and date exercisable.
15	Dividend policy	When reviewing any prospectus of Searchco, confirm whether it contains a statement regarding the dividend policy.

Reconciliation of share certificates

In addition to the other matters covered in the corporate review, in a share purchase transaction it is important to know the whereabouts of the issued share certificates so that they may be surrendered for cancellation on closing. Therefore, it is prudent to reconcile the cancelled and issued share certificates, to ensure that the cancelled share certificates have been duly endorsed for transfer on the reverse or otherwise surrendered for cancellation, and to ensure that all share certificates issued by Searchco have been accounted for.

CORRECTIVE OR REMEDIAL ACTION

Once you have completed the corporate review and finalized the corporate review memo, you should discuss with the supervising lawyer the nature and significance of each of the significant corporate deficiencies disclosed in the memo. In particular, you should consider the potential impact on the commercial transaction and on the form of legal opinion required to be given as part of the transaction. You should then agree on the suggested corrective action to be taken to address and rectify each of the significant corporate deficiencies and outstanding corporate matters.

Depending on the extent, nature, and complexity of the deficiencies identified in the corporate review memo, a number of different means of corrective or remedial action should be considered.

Passage of rectification resolutions

Ideally, if the current board of directors of Searchco has been validly and properly elected and the current shareholders hold valid title to the shares registered in their name, as disclosed by the review of the corporate records, corporate deficiencies may be rectified and outstanding corporate matters may be addressed by the passage of a corporate resolution. It may be appropriate for a joint omnibus resolution to be passed by the current directors and shareholders and for each of the specific corporate deficiencies and outstanding corporate matters to be addressed and rectified. It would also be useful to set out in the same joint rectification resolutions the current corporate structure of Searchco, and for the structure to be approved, ratified, and confirmed by the current directors and shareholders. Approval of the structure effectively creates a "fresh" starting point and clarifies, on a going-forward basis, the corporate structure of Searchco. Sample joint rectification resolutions are set out in figure 2.8 at the end of the chapter.

Statutory declaration

If one of the current directors or officers of Searchco has been associated with the corporation for a number of years, particularly during the period when significant corporate deficiencies occurred, it may be appropriate to have that person make a statutory declaration, to the best of his or her knowledge, belief, and recollection, on the basis of his or her review of the internal files and records, financial statements, and any other relevant documents of Searchco, as to what corporate action, steps, and/or resolutions were intended to have been taken or passed as of the material dates.

Similarly, if the minute books and corporate records of Searchco have been lost or misplaced and cannot be located, it may be appropriate to have a long-time director or officer make a statutory declaration confirming, to the best of his or her knowledge, belief, and recollection, the corporate structure of the corporation. The persons identified as the directors and shareholders of Searchco should then be able to rely on the declaration, and could pass a joint omnibus resolution confirming the corporate structure. A statutory declaration would be particularly useful if the directors and shareholders were not associated with Searchco when the corporate deficiencies arose. A sample statutory declaration is included in figure 2.8 at the end of the chapter.

Court order

Both the CBCA and the OBCA permit a corporation or a shareholder of a corporation or any aggrieved person to apply to the court for an order to rectify certain registers or records if the name of a person is alleged to be, or to have been, wrongly entered or retained in or wrongly deleted or omitted from the registers or other records of the corporation. Pursuant to such an application, the court may make an order requiring that the registers or other records of the corporation be rectified as it deems fit.

Corrected certificate

OBCA s. 275 provides that an application for a corrected certificate may be made to the Ontario Director in respect of an error contained in any document filed. However, the error must be on the face of the document, must be a clerical error, or must relate to provisions in the articles that do not conform to the OBCA. The Ontario Companies Branch has provided in its Companies Branch Requirements publication of April 3, 2000 some examples of circumstances that may warrant a corrected certificate.

CBCA s. 265 confers more discretionary authority on the federal Director than OBCA s. 275 does on the Ontario Director. CBCA s. 265 provides that if the federal Director is satisfied that a correction of an error in articles, a notice, a certificate, or other document would not prejudice any of the shareholders or creditors of the corporation, the Director may correct the document. Corporation Canada's *Policy Statement 2.7* provides that where the error is obvious from the certificate itself, the Director will make the correction as requested (subject to the return of the original certificate and replacement pages, where applicable, and, if the Director deems fit, an accompanying declaration to the effect that the certificate has not yet been used or relied on). For further discussion of the procedure to obtain a corrected certificate, see the companion to this text, Elizabeth Gillis's *Advanced Corporate Legal Procedures*, chapter 13.

KEY TERMS

due diligence
SEDAR

REFERENCES

Statutes

Business Corporations Act (Ontario) (OBCA), RSO 1990, c. B.16, as amended.

Canada Business Corporations Act (CBCA), RSC 1985, c. C-44, as amended.

Corporations Information Act (Ontario) (CIA), RSO 1990, c. C.39, as amended.

Securities Act (Ontario), RSO 1990, c. S.5, as amended.

Other sources

Gillis, Elizabeth A., *Advanced Corporate Legal Procedures* (Toronto: Emond Montgomery, 2004).

Industry Canada, Corporations Canada, "Policy on Correction of CBCA Certificates and Articles," *Policy Statement 2.7*, March 1, 1996.

Ontario Ministry of Government Services, Companies and Personal Property Security Branch, *Corrected Certificate (Business Corporations)*, April 3, 2000.

FORMS AND PRECEDENTS

Figure 2.1: Sample corporate history chart

Figure 2.2: Corporate/commercial search report

Figure 2.3: Due diligence request list

Figure 2.4: Memorandum reporting on corporate review

Figure 2.5: Worksheets for corporate review, including corporate information sheet, register of directors, register of officers, register of shareholders, register of share transfers, reconciliation of share certificates, bylaws, annual proceedings, and material contracts

Figure 2.6: Federal and Ontario corporate legislation

Figure 2.7: Conducting a corporate review — What to look for

Figure 2.8: Sample rectification documents, including resolutions of the directors and shareholders and statutory declaration

REVIEW QUESTIONS

1. Your firm's client, Joe Smith ("the vendor"), proposes to enter into a share purchase agreement with ABCDEF Corporation ("the purchaser") to sell to the purchaser 100 common shares in the capital of GHIJKL Inc. ("Targetco") registered in the name of the vendor ("purchased shares") at the aggregate purchase price of $100,000. The purchase price is to be payable by the purchaser as follows: $60,000 in cash on the closing date with the balance of the purchase price to be paid in full on or before the second anniversary of the closing date.

    The vendor is a resident Canadian who resides in Toronto, Ontario. The registered office address of both the purchaser and Targetco is Hamilton, Ontario. The principal place of business of Targetco is Mississauga, Ontario.

    a. Would you conduct any public searches against the vendor? If so, what searches would you conduct and why?

b. Would you conduct any public searches against the purchaser? If so, what searches would you conduct and why?

c. Would you conduct any public searches against Targetco? If so, what searches would you conduct and why?

d. Where would you conduct the following searches against Targetco?
- *Bulk Sales Act*
- *Bank Act*, s. 427
- *Execution Act*
- litigation

2. Would you ever conduct any due diligence searches against the directors or shareholders of a corporation? If yes, why? If no, why not?

3. Your corporate searches against the vendor in a share purchase transaction have disclosed that the vendor was formed by a series of amalgamations and that the vendor had former and predecessor names as well as French forms of names. As well, the vendor has current registered business names as well as expired registered business names.

a. List all the names of the vendor against which you would conduct your due diligence searches.

b. Should current and expired business names of the vendor be included in your due diligence searches?

c. List the due diligence searches you would conduct against all names of the vendor.

4. The legal name of the borrower in a secured financing transaction is Samuel William Smith; however, you have been advised that it is possible that the borrower is also known as S. William Smith, Bill Smith, Billy Smith, Will Smith, and Samuel Smith. Against which name(s) should you conduct your due diligence searches? Why?

5. What is the purpose of conducting a corporate review of the minute books of a closely held target corporation (whose shares are being sold by the vendor to the purchaser) in a share purchase transaction?

FIGURE 2.1 SAMPLE CORPORATE HISTORY CHART

Acme Incorporated

Former name:
221376 Alberta Inc.

Alberta corporation number:
221376

Continued from Alberta
on March 1, 2000

Acme Incorporated
Date of continuance:
March 1, 2000
Jurisdiction: Ontario
Ontario corporation number: 128365

PREDECESSOR

Brackin Construction Inc.
Former name:
Eden Construction Inc.
Incorporation date: March 17, 1995
Jurisdiction: Ontario
Ontario corporation number: 120268
PREDECESSOR

Smith Construction Inc.
Incorporation date:
April 30, 1978
Jurisdiction: Ontario
Ontario corporation number: 63085

PREDECESSOR

Amalgamated on February 28, 1997

ABC Corporation
Date of incorporation:
January 20, 1980
Jurisdiction: Ontario
Ontario corporation number: 117456

PREDECESSOR

**Brackin Smith
Construction Inc.**
Date of amalgamation:
February 28, 1997
Jurisdiction: Ontario
Ontario corporation number: 120008
PREDECESSOR

Amalgamated on December 1, 2001

ABC Corporation
Date of amalgamation: December 1, 2001
Jurisdiction: Ontario
Ontario corporation number: 1336748
Registered business name: ABC
CURRENT

Note: Corporate searches conducted on September 1, 2005.

FIGURE 2.2   CORPORATE/COMMERCIAL SEARCH REPORT

NAME OF LAW FIRM

CORPORATE/COMMERCIAL SEARCH REPORT

Name: ABC Corporation
Former Name: DEF Corporation

A.   **CORPORATE**

❏   *Business Corporations Act* **(Ontario) and** *Corporations Information Act* **(Ontario)**

❏   *Canada Business Corporations Act*

Date of Search: _____
Jurisdiction: _____

We conducted a corporate search of the records of the Companies and Personal Property Security Branch of the Ontario Ministry of Government Services (**or Industry Canada,** as the case may be). Attached is a copy of the Corporation Profile Report for the Corporation which was produced by the indicated government authority on the above-noted date.

B.   *PERSONAL PROPERTY SECURITY ACT* **("PPSA") (ONTARIO)**

(a)   **Corporation - Current Name**

Date of Search: _____
Currency Date: _____

❏   The certified PPSA enquiry response, with information current to the currency date, which was obtained with respect to the Corporation under its current name disclosed no registrations made under the former *Corporation Securities Registration Act* (Ontario) and the following families of registrations filed under the PPSA which appear to affect the Corporation under its current name.

File No.	Debtor	Secured Party	Registration No.	Expiry Date	General Collateral Description

(b)   **Corporation - Former Name**

Date of Search: _____
Currency Date: _____

❏   The certified PPSA enquiry response, with information current to the currency date, which was obtained with respect to the Corporation under its former name disclosed no registrations made

---

FIGURE 2.2 CONTINUED

under the former *Corporation Securities Registration Act* (Ontario) and the following families of registrations filed under the PPSA which appear to affect the Corporation under its former name:

File No.	Debtor	Secured Party	Registration No.	Expiry Date	General Collateral Description

C.   *S.427 BANK ACT* (CANADA)

(a)   **Corporation - Current Name**

Date of Search: _____
Currency Date: _____

❏   Our search disclosed no record of any Notices of Intention to Give Security under s.427 of the *Bank Act* (Canada) registered in the Bank of Canada in the Province of Ontario affecting the Corporation under its current name up to the currency date.

OR

❏   Our search disclosed the following Notice of Intention to Give Security under s.427 of the *Bank Act* (Canada) registered in the Bank of Canada in the Province of Ontario affecting the Corporation under its current name up to the currency date:

Name & Address of Bank: _____
Date: _____
Number: _____

(b)   **Corporation - Former Name**

Date of Search: _____
Currency Date: _____

❏   Our search disclosed no record of any Notices of Intention to Give Security under s.427 of the *Bank Act* (Canada) registered in the Bank of Canada in the Province of Ontario affecting the Corporation under its former name up to the currency date.

OR

❏   Our search disclosed the following Notice of Intention to Give Security under s.427 of the *Bank Act* (Canada) registered in the Bank of Canada in the Province of Ontario affecting the Corporation under its former name up to the currency date:

Name & Address of Bank: _____
Date: _____
Number: _____

FIGURE 2.2 CONTINUED

D.   *BANKRUPTCY AND INSOLVENCY ACT* (CANADA)

(a)   **Corporation - Current Name**

Date of Search: _____
Currency Date: _____

❑   Our search with the Office of the Superintendent of Bankruptcy at Ottawa (which encompasses information for all of Canada) disclosed no record of any bankruptcy or insolvency proceedings involving the Corporation under its current name up to the currency date.

OR

❑   Our search with the Office of the Superintendent of Bankruptcy at Ottawa (which encompasses information for all of Canada) disclosed the following bankruptcy or insolvency proceeding involving the Corporation under its current name up to the currency date:

[insert particulars from Insolvency Search Report]

(b)   **Corporation - Former Name**

Date of Search: _____
Currency Date: _____

❑   Our search with the Office of the Superintendent of Bankruptcy at Ottawa (which encompasses information for all of Canada) disclosed no record of any bankruptcy or insolvency proceedings involving the Corporation under its former name up to the currency date.

OR

❑   Our search with the Office of the Superintendent of Bankruptcy at Ottawa (which encompasses information for all of Canada) disclosed the following bankruptcy or insolvency proceeding involving the Corporation under its former name up to the currency date:

[insert particulars from Insolvency Search Report]

E.   *BULK SALES ACT* (ONTARIO)

(a)   **Corporation - Current Name**

Place of Search: City of Toronto
Date of Search: _____
Currency Date: _____

❑   Our search disclosed no Bulk Sales Affidavits registered with the Superior Court of Justice in the City of Toronto affecting the Corporation under its current name up to the currency date.

OR

❑   Our search disclosed the following Bulk Sales Affidavit registered with the Superior Court of Justice in the City of Toronto affecting the Corporation under its current name up to the currency date:

[insert particulars of Bulk Sales Affidavit filed]

FIGURE 2.2 CONTINUED

(b)   **Corporation - Former Name**

Place of Search: City of Toronto
Date of Search: _____
Currency Date: _____

❏   Our search disclosed no Bulk Sales Affidavits registered with the Superior Court of Justice in the City of Toronto affecting the Corporation under its former name up to the currency date.

OR

❏   Our search disclosed the following Bulk Sales Affidavit registered with the Superior Court of Justice in the City of Toronto affecting the Corporation under its former name up to the currency date:

        [insert particulars of Bulk Sales Affidavit filed]

F.   *EXECUTION ACT* **(ONTARIO)**

(a)   **Corporation - Current Name**

Place of Search: City of Toronto
Date of Certificate: _____

❏   The certificate obtained from the Sheriff at Land Titles in the City of Toronto disclosed no Writs of Execution, Extent or Certificates of Lien affecting the real or personal property of the Corporation under its current name up to the date of the certificate.

OR

❏   The certificate obtained from the Sheriff at Land Titles in the City of Toronto disclosed the following Writ of Execution, Extent or Certificate of Lien affecting the real or personal property of the Corporation under its current name up to the date of the certificate:

        File No.   _____
        In Favour of: _____
        Amount: _____
        Date: _____

(b)   **Corporation - Former Name**

Place of Search: City of Toronto
Date of Certificate: _____

❏   The certificate obtained from the Sheriff at Land Titles in the City of Toronto disclosed no Writs of Execution, Extent or Certificates of Lien affecting the real or personal property of the Corporation under its former name up to the date of the certificate.

OR

FIGURE 2.2   CONCLUDED

❏ The certificate obtained from the Sheriff at Land Titles in the City of Toronto disclosed the following Writ of Execution, Extent or Certificate of Lien affecting the real or personal property of the Corporation under its former name up to the date of the certificate:

File No.   _____

In Favour of: _____

Amount: _____

Date: _____

Note: The above-noted search results are subject to the accuracy of the information provided by the relevant government authority.

FIGURE 2.3 DUE DILIGENCE REQUEST LIST

DUE DILIGENCE REQUEST LIST

A.   Corporate and Background Information

1   Intercorporate organizational chart illustrating all related, affiliated, and subsidiary companies of the Corporation

2   Description of Corporation's business operations

3   Press releases, articles, brochures, and other marketing materials issued by the Corporation

4   Particulars of each jurisdiction in which the Corporation owns property, leases property, has employees, or otherwise carries on business, including all jurisdictions where the Corporation is licensed or qualified to do business

5   Particulars of all executive officers, directors, and senior employees of the Corporation and each of its subsidiaries, and of the auditor of the Corporation

6   List of all business names or assumed names under which the Corporation carries on business or has carried on business

B.   Real Property

7   Real property documents including deeds, title surveys, leases, subleases, appraisals, or valuations of real property owned or leased by the Corporation or by its subsidiaries

8   Mortgages, deeds of trust, leasehold mortgages, or any other charges or encumbrances in respect of the real property

9   List of expropriation orders pending or threatened against the real property

10   Security interests, liens, and encumbrances

11   Zoning and building codes

12   Description of current use of real property owned or leased by the Corporation

C.   Personal Property

13   Schedule of all machinery, equipment, vehicles, and other tangible personal property owned by the Corporation and particulars of any contracts, agreements, and commitments relating to personal property and copies of documents of title in respect thereof

14   List of inventory of the business of the Corporation as of the most recent available date

15   Schedule of all warehouses or other locations where assets of the Corporation are stored

16   Details of any security interests granted by the Corporation with respect to tangible personal property, including liens and encumbrances

D.   Intellectual Property

17   List of all trademarks and trade names owned by or licensed to the Corporation, all copyrights of the Corporation, agreements with respect to patented or unpatented information, and all patents and industrial design registrations and all related applications of the Corporation

FIGURE 2.3 CONTINUED

DUE DILIGENCE REQUEST LIST

18 Particulars of any infringement of any third-party rights, or claim of such infringement, in connection with any intellectual property owned by the Corporation

19 Any agreements between employees of the Corporation and any third person requiring such employee to assign any interest in inventions or trade secrets or to keep any trade secrets confidential or containing any prohibition or competition or solicitation of customers

20 All licences held by the Corporation (details of parties, term, renewal/termination rights, assignability provisions, etc.)

E. Material Contracts to Which the Corporation or a Subsidiary Is a Party

21 Significant supply contracts, sales contracts with third parties, and equipment and service lease agreements

22 Any agreements for the sale of any assets out of the ordinary course of business and any agreements that cannot be cancelled without penalty within 30 days

23 Insurance policies (property, auto, liability, directors and officers, key-man, etc.), management service, consulting, or any other similar contracts

24 Any contracts or instruments that materially and adversely affect the business practices, operations, or condition of the Corporation or any of its subsidiaries or any of their respective assets or property

25 Any contracts, agreements, or documents with a director, officer, or shareholder of the Corporation

26 All agreements, contracts, or commitments that might reasonably be expected to have a potential adverse impact on the business or operations of the Corporation or any of its subsidiaries including any contracts, instruments, judgments, or decrees that materially and adversely affect the business practices, operations, or condition of the Corporation or any of its subsidiaries or any of the assets or property of the Corporation or any of its subsidiaries

27 Any other material contract or agreement requiring the consent of a third party to the proposed commercial transaction or any agreement as to which a default may occur as a result of the proposed transaction

28 Any other document or information that is significant with respect to the business of the Corporation or that should be considered and reviewed in order to disclose the business of the Corporation and financial condition to prospective investors

F. Intellectual Property

29 Particulars of all institutional loans and lines of credit (including names of lenders, facility, amounts authorized, principal amounts outstanding, interest rates, security given, etc.)

30 List of all intercorporate and related-party loans, guarantees made by the Corporation or by its directors, officers, or shareholders

31 Copies of all agreements and documents relating to loans and other credit arrangements

FIGURE 2.3 CONCLUDED

DUE DILIGENCE REQUEST LIST

G. Litigation and Governmental Regulation

32   Particulars of parties, nature of litigation proceedings, amounts claimed, current status, date of commencement, relief sought, and any legal opinions rendered concerning any active, pending, or threatened actions, including civil suits, criminal actions involving the Corporation, any of its subsidiaries, or any of the directors, officers, or employees

33   Copies of all court orders, judgments, settlement agreements, and other agreements to which the Corporation is a party or by which it is bound

34   Any permits or licences issued by any governmental body and a summary of all such permits or licences that the Corporation should have but does not

H. Federal and Tax

35   Copies of federal, provincial, and foreign tax returns filed by the Corporation

36   All audited and/or unaudited financial statements of the Corporation (including consolidated financial statements) including balance sheets, income statements, and statements of changes in financial position

37   List of all fixed assets of the Corporation and its subsidiaries together with any depreciation schedule

I. Labour and Employee Matters

38   List of all employees of the Corporation and particulars of their respective employment histories and terms of employment, duties and responsibilities, salaries, etc., and copies of employment agreements, consulting agreements, and confidentiality agreements

39   Copies of all employee manuals and other documents relevant to employment policies and practices

40   All collective bargaining agreements and related agreements with any labour organization or union

41   Copies of any labour relations board complaints or court proceedings, investigations, claims, grievances, or arbitrations involving the Corporation in the past 5 years with respect to employment or labour matters

J. Pension and Labour Information

42   Copies of all agreements, contracts, or commitments relating to the employment of any person by the Corporation or any subsidiary, including, without limitation, employee benefit plans, deferred compensation plans, profit-sharing plans, employee stock purchase plans, stock option plans, life insurance programs, severance pay plans, and executive compensation

FIGURE 2.4   SAMPLE MEMORANDUM REPORTING ON CORPORATE REVIEW

MEMORANDUM

TO: _____

FROM: _____

DATE: _____

RE: Corporate Review of ABC Corporation (the "Corporation")

_____

A.   CORPORATE REVIEW

Further to your instructions of _____, on _____ I completed my corporate review of the corporate records of the Corporation. In this connection, please note the following:

B.   PURPOSE AND SCOPE OF REVIEW

You have asked me to confirm the validity of the issued and outstanding common shares in the capital of the Corporation, which shares are being purchased by our client pursuant to a share purchase agreement, as well as the validity of the election of directors. As part of this corporate review, you have also asked me to identify any corporate deficiencies which may need to be rectified prior to the closing of this share purchase transaction and to list any and all material transactions or contracts disclosed in the minute books as part of this review.

C.   MATERIALS REVIEWED

In support of the corporate review of the corporate records of the Corporation, I reviewed the following:

(a)   Two minute books of the Corporation (which cover the period from _____ to _____);

(b)   One share certificate book for the common shares and preference shares of the Corporation;

(c)   Ontario Corporation Profile Report in respect of the Corporation which was produced by the Ministry of Government Services ("**Ontario Ministry**") on _____;

(d)   Ontario Corporate Document List in respect of the Corporation which was produced by the Ontario Ministry on _____; and

(e)   Charter documents copied from the microfiche in respect of the Corporation which was obtained from the Ontario Ministry on _____.

For your reference, the above-noted materials accompany this memorandum.

D.   RESULTS OF CORPORATE REVIEW

Based on my corporate review of the corporate records of the Corporation, I note the following:

1.   **Board of Directors**: The current directors of the Corporation have been properly elected and they are as follows:

Name of Director	Date of First Election	Resident Canadian Status

FIGURE 2.4 CONTINUED

2. **Officers**: The current officers of the Corporation have been properly appointed to the indicated offices and they are as follows:

Office Held	Name	Date of First Appointment

3. **Issued and Outstanding Shares**: Subject to verification that the aggregate subscription prices have been paid in full to the Corporation, the _____ common shares and the _____ preference shares in the capital of the Corporation have been properly issued to the following persons as fully paid and non-assessable:

Shareholder	No. & Class of Shares	Agg. Consideration	Share Cert.
		$	
		$	
		$	

Sample Deficiency

*Note: Each shareholder has signed a proxy, dated November 5, 2001, designating _____ as its nominee to attend and act on its behalf at shareholders' meetings; **PROVIDED**, however, that the proxy is only exercisable in the event of default by the shareholder pursuant to a Stock Pledge Agreement dated as of _____ between each shareholder and _____. This proxy is irrevocable and may only be cancelled upon satisfaction of the conditions set out in paragraph _____ of the Stock Pledge Agreement. There is no notation in the share records or anywhere else in the corporate records of the Corporation which reflect the pledge of any of the issued shares pursuant the Stock Pledge Agreement.

Suggested Action: We should request a copy of this Stock Pledge Agreement to determine the terms and particulars of the share pledge.

4. **Share Transfers**: All share transfers have been properly approved in compliance with the share transfer restrictions contained in the articles of the Corporation.

5. **Reconciliation of Share Certificates**: All old share certificates have been marked **CANCELLED**, have been duly endorsed for transfer on their respective reverse sides and are filed in the share certificate books of the Corporation. The share registers and ledgers confirm the old share certificates that had been issued as well as the share certificate numbers of the currently issued and outstanding share certificates, as more particularly identified in Item 3 above.

Sample Deficiency

Please note my comments in Items 3 and 16 of this memo. I confirm that none of the issued share certificates are filed in the share certificate books and, accordingly, we should follow-up with the client soon to ascertain the status and whereabouts of these outstanding share certificates.

FIGURE 2.4 CONTINUED

6. **Minute Book Registers and Ledgers**: All minute book registers and ledgers with respect to the changes in the directors, officers, issued common shares and issued preference shares are complete and accurately reflect the corporate information contained in the minute books.

7. **Annual Proceedings**: The Corporation is up to date in conducting its annual proceedings. The last annual proceedings were conducted on _____ to approve the financial statements of the Corporation for the financial year ended _____.

8. **By-laws**: All the by-laws of the Corporation have properly been made by the directors and confirmed by the shareholders. The following are all the by-laws of the Corporation:

By-law Number	Nature of By-law	Date Made by Directors	Date Confirmed by Shareholders

9. **Charter Documents**: I have compared the copies of all the charter documents of the Corporation filed in the minute books against the copies obtained from the microfiche of the Corporation and they are identical. Each of the charter documents has been properly authorized and approved by special resolution duly passed by the shareholders of the Corporation. The charter documents of the Corporation are comprised of the following:

Charter Document	Nature of Charter Document	Effective Date	Date Authorized by Shareholders

10. **Signed Corporate Resolutions and Meetings**: Except as set out in Item 15 below, all other corporate resolutions contained in the minute books of the Corporation have been originally signed by all the directors and shareholders of the Corporation as of the respective dates that they were passed. There is no information in the minute books which seem to indicate that any corporate proceedings had been conducted by way of board meetings or shareholders' meetings.

11. **No Extra-Provincial Registrations**: There is no evidence in the Corporation's minute books that the Corporation is licensed or registered to carry on business in any province outside the Province of Ontario. The information in the minute books seems to support the search assistant's NIL search results that there is no record on the public government files indicating that the Corporation is registered to carry on business in any jurisdiction outside the Province of Ontario.

12. **No Shareholders' Agreement**: There is no evidence in the Corporation's minute books that the shareholders have entered into any shareholders' agreement with respect to the business and affairs of the Corporation.

FIGURE 2.4 CONTINUED

13. **Corporate Summary**: For your reference, attached is a Corporate Information Sheet which contains a brief summary of the corporate information for the Corporation contained in the minute books as at the date of this memorandum.

14. **Backup Supporting Notes**: For your reference, attached is a copy of my back-up supporting notes in connection with my corporate review of the corporate records of the Corporation.

E.   SAMPLE CORPORATE DEFICIENCIES

Sample Deficiency

15. **Partially-signed Board Resolution:** The minute book contains 3 partially-signed board resolutions as follows:

Date of Board Resolution	Description of Board Resolution	Missing Director Signatures

Suggested Action: To complete the corporate records of the Corporation, a duplicate counterpart of the above-noted partially-signed board resolutions should be circulated for signature to the indicated directors and returned for filing into the minute books.

Sample Deficiency

16. **Form of Common Share Certificate**: The form of approved specimen share certificate as well as the issued share certificates for the common shares of the Corporation do not indicate that there are rights, privileges, restrictions and conditions attaching to each class of shares pursuant to subsection 56(2) of the *Business Corporations Act* (Ontario).

Suggested Action: A new form of specimen share certificate for the common shares should be approved by board resolution so that it is in compliance with the provisions of the *Business Corporations Act* (Ontario). In light of the contemplated share purchase transaction, however, it is probably not necessary to issue replacement share certificates to the selling shareholders prior to the closing.

Sample Deficiency

17. **Corporate Annual Return Filings**: According to the Ontario Corporate Document List which was produced by the Ontario Ministry on _____, the Corporation is in default of filing its 2000 Ontario corporate annual return under the *Corporations Information Act* (Ontario). This outstanding Ontario corporate annual return should have been filed with the Ontario Ministry by June 30, 2001 in respect of its December 31, 2000 financial year end. I confirm that the 2001 Ontario corporate annual return has been filed with the Ontario Ministry.

Suggested Action: The Corporation should complete and file the outstanding 2000 Ontario corporate annual return so that its corporate filings are brought up to date under the *Corporations Information Act* (Ontario).

FIGURE 2.4   CONCLUDED

F.   MISCELLANEOUS CORPORATE MATTERS

18.   **Dividends**: By board resolution dated as of the indicated dates, dividends were declared payable on the preference shares of the Corporation, all in compliance with the share conditions attached to the preference shares of the Corporation as set out in the Certificate and articles of incorporation of the Corporation, dated _____.

Date of Board Resolution	Amount of Dividend per Preference Share	Aggregate Dividend	Payable to
	$	$	
	$	$	
	$	$	

19.   **Approval   of   Lease   Agreement**: By   board   resolution   of   the   Corporation,   dated _____, the directors authorized and approved a lease agreement made as of _____ between _____ as lessor and the Corporation as lessee in respect of the property municipally known as _____. A copy of the lease agreement is filed in the Corporation's minute books. In the event that you have not yet seen a copy of the Lease Agreement, I have attached a copy for your consideration. It appears that the leased premises referred to in the Lease Agreement is where the Corporation currently has its business address.

_____

Please let me know if you have any questions regarding my corporate review of the corporate records of the Corporation or any instructions with respect to the preparation of rectification resolutions.

FIGURE 2.5   WORKSHEETS FOR CORPORATE REVIEW

CORPORATE REVIEW
CORPORATE INFORMATION SHEET

Date of Review: _____   Reviewed By: _____

Current Corporate Name	English Form:		
	French Form:		
Former Names			
Date of Incorporation			
Dates of Amendment			
Jurisdiction			
Corporation No.			
Registered Office Address			
Authorized Share Capital	Class of Shares	Number Authorized	Voting?
Financial Year End			
Number of Directors			
Current Directors			
Quorum *(board meetings)*			
Current Officers	Office Held	Name	
Banking Arrangements			
Last Annual Proceedings	Financial Statements Approved	Date of Approval	
Issued Share Capital	Shareholder	No. & Class of Shares	Cert. No.
Share Transfer Restrictions			
Quorum *(shareholder meetings)*			
By-laws	By-law No.	Nature of By-law	Effective Date
General Signing Authority			
Registered Business Names	Business Name	BIN	Registration Date	Expiry Date
Extra-Provincial Registrations	Province	Registration No.	Registration Date
Shareholders' Agreement?			
Corporate Seal?			
Other Information			
Date of Last Document in Minute Book			

FIGURE 2.5 CONTINUED

CORPORATE REVIEW
REGISTER OF DIRECTORS

Date of Review: _____   **Reviewed By:** _____

	Period Covered	
	From:	To:
Flexible Number of Directors:		
Fixed Number of Directors:		
Quorum:		

Director	Res. CDN?	Date Elected	Date Ceased
		Date:	Date:
		Consent Signed?	Resignation?
		Date:	Date:
		Consent Signed?	Resignation?
		Date:	Date:
		Consent Signed?	Resignation?
		Date:	Date:
		Consent Signed?	Resignation?
		Date:	Date:
		Consent Signed?	Resignation?
		Date:	Date:
		Consent Signed?	Resignation?

FIGURE 2.5 CONTINUED

CORPORATE REVIEW
REGISTER OF OFFICERS

Date of Review: _____   **Reviewed By:** _____

Office Held	Name	Date Appointed	Date Ceased
		Date:	Date:
			Resignation?
		Date:	Date:
			Resignation?
		Date:	Date:
			Resignation?
		Date:	Date:
			Resignation?
		Date:	Date:
			Resignation?
		Date:	Date:
			Resignation?
		Date:	Date:
			Resignation?
		Date:	Date:
			Resignation?
		Date:	Date:
			Resignation?
		Date:	Date:
			Resignation?
		Date:	Date:
			Resignation?

FIGURE 2.5 CONTINUED

CORPORATE REVIEW
REGISTER OF SHAREHOLDERS

Date of Review: _____   **Reviewed By:** _____

Authorized Number: _____   **Class of Shares:** _____

Note: It is very useful to restate or "freeze-frame" the total number of issued shares as at a particular date so that you can determine how many shares are issued and outstanding as of a particular date.

Date	Name	No. of Shares Held

FIGURE 2.5   CONTINUED

CORPORATE REVIEW
REGISTER OF SHARE TRANSFERS

Date of Review: _____   Reviewed By: _____

SHARE TRANSFER RESTRICTIONS: _____

CLASS OF SHARES: _____

Transfer No.	Date	Class of Shares	Certificates Surrendered		Transferor Transferred From	Transferee Transferred To	New Certificates Issued	
			No.	Shares			No.	Shares

FIGURE 2.5 CONTINUED

CORPORATE REVIEW
RECONCILIATION OF SHARE CERTIFICATES

Date of Review: _____   Reviewed By: _____

Authorized Number: _____   Class of Shares: _____
Lien Provision? _____   Legend Required? _____

Cert. No.	Shareholder	No. of Shares	Status

FIGURE 2.5 CONTINUED

CORPORATE REVIEW
BY-LAWS

Date of Review: _____   **Reviewed By:** _____

No.	Nature of By-law	Made by Directors	Confirmed by Shareholders	Comments

FIGURE 2.5   CONTINUED

CORPORATE REVIEW
ANNUAL PROCEEDINGS

Date of Review: _____   **Reviewed By:** _____

	Financial Statements	Date Approved by Directors	Date Rec'd by Shareholders	Dividends or Bonuses?	Comments
1					
2					
3					
4					
5					
6					
7					
8					
9					
10					
11					
12					
13					
14					
15					
16					
17					
18					
19					
20					
21					

FIGURE 2.5   CONCLUDED

CORPORATE REVIEW
MATERIAL CONTRACTS

Date of Review: _____   **Reviewed By:** _____

Summary	Description
Type of Agreement	
Parties to Agremment	
Date	
Brief Summary	
Value	
Term of Agreement	
Assignment Provision	
Termination Provision	
Consent Requirements	
General Comments	

FIGURE 2.6   FEDERAL AND ONTARIO CORPORATE LEGISLATION

Canada

Period Covered by Statute	Statute	Abbreviation
1988 to present December 12, 1988 to present	***Canada Business Corporations Act***, RSC 1985, c. C-44, s. 1; as amended by SC 1994, c. 24, s. 1	**CBCA**
1975 to 1988 December 15, 1975 to December 12, 1988	***Canada Business Corporations Act***, SC 1974-75-76, c. 33, as amended by SC 1976-77, c. 52, Sched.; SC 1978-79, c. 9; SC 1978-79, c. 11; SC 1980, c. 43; SC 1980-82, c. 47; SC 1980-82, c. 115; RSC 1985, c. C-44, s. 187; SC 1986, c. 35, s. 14; SC 1988, c. 2, s. 19	
1965 to 1975 July 1, 1965 to December 15, 1975	***Canada Corporations Act***, RSC 1952, c. 53; renamed SC 1964-65, c. 52, s. 2; RSC 1970, c. C-32, as amended by RSC 1970, c. 10 (1st Supp.); SC 1970-71-72, c. 43, s. 3(2); SC 1972, c. 17, s. 2(2); SC 1978-79, c. 11, s. 10(1); SC 1985, c. 26, ss. 35, 36, 85, 86, 87; SC 1986, c. 26, ss. 51-55; SC 1986, c. 35, s. 14	**Old CCA**
1934 to 1965 September 15, 1934 to July 1, 1965	***Companies Act, 1934***, RSC 1934, c. 33; RSC 1952, c. 53	**Old 1934 CA**
1928 to 1934 February 1, 1928 to September 15, 1934	***The Companies Act***, RSC 1927, c. 27	**Old 1928 CA**

FIGURE 2.6 CONCLUDED

Ontario

Period Covered by Statute	Statute	Abbreviation
1991 to present December 31, 1991 to Present	***Business Corporations Act***, RSO 1990, c. B.16, as amended by SO 1993, c. 16, s. 2; SO 1994, c. 17, s. 30; SO 1994, c. 27, ss. 71(1) and (43); SO 1998, c. 18, Sched. E, ss. 20 to 32; SO 1999, c. 6, s. 3; SO 1999, c. 12, Sched. F, ss. 1-9; SO 2000, c. 26, Sched. B, s. 3; SO 2000, c. 42, Sched., ss. 1 and 2; SO 2001, c. 8, ss. 1 and 2; SO 2001, c. 9, Sched. D, s. 2; SO 2001, c. 23, s. 6; SO 2002, c. 8, Sched. I, s. 2	**OBCA**
1983 to 1991 July 29, 1983 to December 31, 1991	***Business Corporations Act***, 1982, SO 1982, c. 4, as amended by SO 1986, c. 57; SO 1986, c. 64, s. 3; SO 1993, c. 16, s. 2; SO 1994, c. 17, s. 30; SO 1994, c. 27, s. 71; SO 1998, c. 18, Sched. E, ss. 20, 22-32; SO 1999, c. 6, s. 3; SO 1999, c. 12, Sched. F, ss. 1-9; SO 2000, c. 26, Sched. B, s. 3; SO 2000, c. 42, Sched., ss. 1, 2; SO 2001, c. 8, ss. 1, 2; SO 2001, c. 9, Sched. D, s. 2; SO 2001, c. 23, s. 6	
1971 to 1983 January 1, 1971 to July 29, 1983	***The Business Corporations Act***, RSO 1970, c. 53; RSO 1980, c. 54, as amended by SO 1981, c. 66, Sched. Item 1; repealed SO 1982, c. 4, s. 277	**Old OBCA**
1954 to 1971 April 30, 1954 to January 1, 1971	***The Corporations Act***, 1953, SO 1953, c. 19; RSO 1960, c. 71; RSO 1970, c. 89, as amended by SO 1971, Vol. 2, c. 25; SO 1971, Vol. 2, c. 98, s. 4(1); SO 1973, c. 104; SO 1976, c. 68; SO 1978, c. 29; SO 1979, c. 80	**Old 1954 CA**
1912 to 1954 August 1, 1912 to April 30, 1954	***Companies Act***, SO 1912, c. 31; RSO 1914, c. 178; RSO 1937, c. 251; RSO 1950, c. 59	**Old 1912 CA**

FIGURE 2.7   CONDUCTING A CORPORATE REVIEW — WHAT TO LOOK FOR

Note: The information contained in this chart is not intended to be exhaustive or comprehensive but is intended to serve as a guide to assist you in conducting a corporate review. If the corporate review covers a period before the enactment of the current CBCA and OBCA, for confirmation, you should refer to the relevant federal and Ontario corporate statutes that were in force as of the material dates. The statutes and amendments thereto are listed in figure 2.6.

What To Look For	Comments
A. Charter Documents	
1 Corporate Name Confirm the current corporate name of the corporation, any former names, and whether the corporation has a French version of its corporate name.	*Canada* **From July 1, 1965 to December 15, 1975**, the Old CCA specifically provided that a company may have a name consisting of a separated or combined French and English form of name and that it could use and be legally designated by either the French or English form of its name or both forms. *Ontario* **From April 30, 1954 to January 1, 1971**, the Old 1954 CA provided that, subject to that statute, a corporation was permitted to use its name in such form and in such language as the letters patent or supplementary letters patent provide.
2 Restrictions on Business Determine whether there are any restrictions on the business that the corporation may carry on or powers that it may exercise. *Comments* If the "objects" clause (being the business objectives of the corporation) was included in the charter documents but was not removed in subsequent amendments to the charter, the corporation is still restricted in the business that it may carry on, and the restriction may need to be deleted prior to the completion of a purchase and sale transaction, as appropriate.	*Canada* **Before December 15, 1975** under the Old CCA and predecessor statutes, federal corporations were required to include an "objects" clause in their charter documents. **From December 15, 1975 to the present** under the CBCA, federal corporations have had the capacity and, subject to the CBCA and its articles, the rights, powers, and privileges of a natural person. *Ontario* **Before July 29, 1983** under the Old OBCA and predecessor statutes, Ontario corporations were required to include an "objects" clause in their charter documents. **From July 29, 1983 to the present** under the OBCA, Ontario corporations have had the capacity and, subject to the OBCA and its articles, the rights, powers, privileges of a natural person.

FIGURE 2.7 CONTINUED

What To Look For	Comments
3 **Incorporators/Applicants as First Directors** Determine whether the corporate resolutions reflect the incorporators as the first directors. Confirm that the corporation had the requisite minimum number of directors as set out in the charter documents. Check to see if the consents of first directors who are not incorporators or applicants are attached to the charter documents or kept at the registered office address of the corporation, as appropriate.	***Canada*** **From July 1, 1965 to December 15, 1975** under the Old CCA, a minimum of 3 applicants were required to be set out in the application for letters patent, all of whom must be individuals of at least 21 years of age, who were to be the first directors of the company. **From December 15, 1975 to the present** under the CBCA, a non-distributing corporation is required to have a minimum of 1 director and a distributing corporation is required to have a minimum of 3 directors, at least 2 of whom are not officers or employees of the corporation or any of its affiliates. ***Ontario*** **From April 30, 1954 to January 1, 1971** under the Old 1954 CA, a minimum of 3 applicants were required to be set out in the charter documents, all of whom must be individuals of at least 18 years of age, who were to be the first directors of the company. **From January 1, 1971 to July 29, 1983** under the Old OBCA, at least 1 person, whether a body corporate or an individual at least 18 years of age, was permitted to be an incorporator, and if the articles named as a first director a person who was not an incorporator, the written consent to act as a first director was required to be attached to the articles of incorporation. A non-offering corporation was required to have at least 1 director, and an offering corporation was required to have at least 3 directors, at least 2 of whom were not officers or employees of the corporation or any of its affiliates.

FIGURE 2.7 CONTINUED

What To Look For	Comments
4 **"Private Company" Provisions** Determine whether the non-offering corporation's charter contained the requisite "private company" restrictions to exempt it from the registration and prospectus requirements under the relevant provincial securities legislation. **Before November 30, 2001**, the following restrictions were required to be included in the corporation's articles for the corporation to be deemed to be a "private company" pursuant to the *Securities Act* (Ontario) and to be exempt from the registration and prospectus requirements of that statute: a. a restriction on the transfer of shares (e.g., board or shareholder approval required); b. prohibition of sale of the corporation's securities to the public; and c. a limit of 50 on the number of shareholders of the corporation (excluding employees and former employees). **Effective November 30, 2001**, the "private company" exemption was eliminated in Ontario under OSC Rule 45-501 and was replaced by the closely held issuer exemption, accredited investor exemption, and other exemptions. As a result, effective as of and from November 30, 2001 items (b) and (c) above were no longer required to be included in the corporation's articles in order to be exempt from the registration and prospectus requirements of the *Securities Act* (Ontario); however, the share transfer restriction set out in item (a) above is still required to be included in the charter documents or, alternatively, in a shareholder agreement.	*Canada* **From July 1, 1965 to December 15, 1975** under the Old CCA, a statement as to whether the company was to be a public company or a private company was required to be set out in the charter documents, and if the company was to be a private company, the share transfer restrictions were also required to be set out in the charter documents. This provision was eliminated when the CBCA came into force on December 15, 1975. *Ontario* **From April 30, 1954 to January 1, 1971**, the term "private company" was a defined term in the Old 1954 CA. If the corporation was a "private company," the charter documents were required to contain a statement to that effect as well as a restriction on the transfer of the corporation's shares. **On January 1, 1971**, "private company" ceased to be a defined term under the Old OBCA, but it was a defined term in the *Securities Act* (Ontario). Until November 30, 2001, an Ontario corporation was deemed to be a "private company" if it met the criteria set out in the *Securities Act* (Ontario).

FIGURE 2.7   CONTINUED

What To Look For	Comments
5 Authorized Capital ***Capitalization*** Determine whether there are any limitations on the maximum consideration for which shares may be issued. If the letters patent contained a limitation on the maximum consideration for which shares could be issued and this limitation has not been removed in subsequent amendments to the charter documents, the corporation is still restricted from issuing shares in excess of this maximum consideration. Therefore, in conducting your corporate review, confirm whether this limitation affects on the validity of the issuance of shares that may have inadvertently been issued for consideration in excess of the maximum provided for in the charter documents. ***Fixed Number of Shares Authorized To Be Issued*** Determine whether the charter documents provide for a fixed or maximum number of shares that the corporation is authorized to issue. If the charter documents contain a limitation on the maximum number of shares that the corporation is authorized to issue and this limitation has not been removed in subsequent amendments to the charter documents, the corporation is still restricted from issuing shares in excess of this maximum number of shares. Therefore, in conducting your corporate review, confirm that the number of shares issued by the corporation does not exceed the fixed or maximum number of authorized shares set out in the charter documents.	***Canada*** **From July 1, 1965 to December 15, 1975** under the Old CCA, the letters patent were required to set out: a. the authorized capital of any classes of shares into which the authorized capital was to be divided and the number of shares of each class; and b. where the shares of a class were to be without par value, the maximum consideration for which each share or the maximum aggregate consideration for which all shares of the class could be issued. ***Ontario*** **From April 30, 1954 to January 1, 1971** under the Old 1954 CA, the letters patent were required to set out: a. the authorized capital and the classes of shares, if any, into which the authorized capital was to be divided, and the number of shares of each class; or b. where the shares were to be without par value, the maximum consideration, if any, for which each share or the maximum aggregate consideration, if any, for which all the shares of each class could be issued. Under the Old 1954 CA, the filing fee for incorporation in Ontario was based on a sliding scale, dependent on the dollar amount of capital requested in the application for incorporation. The minimum filing fee was for aggregate consideration of $40,000 and, accordingly, it was quite common for corporations to contain a $40,000 aggregate maximum consideration restriction in their letters patent.

FIGURE 2.7 CONTINUED

What To Look For	Comments

6 **Share Attributes Attaching to Shares**
 	
Determine the rights, privileges, restrictions, and conditions attaching to each class or series of shares and, in particular, note the following matters:
 	
a. voting rights and whether there is more than one vote attached to any particular class of shares;
 	
b. whether there is a provision entitling the non-voting shares to become voting in the event, for example, of failure of the corporation to pay dividends for a specific period of time;
 	
c. the priority of classes of shares with respect to the declaration and payment of dividends and on voluntary dissolution or winding up;
 	
d. whether the shares are entitled to be redeemed by the corporation and/or by the holder thereof, the redemption price to be paid, and the redemption procedure (including notice requirements); and
 	
e. whether any class of shares is authorized to be issued in one or more series.
	Canada
	
	From December 15, 1975 to the present under the CBCA:
	
	a. Where a corporation has only one class of shares, the rights of the holders thereof are equal in all respects and include the right to:
	
	  i. vote at any meeting of shareholders;
	
	  ii. receive any dividend declared by the corporation; and
	
	  iii. receive the remaining property of the corporation on dissolution.
	
	b. The articles may provide for more than one class of shares and, if they so provide:
	
	  i. the rights, privileges, restrictions. and conditions attaching to the shares of each class shall be set out therein; and
	
	  ii. the rights set out in item (a) above shall be attached to at least one class of shares but all such rights are not required to be attached to any one class.
	
	c. The articles may authorize the issue of any class of shares in one or more series and may authorize the directors to fix the number of shares in each series and to determine the designation, rights, privileges, restrictions, and conditions attaching to the shares of each series, subject to the limitations set out in the articles.
	
	Ontario
	
	From January 1, 1971 to July 29, 1983 under the Old OBCA, if a company has more than one class of shares:
	
	a. one class shall be designated as common shares and the other class or classes of shares shall be preference shares howsoever designated (but this requirement does not apply to shares authorized before April 30, 1954);
	
	b. the charter documents shall provide that the preference shares of a class confer upon the holders thereof a preference or right over the holders of shares of another class, either preference or common, and such preference or right may be in respect of dividends, repayment of capital, the right to elect part of the board of directors, or the right to convert such shares into shares of another class or into securities; and
	
	c. preference shares without par value do not have a preference in respect of the repayment of capital and are not subject to redemption or purchase for cancellation.
	
	From July 29, 1983 to the present under the OBCA:
	
	a. where a corporation has only one class of shares, the rights of the holders thereof are equal in all respects and include the rights to vote at all meetings of shareholders and to receive the remaining property of the corporation upon dissolution; and
	
	b. where the articles provide for more than one class of shares, the rights, privileges, restrictions, and conditions attaching to each class of shares shall be set out therein and the entitlement to vote and to receive the remaining property of the corporation upon dissolution shall be attached to at least one class of shares, but both such rights are not required to be attached to any one class.

FIGURE 2.7 CONTINUED

What To Look For	Comments
7 Number of Directors Determine that the corporation had the requisite minimum number of directors as set out in the charter documents. Determine whether the charter documents of the corporation provide for a fixed number of directors or, alternatively, a flexible number of directors in accordance with the applicable statute in force as of the material date.	**Canada** **From July 1, 1965 to December 15, 1975** under the Old CCA, a minimum of 3 directors were required to be named in the application for letters patent. **From December 15, 1975 to the present** under the CBCA, a non-distributing corporation is required to have a minimum of 1 director and a distributing corporation is required to have a minimum of 3 directors, at least 2 of whom are not officers or employees of the corporation or any of its affiliates. **Ontario** **From April 30, 1954 to January 1, 1971** under the Old 1954 CA, a minimum of 3 applicants were required to be set out in the charter documents, all of whom must be individuals of at least 18 years of age, who were to be the first directors of the company. **From January 1, 1971 to July 29, 1983** under the Old OBCA: a. the class and number of shares, if any, to be taken by each incorporator and the amount to be paid for such shares were required to be set out in the charter documents; and b. at least 1 person, whether a body corporate or an individual at least 18 years of age, was permitted to be an incorporator, and if the articles named as a first director a person who was not an incorporator, the written consent to act as a first director was required to be attached to the articles of incorporation. **From July 29, 1983 to the present** under the OBCA, a non-offering corporation is required to have a minimum of 1 director and an offering corporation is required to have a minimum of 3 directors, at least 1/3 of whom shall not be officers or employees of the corporation or any of its affiliates.
8 Other Provisions Determine whether there are any other provisions set out in the charter documents that may affect the corporate review. Examples of these other provisions are: a. borrowing provisions; b. lien provision (for shareholder indebtedness); c. use of corporate name in another language; d. pre-emptive right (restricting the issue of additional shares from treasury unless such shares are offered pro rata to existing shareholders); e. entitlement of holders of fractional shares to exercise voting shares and receive dividends in respect of such fractional shares; f. cumulative voting rights by directors.	**Canada** **From July 1, 1965 to December 15, 1975** under the Old CCA, the charter documents could include any provision that could be contained in any bylaw of the company. **From December 15, 1975 to the present** under the CBCA, the charter documents could include any provisions permitted by the CBCA or by law to be set out in the bylaws of the corporation. **Ontario** **From April 30, 1954 to January 1, 1971** under the Old 1954 CA, the charter documents could include any provision that could be the subject of a bylaw of the company. **From January 1, 1971 to the present** under both the Old OBCA and the OBCA, the charter documents could include any provisions permitted by the Old OBCA or the OBCA or permitted by law to be set out in the bylaws of the corporation.

FIGURE 2.7 CONTINUED

What To Look For	Comments
9 Head Office/Registered Office Address Determine the location or place of the registered office and, within such location or place, determine the registered office address of the corporation. Determine if all changes to the location or place of the registered office and to the registered office address were made in accordance with the applicable statute in force as of the material date. For federal corporations, prior to December 15, 1975, "registered office" was known as "head office." Similarly, for Ontario corporations, prior to July 29, 1983, "registered office" was known as "head office."	*Canada* **From July 1, 1965 to December 15, 1975** under the Old CCA, the corporation was required to have its head office in the "place" within Canada set out in the letters patent. The corporation was permitted, by bylaw, to change the place of the head office, and a certified copy of such bylaw was required to be filed with the minister under the Old CCA and notice thereof published in the *Canada Gazette.* **From December 15, 1975 to November 24, 2001** under the CBCA, the corporation was required to have a registered office in the place within Canada specified in its articles and the registered office address was required to be within such place set out in the articles. The directors were authorized to change the registered office address within the place set out in the articles, and a Notice of Change of Registered Office in prescribed form was required to be filed with the Director under the CBCA, within 15 days of any change of registered office address. To change the address of the registered office, as set out in the articles, to another place, articles of amendment in prescribed form were required to be authorized by special resolution of the shareholders and filed with the Director under the CBCA. **From November 24, 2001 to the present** under the CBCA, the articles of the corporation are no longer required to state the "place" but, rather, only the province or territory in Canada where the registered office is situated. *Ontario* **From April 30, 1954 to January 1, 1971** under the Old 1954 CA, the corporation was required at all times to have a head office in the place within Ontario set out in the letters patent. The corporation was permitted, by special resolution, to change the location of its head office to another place in Ontario. **From January 1, 1971 to July 29, 1983** under the Old OBCA, a corporation was required to have its head office in the municipality or geographic township set out in the articles of incorporation. The corporation was permitted, by special bylaw, to change the location of its head office to another municipality or geographic township in Ontario. **From July 29, 1983 to November 28, 1986** under the OBCA, the corporation was permitted to change the municipality or geographic township in which its registered office was located by articles of amendment authorized by special resolution and filed with the minister under the OBCA. **From November 27, 1986 to the present** under the OBCA, the corporation was permitted to change the municipality or geographic township in which its registered office is located by special resolution rather than by articles of amendment.

FIGURE 2.7 CONTINUED

What To Look For	Comments

B. Organizational Minutes and Resolutions

10   Constitution and Qualification of Board of Directors

CCA/CCBA Corporation

Determine whether the board of directors of the corporation has been properly and validly elected and that each director is duly qualified to act as a director of the corporation in accordance with the requirements of the governing federal statute in force at the particular time. You should note, among other things, the following:

a. whether the board of directors meets the resident Canadian quorum requirements of the governing federal statute in force at the particular time;

b. whether the directors were or are required to hold qualifying shares of the corporation;

c. whether the director consented in writing to act as a director in accordance with the governing statute or was present at the meeting at which he was elected; and

d. whether the board of directors has the requisite number of directors in accordance with the charter documents and/or governing federal statute in force at that time.

Comments

Qualifying Shares Held by Directors

Effective December 15, 1975, the CBCA eliminated the requirement under the Old CCA for directors to hold qualifying shares. Specifically, the CBCA provides that, unless the articles otherwise provide, a director of a corporation is not required to hold shares issued by the corporation.

Resident Canadian Quorum Requirement for Directors

Effective from December 15, 1975 to November 24, 2001 under the CBCA, a majority of directors on the board of directors and a majority of the directors on the

Canada

From July 1, 1965 to December 15, 1975 under the Old CCA:

a. The board of directors was required to consist of a fixed number of directors (a specified number of directors), not fewer than 3 individuals, all of whom were required to be at least 21 years of age.

b. Each director of the corporation was required to hold a qualifying share issued by the corporation within 10 days of his or her election or appointment as a director. (If such person failed to become a shareholder within that 10-day period, he or she thereupon ceased to be a director.)

c. An undischarged bankrupt was ineligible to act as a director, and if any director became a bankrupt, he or she thereupon ceased to be a director.

From December 15, 1975 to November 24, 2001 under the CBCA:

a. The board of directors was required, for a non-distributing corporation, to consist of 1 or more directors and, for a distributing corporation, not fewer than 3 directors, at least 2 of whom were not officers or employees of the corporation or any of its affiliates.

b. Except as provided below, a majority of the directors was required to be resident Canadian. Exception: This requirement did not apply to a holding corporation that earned in Canada, directly or indirectly through its subsidiaries, less than 5% of the gross revenues of the holding corporation and its subsidiary corporations.

c. A director is required to be an individual who is at least 18 years of age and of sound mind, and who does not have the status of a bankrupt.

d. Unless the articles otherwise provide, a director of a corporation is not required to hold qualifying shares issued by the corporation.

Effective November 24, 2001 to the present under the CBCA:

a. The board of directors is required, for a non-distributing corporation, to consist of 1 or more directors and, for a distributing corporation, not fewer than 3 directors, at least 2 of whom are not officers or employees of the corporation or any of its affiliates.

b. Unless the articles otherwise provide, a director of a corporation is not required to hold qualifying shares issued by the corporation.

c. A director is required to be an individual who is at least 18 years of age and of sound mind, and who does not have the status of a bankrupt.

d. Except as provided below, at least 25% of the directors must be resident Canadians; however, if the corporation has fewer than 4 directors, at least 1 director must be a resident Canadian. **Exception:** For corporations involved in uranium mining or book publishing or distribution, or where required by an act of Parliament, a majority of directors must be resident Canadians. If such a corporation has fewer than 3 directors, at least 1 director must be a resident Canadian.

e. A director elected or appointed is deemed not to have been elected or appointed as a director unless

i. he or she was present at the meeting at which he or she was elected or appointed and did not refuse such election or appointment; or

ii. if he or she was not present at the meeting, either he or she consented in writing to act as a director before the election or appointment or within 10 days thereafter, or he has acted as a director pursuant to the election or appointment.

FIGURE 2.7 CONTINUED

What To Look For	Comments

executive committee were required to be "resident Canadians." This definition included Canadian citizens ordinarily resident in Canada and landed immigrants.
 	
Effective from November 24, 2001 to the present, the minimum requirement for resident Canadian directors has been reduced from 51% to 25% unless the corporation is involved in uranium mining or book publishing or distribution, or where required by an act of Parliament. In addition, the requirement for resident Canadian representation on board committees (such as the executive committee) has been completely eliminated.
 	
OBCA Corporation
 	
Determine whether the board of directors of the corporation has been properly and validly elected and that each director is duly qualified to act as a director of the corporation in accordance with the requirements of the governing Ontario statute in force at the particular time. You should note, among other things, the following:
 	
a. whether the board of directors meets the resident Canadian quorum requirements of the governing Ontario statute in force at the particular time;
 	
b. whether the directors were or are required to hold qualifying shares of the corporation;
 	
c. whether the director consented in writing to act as a director in accordance with the governing statute or was present at the meeting at which he or she was elected;
 	
d. whether the board of directors has the minimum requisite number of directors in accordance with the charter documents and/or governing Ontario statute in force at that time.
	Ontario
	
	From January 1, 1971 to July 29, 1983 under the Old OBCA:
	
	a. The board of directors was required to consist of a fixed number of directors (a specified number of directors) — at least 1 director for a non-offering corporation and at least 3 directors for an offering corporation.
	
	b. A majority of the directors of a corporation other than a non-resident corporation were required to be resident Canadians.
	
	c. A director was required to be at least 18 years of age.
	
	d. A person elected or appointed as a director was not a director unless
	
	  i. he or she was present at the meeting at which he or she was elected or appointed and did not refuse at that meeting to act as a director, or
	
	  ii. if he or she was not present at the meeting, he or she consented in writing to act as a director within 10 days of his or her election or appointment.
	
	(This requirement was eliminated under the OBCA on July 29, 1983 but reintroduced on March 1, 1995.)
	
	Effective as of the indicated dates under the OBCA:
	
	a. **From July 29, 1983 to the present:**
	
	  i. The board of directors shall consist of at least 1 individual for a non-offering corporation and at least 3 individuals for an offering corporation.
	
	  ii. At least 1/3 of the directors of an offering corporation shall not be officers or employees of the corporation or any of its affiliates.
	
	  iii. Unless the articles provide otherwise, a director of a corporation is not required to hold qualifying shares issued by the corporation.
	
	  iv. A director is required to be an individual who is at least 18 years of age and of sound mind, and who does not have the status of a bankrupt.
	
	  v. A majority of the directors of a corporation other than a non-resident corporation shall be resident Canadians, but where a corporation has fewer than 3 directors, at least 1 director shall be a resident Canadian.
	
	  vi. Until the first meeting of shareholders, the first directors named in the articles cannot resign unless, at the time that the resignation is to be effective, a successor has been elected or appointed.

FIGURE 2.7 CONTINUED

What To Look For	Comments
Comments ***Qualifying Shares Held by Directors*** Although the Old OBCA eliminated on January 1, 1971 the requirement for directors to hold qualifying shares, if the bylaws of the corporation already contained the provision requiring directors to hold qualifying shares and these bylaws were not amended after **January 1, 1971** to remove such requirement, then the directors were still required to hold qualifying shares of the corporation in accordance with its bylaws. **Effective July 29, 1983 to the present**, the OBCA provides that unless the articles provide otherwise, a director of a corporation is not required to hold shares issued by the corporation. ***New Resident Canadian Quorum Requirement for Directors*** **Effective October 1, 1973** under the Old OBCA, the introduction of a new resident Canadian quorum requirement was introduced for directors. A majority of directors on the board of directors and a majority of the directors on the executive committee are required to be resident Canadians, defined as Canadian citizens ordinarily resident in Canada. This definition excluded landed immigrants.	b. **From March 1, 1995 to March 27, 2000**, a director was required to consent in writing within 10 days of his or her election or appointment as a director. **From March 27, 2000 to the present**, written consent by a director was required to be given *before* or within 10 days of appointment or election; however, if the person elected or appointed as a director consents in writing after the 10-day period, such election or appointment is valid.

FIGURE 2.7   CONTINUED

	What To Look For	Comments
11	**Resolutions in Writing**	*Canada*
	First Year of Incorporation of Ontario Corporation Prior to January 1, 1971	**From February 1, 1928 to December 15, 1975** under the Old 1928 CA, the Old 1934 CA, and Old CCA, there was no provision permitting resolutions of the directors and shareholders to be passed by the signature of the directors and/or shareholders in lieu of being passed at a duly called and held meeting of the directors or shareholders.
	For Ontario corporations formed prior to January 1, 1971, check to see if resolutions were signed by the directors and/or shareholders during an Ontario corporation's first year of existence in lieu of being passed at a meeting of the directors and/or shareholders. Thereafter, resolutions were required to be passed at a meeting.	**From December 15, 1975 to the present** under the CBCA, a resolution signed by all the directors entitled to vote on that resolution at a meeting of directors or a committee of directors is as valid as if it had been passed at a meeting of directors or a committee of directors. Similarly, except as otherwise specifically provided by s. 110(2) or 168(5) of the CBCA, a resolution signed by all the shareholders entitled to vote on that resolution at a meeting of shareholders is as valid as if it had been passed at a meeting of the shareholders and satisfies all the requirements of the CBCA relating to that meeting of shareholders.
	There is no corresponding provision for federal corporations.	*Ontario*
	Fully Signed	**From April 30, 1954 to January 1, 1971** under the Old 1954 CA, any bylaw or resolution signed during the first year of existence of the corporation by all its directors or by all its shareholders, as the case may be, was as valid as if passed at a meeting of directors or shareholders duly called, constituted, and held for that purpose. Any bylaw passed at any time during a corporation's existence was required, in lieu of confirmation at a general meeting of shareholders, to be confirmed in writing by all the shareholders entitled to vote at such meeting. Thereafter, corporate proceedings were required to be conducted by the directors and shareholders at duly called and constituted meetings and bylaws could not be passed by written resolution of the directors and/or shareholders, but could be passed only at duly convened meetings of the directors and shareholders.
	Check to see if all resolutions passed by the directors and/or shareholders have been duly signed by all the director or shareholders, as the case may be, entitled to vote on such resolution.	
	Special Resolution	**From January 1, 1971 to the present** under the Old OBCA and the OBCA, a resolution signed by all the directors entitled to vote on that resolution at a meeting of directors or a committee of directors is as valid as if it had been passed at a meeting of directors or a committee of directors. Similarly, except as otherwise specifically provided by s. 123(2) or 149(6) of the OBCA, a resolution signed by all the shareholders entitled to vote on that resolution at a meeting of shareholders (or by their attorney authorized in writing) is as valid as if it had been passed at a meeting of the shareholders and satisfies all the requirements of the OBCA relating to that meeting of shareholders.
	A "special resolution" was a resolution that was not effective until passed by the directors and confirmed with or without variation by at least 2/3 of the votes cast at a general meeting of shareholders duly called for that purpose or by the consent in writing of all the shareholders.	

FIGURE 2.7 CONTINUED

What To Look For	Comments
12 Meetings of Directors Determine whether meetings of the directors were properly called and held. The proper constitution and conduct of a meeting will affect the validity of any resolutions passed or actions agreed to at that meeting. In particular, when reviewing the minutes of a meeting of the board of directors, you should confirm the following: a. whether proper notice of the meeting was given to each director of the corporation pursuant to the bylaws of the corporation or whether notice of such meeting was waived by the directors; b. whether a quorum was present at the meeting in accordance with the quorum requirements of the articles or bylaws and whether the resident Canadian quorum requirements were met; c. whether the meeting was held at a place permitted by the articles, bylaws, or governing statute; and d. whether any director with an interest in any contract or transaction being approved at such meeting has disclosed the nature and extent of that interest and abstained from voting on such contract or transaction. **Comments** You should carefully review the minutes of board meetings to ensure that there has been no loss of quorum from the opening to the end of each meeting. For federal corporations, until December 15, 1975, and for Ontario corporations, until January 1, 1971, directors were required to hold qualifying shares. As a result, it was quite common for the first directors to resign and transfer their qualifying shares to their replacements at a board meeting at which the retiring directors and the replacement directors were present. However, you should carefully read the minutes of this kind of board meeting to ensure that the "turnover" was properly recorded in the minutes and that there was no loss of quorum in the "passing of the baton" from the first directors to their replacements.	**Canada** **From December 15, 1975 to November 24, 2001** under the CBCA: a. After the certificate of incorporation has been issued, a meeting of the directors shall be held at which the directors may make bylaws, adopt forms of share certificates and corporate records, authorize the issuance of shares, appoint officers, appoint an auditor to hold office until the first annual meeting of shareholders, make banking arrangements, and transact any other business. Such meeting may be called by an incorporator or a director by giving not less than 5 days' notice by mail to each director, stating the time and place of the meeting. b. Unless the articles or bylaws provide otherwise, the directors may meet at any place and upon such notice as the bylaws require. c. Subject to the articles or bylaws, a majority of the number of directors or minimum number of directors required by the articles constitutes a quorum at any meeting of directors. Directors, unless otherwise provided for non-resident holding corporations, shall not transact business at a meeting of directors unless a majority of directors present are resident Canadians. However, directors may transact business at a meeting of directors where a majority of resident Canadian directors is not present if a resident Canadian director who is unable to be present approves the business transacted at such meeting, in writing or by telephone or other communications facility, and a majority of resident Canadian directors would have been present had that director been present at the meeting. d. A notice of a meeting of directors shall specify any matter referred to in s. 110(3) (subsequently s. 115(3), which deals with the matters that the directors may delegate) that is to be dealt with at the meeting but, unless the bylaws provide otherwise, need not specify the purpose of the business to be transacted. A director may, in any manner, waive notice of a meeting of directors, and attendance of a director at such a meeting is deemed to be a waiver of notice (except where the director attends the meeting for the express purpose of objecting to the transaction of any business). e. Subject to the bylaws, a director may, if all the directors of the corporation consent, participate in a board meeting or committee meeting by such telephonic or other communications facility as permits all persons participating in the meeting to hear each other, and a director participating by such means is deemed to be present at the meeting. **From November 24, 2001 to the present** under the CBCA, items (a), (b), (d), and (e) remain unchanged; item (c) was amended as follows: Directors, other than directors of a corporation referred to in s. 105(4) of the CBCA (non-resident holding corporation) shall not transact business at a meeting of directors unless at least 25% of the directors present are resident Canadians or, if the corporation has fewer than 4 directors, at least one of the directors present is a resident Canadian (unless the corporation is involved in uranium mining or book publishing or distribution, or where required by an act of Parliament). Directors, unless otherwise provided for non-resident holding corporations, shall not transact business at a meeting of directors unless such resident Canadian quorum is present. However, directors may transact business at a meeting of directors where a majority of resident Canadian directors is not present if a resident Canadian director who is unable to be present approves the business transacted at such meeting, in writing or by telephone or other communications facility and the required number of resident Canadian directors would have been present had that director been present at the meeting.

FIGURE 2.7 CONTINUED

What To Look For	Comments
	Ontario
	From July 29, 1983 to the present under the OBCA:

a. After incorporation, a meeting of the directors shall be held at which the directors may make bylaws, adopt forms of share certificates and corporate records, authorize the issuance of shares, appoint officers, appoint an auditor to hold office until the first annual meeting of shareholders, make banking arrangements, and transact any other business. Such meeting may be called by an incorporator or a director by giving not less than 5 days' notice by mail to each director, stating the time and place of the meeting.

b. Unless the bylaws provide otherwise, a meeting of directors shall be held at the place where the registered office of the corporation is located. Where provided by the bylaws, a meeting of the board of directors may be held at any place within or outside Ontario, but except where the corporation is a non-resident corporation or the articles or bylaws provide otherwise, in any financial year of the corporation a majority of the meetings of the board of directors shall be held at a place within Canada.

c. Subject to the articles or bylaws, a majority of the number of directors or minimum number of directors required by the articles constitutes a quorum at any meeting of directors, but in no case shall a quorum be less than 2/5 of the number of directors or minimum number of directors, as the case may be. If the corporation has fewer than 3 directors, both directors must be present at a meeting of directors to constitute a quorum.

d. Directors, other than directors of a non-resident corporation, shall not transact business at a meeting of directors unless a majority of directors present are resident Canadians. However, directors may transact business at a meeting of directors where a majority of resident Canadian directors is not present if a resident Canadian director who is unable to be present approves the business transacted at such meeting, in writing or by telephone or other communications facility, and a majority of resident Canadian directors would have been present had that director been present at the meeting.

e. In the absence of any other provision in the articles or bylaws, notice of the time and place for the holding of the meeting shall be given to every director by sending the notice 10 days or more before the date of the meeting to the director's latest address. A director may, in any manner, waive notice of a meeting of directors, and attendance of a director at such a meeting is deemed to be a waiver of notice (except where the director attends the meeting for the express purpose of objecting to the transaction of any business).

f. Unless the bylaws provide otherwise, if all the directors present at or participating in the meeting consent, a meeting of directors or committee of directors may be held by such telephonic, electronic, or other communications facility as permits all persons participating in the meeting to communicate with each other simultaneously and instantaneously, and a director participating by such means is deemed to be present at the meeting. If a majority of the directors participating in the meeting are then in Canada, the meeting shall be deemed to have been held in Canada.

FIGURE 2.7   CONTINUED

What To Look For	Comments

13 Meetings of Shareholders
 	
Determine whether meetings of the shareholders were properly called and held. The proper constitution and conduct of a meeting will affect the validity of any resolutions passed or actions agreed to at that meeting. In particular, when reviewing the minutes of a meeting of the shareholders, you should confirm the following:
 	
a. whether proper notice of the meeting was given to each shareholder entitled to receive notice pursuant to the bylaws and the governing statute or whether notice of such meeting was waived by the shareholders;
 	
b. whether a quorum was present at the meeting in accordance with the quorum requirements of the bylaws; and
 	
c. whether the meeting was held at a place permitted by the articles, bylaws, or governing statute.
	Canada
	
	From December 15, 1975 to November 24, 2001 under the CBCA:
	
	a. Meetings of shareholders shall be held at the place within Canada provided in the bylaws or, in the absence of such provision, at the place within Canada that the directors determine. Meetings may be held outside Canada if all the shareholders entitled to vote at that meeting so agree, and a shareholder who attends such meeting is deemed to have so agreed except when he attends the meeting for the express purpose of objecting to the transaction of any business on the grounds that the meeting is not lawfully held.
	
	b. The directors shall call an annual meeting of shareholders not later than 18 months after incorporation and subsequently not later than 15 months after holding the last preceding annual meeting, and may at any time call a special meeting of shareholders.
	
	c. For the purpose of determining shareholders entitled to receive notice of a meeting of shareholders, the directors may fix in advance a date as the record date for such determination of shareholders, but such record date shall not precede by more than 50 days or by less than 21 days the date on which the meeting is to be held.
	
	d. All business transacted at a special meeting of shareholders and all business transacted at an annual meeting of shareholders, except consideration of the financial statements and auditor's report, the election of directors, and the reappointment of the incumbent auditor, is deemed to be special business.
	
	e. Notice of the time and place of a meeting of shareholders shall be sent not less than 21 days and not more than 50 days before the meeting to
	
	   i. each shareholder entitled to vote at the meeting,
	   ii. each director, and
	   iii. the auditor of the corporation.
	
	If a meeting of shareholders is adjourned for less than 30 days, it is not necessary (unless the bylaws provide otherwise) to give notice of an adjourned meeting. Notice of a meeting at which special business is to be transacted shall state the nature of that business in sufficient detail to permit the shareholder to form a reasoned judgment and shall set out the text of any special resolution to be submitted to the meeting.
	
	f. A shareholder and any other person entitled to attend a meeting of shareholders may, in any manner, waive notice of a meeting of shareholders, and attendance at such a meeting is deemed to be a waiver of notice (except where the person attends for the express purpose of objecting to the transaction of any business on the grounds that the meeting was not lawfully called).
	
	g. Unless the bylaws otherwise provide, a quorum of shareholders is present at a meeting of shareholders, irrespective of the number of persons actually present at the meeting, if the holders of a majority of the shares entitled to vote at the meeting are present in person or represented by proxy.
	
	From November 24, 2001 to the present under amendments to the CBCA:
	
	a. A meeting of shareholders may be held at a place outside Canada *if the place is specified in the articles* or all the shareholders entitled to vote at the meeting agree that the meeting is to be held at that place. A shareholder who attends a shareholders' meeting held outside Canada is deemed to have agreed to it being held outside Canada except where the shareholder attends the meeting for the express purpose of objecting to the transaction of any business on the grounds that the meeting is not lawfully held.
	
	b. Unless the bylaws provide otherwise, any person entitled to attend a meeting of shareholders may participate in the meeting by means of a telephonic, electronic, or other communication facility that permits all participants to communicate adequately with each other during the meeting. A person participating in a meeting by such means is deemed for the purpose of the CBCA to be present at the meeting.
	
	c. In the case of a non-distributing corporation, a notice calling a shareholders' meeting may be sent within a shorter period than that specified by the CBCA if so provided in the articles or bylaws.

FIGURE 2.7   CONTINUED

What To Look For	Comments
	Ontario
	From July 29, 1983 to November 1, 2001 under the OBCA:
	a. Subject to the articles and any unanimous shareholder agreement, a meeting of shareholders shall be held at such place in or outside Ontario as the directors determine or, in the absence of such determination, at the place where the registered office of the corporation is located.
	b. The directors shall call an annual meeting of shareholders not later than 18 months after incorporation and subsequently not later than 15 months after holding the last preceding annual meeting, and may at any time call a special meeting of shareholders.
	c. For the purpose of determining shareholders entitled to receive notice of a meeting of shareholders, the directors may fix in advance a date as the record date for such determination of shareholders, but such record date shall not precede by more than 50 days or by less than 21 days the date on which the meeting is to be held.
	d. All business transacted at a special meeting of shareholders and all business transacted at an annual meeting of shareholders, except consideration of the financial statements and auditor's report, the election of directors, and the reappointment of the incumbent auditor, is deemed to be special business.
	e. Notice of the time and place of a meeting of shareholders of a non-offering corporation shall be sent not less than 10 days and not more than 50 days before the meeting to
	i. each shareholder entitled to vote at the meeting,
	ii. each director, and
	iii. the auditor of the corporation.
	If a meeting of shareholders is adjourned for less than 30 days, it is not necessary (unless the bylaws provide otherwise) to give notice of an adjourned meeting. Notice of a meeting at which special business is to be transacted shall state the nature of that business in sufficient detail to permit the shareholder to form a reasoned judgment and shall set out the text of any special resolution to be submitted to the meeting.
	f. A shareholder and any other person entitled to attend a meeting of shareholders may, in any manner, waive notice of a meeting of shareholders, and attendance at such a meeting is deemed to be a waiver of notice (except where the person attends the meeting for the express purpose of objecting to the transaction of any business on the grounds that the meeting was not lawfully called).
	g. Unless the bylaws provide otherwise, the holders of a majority of the shares who are entitled to vote at a meeting of shareholders, whether present in person or represented by proxy, constitute a quorum.
	From November 1, 2001 to the present under amendments to the OBCA:
	Where permitted by the articles or the bylaws, a meeting of shareholders may be held by telephonic or electronic means and a shareholder who, through those means, votes at the meeting or establishes a communications link to the meeting shall be deemed for the purposes of the OBCA to be present at the meeting. A meeting held by such electronic means shall be deemed to be held at the place where the registered office is located.

FIGURE 2.7 CONTINUED

What To Look For	Comments

C. Bylaws

14 Bylaws

General Bylaws

Determine if a bylaw has been properly enacted by the directors and shareholders at a duly convened board and/or shareholders' meeting at which a quorum was present, or, alternatively, has been duly passed by written resolution of the directors and shareholders.

Confirm if the bylaws contain a provision requiring the directors to hold qualifying shares. If this provision was not deleted from the bylaws by a subsequent amending bylaw, then that requirement continued in full force and effect until December 15, 1975 for federal corporations and until July 29, 1983 for Ontario corporations.

Review the general operating bylaw with a view to determining:

a. quorum requirements at board and shareholders' meetings;

b. whether the chair of a meeting has a casting vote;

c. the notice period for calling board and shareholders' meetings;

d. general signing authority;

e. the qualification of officers;

f. the qualification of directors;

g. whether there is a lien provision on shares;

h. the financial year-end;

i. whether the approval of the corporate seal has been included;

j. establishment of any committees; and

k. whether telephonic or other electronic meetings are permitted.

Canada

From July 1, 1965 to December 15, 1975 under the Old CCA, the directors were authorized to make, amend, or repeal bylaws, but every such bylaw, except bylaws made respecting agents, officers, and servants of the corporation, only had force until the next annual meeting of shareholders, and in default of confirmation by the shareholders at such meeting, it ceased to have force.

From December 15, 1975 to the present under the CBCA, unless the articles, bylaws, or unanimous shareholder agreement provide otherwise, the directors may, by resolution, make, amend, or repeal any bylaws that regulate the business or affairs of the corporation. The directors are required to submit a bylaw or an amendment or repeal of a bylaw to the shareholders at the next meeting of shareholders and the shareholders may, by ordinary resolution, confirm, reject, or amend the bylaw, amendment, or repeal. A bylaw or an amendment or repeal of a bylaw is effective from the date of the resolution of the directors until it is confirmed, confirmed as amended, or rejected by the shareholders or until it ceases to be effective under s. 98(4) of the CBCA, and if it is confirmed or confirmed as amended, such bylaw continues in effect in the form in which it was so confirmed. If, however, a bylaw, amendment, or repeal is rejected by the shareholders, or if the directors do not submit a bylaw, amendment, or repeal to the shareholders, it ceases to be effective and no subsequent resolution of the directors to make, amend, or repeal a bylaw having substantially the same purpose or effect is effective until it is confirmed or confirmed as amended by the shareholders.

Ontario

From April 30, 1954 to January 1, 1971 under the Old 1954 CA, the directors were authorized to pass bylaws not contrary to that statute or to the letters patent. Such bylaw and a repeal, amendment, or re-enactment thereof, unless in the meantime confirmed at a general meeting of shareholders duly called for that purpose, was effective only until the next annual meeting of shareholders unless confirmed at that meeting, and in default of such confirmation, it ceased to have effect; and from that time and in that case, no new bylaw of the same or like substance had any effect until confirmed at a general meeting of the shareholders. The shareholders at their general meeting or annual meeting could confirm, reject, amend, or otherwise deal with any bylaw passed by the directors and submitted to them at their meeting for confirmation, but no act done or right acquired under any such bylaw would be prejudicially affected by any such rejection, amendment or other dealing. No bylaw for the payment of the president or of any director was effective until confirmed at a general meeting of the shareholders duly called for that purpose.

From January 1, 1971 to July 29, 1983 under the Old OBCA, unless the articles, bylaws, or unanimous shareholder agreement provided otherwise, the directors could, by resolution, make, amend, or repeal any bylaws that regulated the business or affairs of the corporation. The directors were required to submit a bylaw or an amendment or repeal of a bylaw to the shareholders at the next meeting of shareholders and the shareholders could, by ordinary resolution, confirm, reject, or amend the bylaw, amendment, or repeal. A bylaw or an amendment or repeal of a bylaw was effective from the date of the resolution of the directors until it is confirmed, confirmed as amended, or rejected by the shareholders or until it ceased to be effective under the Old OBCA, and if it was confirmed or confirmed as amended, such bylaw continued in effect in the form in which it was so confirmed. If, however, the bylaw, amendment, or repeal was rejected by the shareholders or if the directors did not submit a bylaw, amendment, or repeal to the shareholders, it ceased to be effective and no subsequent resolution of the directors to make, amend, or repeal a bylaw having substantially the same purpose or effect was effective until it was confirmed or confirmed as amended by the shareholders. A bylaw need not be described as a bylaw in a resolution.

FIGURE 2.7 CONTINUED

What To Look For

Determine which corporate matters were required to be passed by bylaw under the predecessor Ontario and federal statutes, rather than by simple directors' or shareholders' resolutions, and whether any such bylaws were properly enacted by the directors and shareholders. These matters include:

a. the creation and establishment of an executive committee;

b. the remuneration of the president or any director;

c. the increase or decrease in the number of directors;

d. the distribution of the corporation's property on dissolution.

Special Bylaws

Determine if the corporation has enacted any special bylaws. For an Ontario corporation, a "special bylaw" was a bylaw that was not effective until passed by the directors *and* confirmed with or without variation by at least 2/3 of the votes cast at a general meeting of shareholders duly called for that purpose or, in lieu of such confirmation, by the consent in writing of all the shareholders entitled to vote at such meeting. The requirement for special bylaws under the Old OBCA was eliminated on **July 29, 1983.**

D. Corporate Seal

15   Determine whether the corporation was required to have a corporate seal during the material times. Both the CBCA and the OBCA no longer require that a corporation have a corporate seal.

Comments

Canada

From July 1, 1965 to December 15, 1975 under the Old CCA, it was required that the corporation have a corporate seal with its name engraved thereon in both its English and French forms, as applicable.

From December 15, 1975 to November 24, 2001 under the CBCA, an instrument or agreement executed on behalf of a corporation by a director, an officer, or an agent of the corporation is not invalid merely because a corporate seal is not affixed thereto.

From November 24, 2001 to the present under the CBCA, a corporation may, but need not, adopt a corporate seal. A document executed on behalf of a corporation is not invalid merely because a corporate seal is not affixed to it.

Ontario

From April 30, 1954 to July 29, 1983 under the Old 1954 CA and the Old OBCA, a corporation was required to have a corporate seal. Under the Old 1954 CA, if a corporation was a "private company," those words were required to be included in the seal.

From July 29, 1983 to the present under the OBCA, a corporation may, but need not, have a seal.

FIGURE 2.7 CONTINUED

What To Look For	Comments

E. Officers

16. Determine whether the corporation was required to appoint certain officers (such as president and secretary) as may be required by the charter documents, the bylaws, or the governing statute in force as of the particular date.

If the bylaws have never been amended to delete an original requirement for an officer to be a director, and the original requirement therefore still prevails, it may be appropriate to amend such bylaw to delete that original provision, in order to give greater flexibility to the directors in appointing its officers.

Canada

From July 1, 1965 to December 15, 1975 under the Old CCA, in the absence of other provisions in the letters patent or bylaws, the directors were required to elect the president from among themselves and, if so desired, appoint a vice-president and such other officers as they may have determined.

From December 15, 1975 to the present under the CBCA, subject to the articles, the bylaws, or any unanimous shareholder agreement, the directors may designate the offices of the corporation, appoint officers, specify their duties, and delegate to them such powers to manage the business and affairs of the corporation (except such powers set out in s. 115(3) of the CBCA). Subject to the articles, the bylaws, or any unanimous shareholder agreement, two or more offices of the corporation can be held by the same person, and a director can be appointed to any office of the corporation. Therefore, there is no statutory requirement that a corporation have a president or that a director be an officer. *However*, if the bylaws have not been amended to delete the requirement for an officer to be a director, that requirement for an officer to be a director still prevails.

Ontario

From January 1, 1971 to July 29, 1983 under the Old OBCA:

a. The corporation was required to have a president and a secretary and such other officers provided for by bylaw or by resolution of the directors. In the absence of other provisions in the articles or bylaws, the directors were required to elect the president from among the directors, and appoint or elect the secretary and one or more vice-presidents or other officers.

b. If authorized by special bylaw, the corporation was entitled to provide for the election or appointment by the directors from among themselves of a chairman of the board.

c. Unless the articles or bylaws otherwise provided, the president was required to be a director of the corporation and no other officer, except chairman of the board, was required to be a director.

From July 29, 1983 to the present under the OBCA, subject to the articles, the bylaws, or any unanimous shareholder agreement, the directors may designate the offices of the corporation, appoint officers, and specify their duties. Therefore, in contrast to the Old OBCA, there is no statutory requirement that a corporation have a president and/or secretary or for a director to be an officer. *However*, if the bylaws have not been amended to delete the requirement for an officer to be a director, that requirement still prevails.

FIGURE 2.7   CONTINUED

What To Look For

F. Issuance of Shares

17 Confirm whether each issued share in the capital of the corporation has been fully paid for in cash or past services or property. *Note: Property does not include a promissory note made by a person to whom a share is issued or a person who does not deal at arm's length with a person to whom a share is issued.*

If the shares are of no par value, determine whether the directors have fixed the consideration for each such share at the time of the share issuance.

If the shares had par value, determine whether such par value shares were subscribed for and issued for the par value amount.

If there was a maximum consideration attached to a class of shares, determine whether the consideration paid on the issuance of shares exceeded the maximum consideration (unless otherwise increased by articles of amendment or as permitted by the governing statute in force as of the material time).

Confirm that the number of issued shares did not exceed the maximum authorized number of shares provided for in the charter documents.

Confirm that the share issuance has been made in compliance with the provisions of any existing shareholder agreement.

Comments

Canada

From July 1, 1965 to December 15, 1975 under the Old CCA, in the absence of any provisions to the contrary in the letters patent or supplementary letters patent or bylaws, shares in the capital stock of the company, including any shares created by supplementary letters patent increasing the capital stock of the corporation, could be allotted at such times and in such manner and to such persons or class of persons as the directors by resolution determined.

From December 15, 1975 to the present under the CBCA, shares of a corporation shall be in registered form and shall be without nominal or par value. Subject to the articles, the bylaws, and any unanimous shareholder agreement and to the pre-emptive right provided for in s. 28 of the CBCA, shares may be issued at such times and to such persons and for such consideration as the directors may determine. A share shall not be issued until the consideration for the share is fully paid in money, or in property or past service that is not less in value than the fair equivalent of the money that the corporation would have received if the share had been issued for money. The corporation shall add to the appropriate stated capital account the full amount of any consideration it receives for any shares the corporation issues.

From November 8, 1977, if a corporation issues shares in exchange for property of a person or a corporation on a non-arm's-length basis under the *Income Tax Act* (Canada) pursuant to an amalgamation agreement or an arrangement in accordance with the CBCA, or issues shares to shareholders of an amalgamating body corporate, the corporation may add to the stated capital accounts maintained for the shares of the classes or series issued the whole or any part of the amount of the consideration it received in the exchange.

Ontario

From January 1, 1971 to July 29, 1983 under the Old OBCA, where all the shares were without par value or where part of the corporation's shares are with par value and part are without par value, the articles could provide that each share without par value could not be issued for consideration, or the shares of each class of shares without par value could not be issued for aggregate consideration, exceeding in amount or value a stated amount in Canadian or other currency. In addition, the articles could provide that such share or shares may be issued for such greater amount as the board of directors of the corporation determined by board resolution.

From July 29, 1983 to the present under the OBCA, shares of a corporation shall be in registered form and shall be without nominal or par value. Shares with nominal or par value of a corporation incorporated before July 29, 1983 shall be deemed to be shares without nominal or par value. Subject to the articles, the bylaws, any unanimous shareholder agreement, and s. 26 of the OBCA with respect to pre-emptive rights, shares may be issued at such time and to such persons and for such consideration as the directors may determine. A share shall not be issued until the consideration for the share is fully paid in money, or in property or past service that is not less in value than the fair equivalent of the money that the corporation would have received if the share had been issued for money. The directors shall, in connection with the issue of any share not issued for money, determine:

a. the amount of money the corporation would have received if the share had been issued for money; and

b. either

   i. the fair value of the property or past service in consideration of which the share is issued, or

   ii. that such property or past service has a fair value that is not less than the amount of money referred to in item (a) above.

FIGURE 2.7 CONTINUED

What To Look For	Comments
G. Transfers of Shares	

18   Determine whether any incorporators' shares were validly transferred.
 	
Determine whether all share transfers were effected in compliance with the provisions of the charter documents and any existing shareholder agreement (which may require approvals in addition to the approvals set out in the charter documents) and whether share certificates held by the transferor, if any, have been duly endorsed for transfer (either on the reverse side of the share certificate or by separate transfer instrument) and surrendered for cancellation.
 	
Confirm that any rights of first refusal provisions in accordance with the charter documents or pre-emptive rights in accordance with the governing statute have been complied with prior to any transfer to third parties.
 	
Confirm that the minute book registers and ledgers have been updated to reflect each transfer of shares.
 	
Determine whether beneficial and registered ownership have been transferred, not just registered ownership.
 	
If any shares have been or are subject to a pledge, confirm that they have been released from the pledge before the completion of the share transfer.
 	
Confirm that the that the shares of a deceased shareholder are properly recorded in the name(s) of the estate trustees and, thereafter, have been properly transferred to the beneficiary thereof, as appropriate, in compliance with the share transfer restrictions set out in the charter documents and/or in any shareholder agreement.
	Canada
	From July 1, 1965 to December 15, 1975 under the Old CCA:
	
	a. Any transfer of shares must be made in accordance with the restrictions set out in the letters patent or supplementary letters patent;
	
	b. No transfer of shares that has not been paid in full could be made without the consent of the directors. If such transfer was made with the consent of the directors to a person who was not apparently of sufficient means to fully pay up such shares, subject to s. 40(3) of the Old CCA, the directors were jointly and severally liable to the company and its creditors to the same extent as the transferring shareholder.
	
	c. Where a share upon which a call was unpaid was transferred with the consent of the directors, the transferee was liable for the call to the same extent as if he had been the holder when the call was made and the transferor also remained liable for the call until it was paid.
	
	d. Where the letters patent, supplementary letters patent, or bylaws conferred such power on the directors, the directors could decline to permit the registration of a transfer of a fully paid share belonging to a shareholder who was indebted to the corporation (except in the case of shares listed on a recognized stock exchange).
	
	From December 15, 1975 to the present under the CBCA:
	
	a. Any transfer of shares shall be made in accordance with the restrictions set out in the articles of the corporation and any shareholder agreement.
	
	b. On delivery of a security, the purchaser acquires the rights in the security that the transferor had or had authority to convey, except a purchaser who has been a party to any fraud or illegality affecting the security or who, as a prior holder, had notice of an adverse claim.
	
	c. A bona fide purchaser, in addition to acquiring the rights of a purchaser, also acquires the security free from any adverse claim.
	
	d. Where a security in registered form is presented for transfer, the issuer shall register the transfer if:
	
	   i. the security is endorsed by an appropriate person under the CBCA;
	
	   ii. reasonable assurance is given that the endorsement is genuine and effective;
	
	   iii. the issuer has no duty to inquire into adverse claims or has discharged any such duty;
	
	   iv. any applicable law relating to the collection of taxes has been complied with;
	
	   v. the transfer is rightful or is to a bona fide purchaser; and
	
	   vi. any fee for the issue of a share certificate in respect of the transfer has been paid.
	
	Ontario
	From January 1, 1971 to July 29, 1983 under the Old OBCA, the corporation could not impose restrictions on the transfer of shares except such restrictions as were authorized by its articles.
	
	From July 29, 1983 to the present under the OBCA, a corporation shall not impose restrictions on the transfer or ownership of any class or series except such restrictions as are authorized by its articles.

FIGURE 2.7 CONTINUED

What To Look For	Comments
H. Share Certificates	
19 Review the specimen and issued share certificates for the following information:	**Canada**
	From July 1, 1965 to December 15, 1975 under the Old CCA, where there was more than one class of shares, the preferences, rights, conditions, restrictions, limitations, or prohibitions attaching to any class of shares were required to be stated on every share certificate representing that class of shares or by a writing permanently attached to the share certificate, or reference to such preferences, rights, etc., was required to be included on each such share certificate, with a statement that the full text was obtainable on demand from the secretary of the company.
a. Confirm that the form of the share certificate is in compliance with the provisions of the governing statute.	
b. Confirm that the issued share certificates conform with the specimen form of share certificate of that class, as approved by the directors of the corporation.	**From December 15, 1975 to the present** under the CBCA:
	a. A security certificate shall be signed manually by 1 director or officer, or by a registrar, transfer agent, or by a trustee, and any additional signatures may be printed or otherwise mechanically produced.
c. If there is an existing shareholder agreement, determine whether each issued share certificate contains a legend referencing and containing the prescribed wording set out in the shareholder agreement, as appropriate.	b. The certificate shall state on its face the corporation's name, the words "Incorporated under the *Canada Business Corporations Act*," the name of the person to whom it was issued, and the number and class of shares and the designation of any series.
	c. If the share certificate was issued before the corporation became subject to the CBCA or becomes subject to a restriction on its transfer, a lien in favour of the corporation, a unanimous shareholder agreement, or an endorsement in respect of a dissenting shareholder under s. 184(1) of the CBCA, the foregoing restrictions are ineffective against a transferee of the security who has no actual knowledge of it unless it or a reference to it is noted conspicuously on the security certificate. If a corporation continued under the CBCA has outstanding security certificates and if the words "private company" appear on the certificates, those words are deemed to be a notice of a restriction, lien, agreement, or endorsement.
d. Confirm that any restrictions on share transfers, any lien provisions, and references to the rights, privileges, restrictions, and conditions of each class, if any, are noted on the share certificate.	d. If the corporation is authorized to issue shares of more than one class or series, the rights, privileges, restrictions, and conditions attached thereto or reference to such rights, privileges, etc., shall be attached to such security certificate, with a statement that the corporation will furnish to a shareholder on demand and without charge a full copy of the text thereof.

FIGURE 2.7 CONTINUED

What To Look For	Comments
	Ontario

From January 1, 1971 to July 29, 1983 under the Old OBCA, in addition to item (a) under the CBCA above:

a. Every share certificate shall state on its face the name of the corporation, the words "Incorporated under the law of the Province of Ontario" or words of like effect, the name of the person to whom it was issued and the number and class of shares represented thereby, and whether the shares are with par value or without par value and, if with par value, the par value thereof.

b. Every share certificate shall state on the certificate or have attached thereto a legible statement of the preferences, rights, conditions, restrictions, prohibitions, or limitations attaching to that class of shares or legibly state that there are preferences, rights, etc., attaching to that class and that a copy of the full text thereof is obtainable on demand and without fee from the corporation.

c. If the articles or bylaws provide that a corporation has a lien, the right of the corporation to the lien shall be noted on every share certificate issued by the corporation.

d. Any share transfer restrictions shall be stated on the certificate, either by attaching thereto a legible statement of the restrictions on the right to transfer the shares, or by stating on the certificate that there are restrictions on the right to transfer the shares and that a copy of the full text thereof is obtainable on demand and without fee from the corporation.

From July 29, 1983 to the present under the OBCA:

a. A security certificate shall be signed manually by at least 1 director or officer of the corporation or by a registrar, transfer agent, branch transfer agent, or issuing or other authenticating agent of the corporation, or by a trustee who certifies it in accordance with a trust indenture, and any additional signatures required on a security certificate may be printed or otherwise mechanically reproduced thereon.

b. The corporation shall state on the face of each share certificate the name of the corporation and the words "Incorporated under the law of the Province of Ontario" or words of like effect, the name of the person to whom it was issued, and the number and class of shares and the designation of any series that the certificate represents. Where the articles restrict the issuance, transfer, or ownership of shares of any class or series, such restriction shall be noted conspicuously on every share certificate evidencing a share that is subject to such restriction, with a statement that the corporation will furnish to a shareholder on demand and without charge a full copy of the text thereof.

c. Where the corporation is authorized to issue shares of more than one class or series, the corporation is required to state on each share certificate:

   i. the rights, privileges, restrictions, and conditions attaching to the shares of each class and series; or

   ii. that the class or series of shares has rights, privileges, restrictions, or conditions attached thereto and that the corporation will furnish to a shareholder on demand and without charge a full copy of the text thereof; and

   iii. the authority of the directors to fix such rights, privileges, etc.

FIGURE 2.7 CONTINUED

What To Look For	Comments
I. Annual Meetings or Annual Proceedings	
20 Determine whether the corporation has conducted its annual business by holding an annual meeting or, alternatively in lieu thereof (and when permitted by statute), by signing resolutions within 18 months of the date of incorporation and within 15 months thereafter. If the annual proceedings were conducted by way of meetings of the directors and/or shareholders, determine that the corporation has complied with the notice and quorum requirements in accordance with its bylaws and the governing statute in force at the material date. In particular, confirm the following: a. that the financial statements of the corporation for each financial year-end have been approved by the directors and submitted to the shareholders in accordance with the time requirements set out in the governing statute; b. that the annual election of directors has been included (except in the case where the term of office of a director is more than 1 year); c. that the shareholders have appointed an auditor for the ensuing year or, alternatively, that all the shareholders (both voting and non-voting) have waived the requirement to appoint an auditor; d. that each new director elected has signed a Consent to Act as a Director and is duly qualified to act as a director of the corporation; and e. that the newly elected directors have appointed new officers for the ensuing year in accordance with the bylaws.	***Canada*** **From July 1, 1965 to December 15, 1975** under the Old CCA, an annual meeting of shareholders was required to be held at some date not later than 18 months after the incorporation of the corporation and subsequently at least once in every calendar year and not more than 15 months after the holding of the last preceding annual meeting. There was no provision in the Old CCA (or in any predecessor statute) permitting resolutions of the directors and shareholders to be passed by the signature of the directors and/or shareholders in lieu of being passed at a duly called and held annual meeting. **From December 15, 1975 to November 24, 2001** under the CBCA, the directors were required to call an annual meeting of shareholders no later than 18 months after the date of formation of the corporation and subsequently no later than 15 months after holding the last preceding annual meeting. In lieu of the holding of an annual meeting, the CBCA permitted the annual proceedings to be conducted and passed by the signature of the directors and all the shareholders entitled to vote thereon. **From November 24, 2001 to the present**, a new provision requires that an annual meeting shall be held no later than 6 months after the end of the corporation's preceding financial year. ***Ontario*** **From April 30, 1954 to January 1, 1971** under the Old 1954 CA, an annual meeting of shareholders was required to be held at some date not later than 18 months after the incorporation of the corporation and subsequently at least once in every calendar year and not more than 15 months after the holding of the last preceding annual meeting. There was no provision in the Old 1954 CA (or in any predecessor statute) permitting annual resolutions of the directors and shareholders to be passed by the signature of the directors and/or shareholders in lieu of being passed at a duly called and held annual meeting. **From January 1, 1971 to the present** under the Old OBCA and the OBCA, the directors are required to call an annual meeting of shareholders no later than 18 months after the date of formation of the corporation and subsequently no later than 15 months after holding the last preceding annual meeting. In lieu of holding an annual meeting, the Old OBCA permitted and the OBCA permits the annual proceedings to be conducted and passed by the signature of the directors and all the shareholders entitled to vote thereon.

FIGURE 2.7   CONCLUDED

What To Look For	Comments

J. Minute Book Registers and Ledgers
 	
21   Review the minute book registers and ledgers to confirm that the appropriate directors' register, the shareholders' registers, and the transfer registers are complete and accurately reflect the corporate information contained in the corporate records of the corporation with respect to the directors and the issued share capital of the corporation.
 	
Determine whether the minute books of the corporation contain all the corporate records required to be kept and maintained under the OBCA and the CBCA.
 	
Comments
 	
Under the CBCA and the OBCA, a corporation or appointed transfer agent is not required to produce any share certificate 6 years from the date of its cancellation.
	Canada
	
	From December 15, 1975 to the present under the CBCA, a corporation is required to prepare and maintain at its registered office, or at such other place in Canada designated by the directors, records containing:
	
	a. the articles, bylaws, and all amendments thereto, and any unanimous shareholder agreement;
	
	b. minutes of meetings and resolutions of shareholders;
	
	c. copies of all notices in respect of the directors and changes in directors; and
	
	d. a securities register with a record of the securities issued by the corporation showing with respect to each class or series of securities:
	
	    i. the names (in alphabetical order) of persons, together with their respective latest known addresses, who are or have been security holders;
	
	    ii. the number of securities held by each security holder; and
	
	    iii. the date and particulars of the issue and transfer of each security.
	
	In addition to the above, the corporation shall prepare and maintain adequate accounting records and records containing minutes of meetings and resolutions of the directors and any committee thereof.
	
	Ontario
	
	From July 20, 1983 to the present under the OBCA, a corporation is required to prepare and maintain at its registered office, or at such other place in Ontario designated by the directors:
	
	a. the articles, bylaws, and all amendments thereto, and a copy of any unanimous shareholder agreement known to the directors;
	
	b. minutes of meetings and resolutions of shareholders;
	
	c. a register of directors (setting out the names and residence addresses of all persons who are or have been directors of the corporation with the dates that they became and ceased to be director);
	
	d. a securities register with a record of the securities issued by the corporation showing with respect to each class or series of securities:
	
	    i. the names (in alphabetical order) of persons, together with their respective addresses, who are or have been within 6 years registered as:
	
	        • shareholders together with the number and class of shares registered in their names;
	
	        • holders of debt obligations together with class or series and principal amount of such debt obligations; or
	
	        • holders of warrants of the corporation (other than warrants exercisable within 1 year from the date of issue); and
	
	    ii. the date and particulars of the issue of each such security and warrant;
	
	e. a transfer register in which all transfers of shares and the date and other particulars of each transfer are set out.
	
	In addition to the above, the corporation shall prepare and maintain adequate accounting records and records containing minutes of meetings and resolutions of the directors and any committee thereof.

FIGURE 2.8   SAMPLE RECTIFICATION DOCUMENTS

RESOLUTIONS OF THE DIRECTORS AND SHAREHOLDERS

OF

_____

(the "Corporation")

I.   **RECTIFICATION**

RECITALS:

(A)   On review of the corporate records of the Corporation, it was noted that there were certain corporate deficiencies and outstanding corporate matters which were not approved and/or passed in compliance with the Corporation's by-laws and/or the *Business Corporations Act* (Ontario).

(B)   To complete and correct the corporate records of the Corporation and bring them up to date, it is in order for these corporate deficiencies and outstanding corporate matters to be rectified and ratified at this time, to the fullest extent possible and, for greater certainty, for the corporate structure of the Corporation to be approved, ratified and confirmed for all purposes.

RESOLVED that in spite of any corporate deficiencies or irregularities in the corporate proceedings of the Corporation, all acts and corporate proceedings taken or reported to have been taken to the date hereof by the directors, officers and/or shareholders of the Corporation or persons acting as such directors, officers or shareholders of the Corporation, as disclosed by the books and records and financial statements of the Corporation and amended by these resolutions, except for willful neglect and fraud, are approved, ratified, adopted and confirmed for all purposes including, without limitation, the following resolutions:

II.   **CONFIRMATION OF CORPORATE STRUCTURE**

RESOLVED that in spite of any corporate deficiencies or irregularities in the validity of the election of directors, the appointment of officers and the issuances and/or transfers of shares in the capital of the Corporation, the directors and shareholders of the Corporation, for greater certainty, hereby jointly approve, ratify and confirm the following corporate structure of the Corporation for all purposes:

Current Issued Shareholding

The current issued and outstanding share capital of the Corporation as at the date hereof is as follows:

Name of Shareholder	No. & Class of Shares
TOTAL	

Current Directors

The following persons, both of whom are resident Canadians as defined in the *Business Corporations Act* (Ontario), are all the directors of the Corporation as at the date hereof:

_____

_____

FIGURE 2.8   CONTINUED

<u>Current Officers</u>

The following persons are all the officers of the Corporation who hold the indicated offices of the Corporation as at the date hereof:

Office held	Name

The foregoing resolutions are hereby signed by all the directors of the Corporation. These resolutions may be signed and delivered in counterpart and/or by electronic facsimile.

DATED: _____

_____   _____

The foregoing resolutions are hereby signed by all the shareholders of the Corporation entitled to vote thereon. These resolutions may be signed and delivered in counterpart and/or by electronic facsimile.

DATED: _____

_____   _____

FIGURE 2.8   CONTINUED

STATUTORY DECLARATION

CANADA	) **IN THE MATTER** of the *Business*
PROVINCE OF ONTARIO	) *Corporations Act* (Ontario) and
	) of _____

I, _____ of the City of _____ in the Province of Ontario, **DO SOLEMNLY DECLARE** as follows:

1.   I was the incorporator and first director, the President and a shareholder of _____ (the "**Corporation**") which was formed under the *Business Corporations Act* (Ontario) (the "**Act**") on _____ ("**Incorporation Date**"). Since the Incorporation Date, I have continued to be a director, the President and a shareholder of the Corporation and, as such, I have knowledge of the business and affairs of the Corporation.

2.   I understand that, through inadvertence, the minute books of the Corporation containing the original articles, by-laws, corporate minutes and signed resolutions, directors' and officers' registers as well as the share records and ledgers have been lost or misplaced and, after a thorough search of the offices of the Corporation, the accountants of the Corporation and the former solicitors of the Corporation, cannot be found or located.

3.   To assist the solicitors of the Corporation in preparing the necessary corporate resolutions to reconstitute the corporate records and minute books of the Corporation, I have been asked to confirm, to the best of my knowledge and belief, the corporate structure of the Corporation as well as changes in its corporate structure from the Incorporation Date to the date hereof. In support of the making of this Statutory Declaration, I have reviewed our office files and records as well as the following documents which have been shown to me but do not form part of this statutory declaration:

   (a)   Copy of the Certificate and articles of incorporation of the Corporation obtained from the microfiche certified by the Director appointed under the Act on _____;

   (b)   Copies of the financial statements of the Corporation for each of the financial years ended _____;

   (c)   Corporate Document List and Corporation Profile Report produced by the Ontario Companies and Personal Property Security Branch of the Ministry of Government Services on _____;

   (d)   Copies of filed Form 1 Notices obtained from the microfiche certified by the Director appointed under the Act on _____;

   (e)   Shareholders Agreement dated as of _____ made between _____, _____, _____ and _____;

   (f)   Copies of share certificates issued to the current shareholders of the Corporation; and

   (g)   _____,

   (collectively, the "**Available Corporate Information**").

4.   To the best of my knowledge and belief, I confirm and acknowledge the following information based on the Available Corporate Information, my recollection of the following matters and otherwise:

FIGURE 2.8 CONTINUED

A.   **ISSUED SHARE CAPITAL**

(a)   The following shares were purportedly issued to the indicated shareholders of the Corporation, as fully paid and non-assessable, effective as of the indicated dates:

Effective Date	Shareholder	No. & Class of Shares	Aggregate Issue Price

(b)   The following share transfers of the Corporation were purportedly effected on the indicated dates:

Effective Date	Transferor	Transferee	No. & Class of Shares

(c)   The current issued share capital of the Corporation as at the date hereof is as follows:

Shareholder	No. & Class of Shares	Percentage Equity Interest

B.   **DIRECTORS**

(a)   The following persons purportedly held office as directors of the Corporation, effective as of the indicated dates:

Name of Director	Res. CDN?	Date of Election	Date Ceased

(b)   The following persons are all the current directors of the Corporation as at the date hereof:

FIGURE 2.8 CONTINUED

C.   **OFFICERS**

(a)   The following persons were purportedly appointed to the indicated offices of the Corporation, effective as of the indicated dates:

Office Held	Name of Officer	Date of Appointment	Date Ceased

(b)   The following persons are all the officers of the Corporation and hold the indicated offices of the Corporation as at the date hereof:

Office	Name of Officer
President	_____
Vice-President	_____
Secretary-Treasurer	_____

D.   **REGISTERED OFFICE**

(a)   The Corporation's former registered office address, as indicated in the articles of incorporation of the Corporation certified on _____, was located at _____. Since that date, the Corporation has changed its registered office address to the following addresses, effective as of the indicated dates:

Registered Office Address	From	To

(b)   The current registered office address of the Corporation, as at the date hereof, is located at the following address:

_____

_____

FIGURE 2.8 CONCLUDED

E.   **BANKING ARRANGEMENTS**

The Corporation currently maintains its banking arrangements at _____
and the current signing authority for the execution of cheques, notes and other negotiable instruments on behalf of the Corporation is as follows: _____
_____.

The Corporation does not maintain bank accounts with any other financial institution, other than its bank account at _____.

F.   **FINANCIAL YEAR-END**

The Corporation's first financial year terminated on _____ and on _____ on each year thereafter. The Corporation's last completed financial year end was _____.

G.   **CONSENT TO AUDIT EXEMPTION**

All the shareholders of the Corporation have waived the audit requirements of the Act in respect of each financial year-end of the Corporation, commencing from the Incorporation Date.

H.   **DIVIDENDS**

The Corporation has never declared any dividends on any of its issued shares from the date of its incorporation up to the date hereof.

I.   **OTHER MATTERS**

[INSERT APPROPRIATE TEXT]

AND I make this solemn declaration conscientiously believing it to be true and knowing that it is of the same force and effect as if made under oath and by virtue of the *Canada Evidence Act.*

DECLARED before me at the City of   )
_____, in the Province of Ontario   )
this _____ day of _____, _____   )
)
_____   )   _____
A Notary Public in and for the Province   )
of Ontario   )

CHAPTER 3

Corporate reorganizations: Amalgamations, dissolutions/windups, and rollovers

Sue Kavanagh, Perley-Robertson, Hill & McDougall LLP

CHAPTER OVERVIEW

This chapter discusses various types of corporate reorganizations — namely, amalgamations, dissolutions and windups, and rollovers — under the federal and Ontario corporate statutes and the federal *Income Tax Act*. The procedures and documents required to effect each type of reorganization are described. The chapter highlights some important tax consequences of these corporate reorganizations.

CHAPTER OBJECTIVES

After completing this chapter, you should be able to:
1. Explain the difference between an amalgamation, a dissolution, a windup, and a rollover.
2. Identify the methods of amalgamation available and explain when it is appropriate to use each of these methods.
3. Identify and complete the documents required for amalgamation.
4. Identify the methods of dissolution provided for in the CBCA and the OBCA and describe an appropriate plan of action for dissolution.
5. Identify and complete the documents required for dissolution.

6. Review the practical aspects of rollovers and their application in a typical transaction.

7. List the requirements to be met for a rollover of assets under s. 85 of the ITA.

8. Explain the difference between paid-up capital and stated capital.

9. List the information to be included in a rollover agreement.

10. Identify and complete the documents required for a typical s. 85 rollover.

11. Identify and complete the documents required for a typical reorganization of capital under s. 86 of the ITA.

AMALGAMATION

Introduction

Amalgamation is the process whereby two or more corporations ("amalgamating" or "predecessor" corporations) join to become a single corporate entity (the "amalgamated" corporation).

Under corporate statutes, when an amalgamation takes place, the predecessor corporations do not cease to exist but continue in the amalgamated corporation. The analogy of "a river formed by the confluence of two streams, or the creation of a single rope through the inter-twining of strands"[1] is often used to describe this concept of continuing existence. Under the *Income Tax Act* (Canada) (ITA), however, an amalgamated corporation is generally treated as a new corporation rather than a continuation of the amalgamating corporations.

BUSINESS REASONS FOR AMALGAMATION

If two or more corporations have common ownership, it may be desirable to combine them into one legal entity. This could eliminate or reduce administrative inefficiencies and unnecessary costs, including:

- the cost of separate financial statements for each corporation in the group, especially if they are audited;

- duplication of legal and other expenses incurred to maintain the status of each corporation (that is, the cost of annual meetings and registration fees necessary to carry on business in several provinces); and

- directors' fees and related expenses (such as indemnity insurance) where an amalgamation reduces the number of directors.

TAX REASONS FOR AMALGAMATION

A typical tax reason for amalgamating is to maximize the use of losses within a corporate group. For example, if one corporation in a group has tax losses and other corporations in the group have taxable profits, it may be desirable to merge the loss corporation with one or more of the profitable corporations.

General planning considerations

There are several important points to keep in mind when planning for an amalgamation:

1. The amalgamating corporations must be governed by the same corporate statute. For example, if a corporation incorporated under the *Business Corporations Act* (Ontario) (OBCA) wishes to amalgamate with a corporation incorporated under the *Canada Business Corporations Act* (CBCA), and the amalgamated corporation is to be governed by the CBCA, it will be necessary for the OBCA corporation to apply for **continuance** as a CBCA corporation before the amalgamation can proceed. The procedure for continuance of a corporation under the laws of another jurisdiction is described in chapter 14 of the companion text by Gillis, *Advanced Corporate Legal Procedures*.

   continuance
   a procedure that allows a corporation governed by the laws of one jurisdiction to leave that jurisdiction and to continue and become governed by the laws of another jurisdiction

2. Tax-planning considerations include structuring the reorganization to qualify as an amalgamation under s. 87 of the ITA. Generally, s. 87 provides for a rollover on amalgamation of many, if not all, tax accounts and tax bases of the amalgamating corporations to the new corporation with few, or no, tax consequences. To qualify for this treatment, the amalgamation must meet the following conditions (ITA s. 87(1)):

   a. There must be a merger of two or more corporations, each of which was, immediately before the merger, a taxable Canadian corporation (as defined in s. 89(1) of the ITA), to form one corporate entity.

   b. All of the property of the predecessor corporations immediately before the merger becomes property of the new corporation by virtue of the merger.

   c. All of the liabilities of the predecessor corporations immediately before the merger become liabilities of the new corporation by virtue of the merger.

   d. All of the shareholders who owned shares of the capital stock of any predecessor corporation immediately before the merger receive shares of the capital stock of the new corporation as a result of the merger.

3. On amalgamation, the property of the amalgamating corporations becomes and continues to be the property of the amalgamated corporation, and the amalgamated corporation becomes and continues to be liable for the obligations of each of the amalgamating corporations. Prior to amalgamation, existing agreements under which any amalgamating corporation may be bound should be reviewed to determine whether consents of any party to the amalgamation are required. For example, the provisions of a debenture, bank loan, or guarantee may require consent.

4. Another early planning consideration is the conversion value of existing shares of the respective amalgamating corporations in exchange for new shares of the amalgamated corporation at the time of amalgamation. In particular, it is important to ensure that no shareholder of a predecessor corporation ends up with shares of the amalgamated corporation that have a lesser value than the predecessor shares. A valuation of each amalgamating corporation may be necessary so that the new shares can be designed to maintain the relative values of the predecessor shares. The following example illustrates how valuation can affect the decision on the conversion of shares.

Shareholder A holds 100 common shares of A Corp and shareholder B holds 100 common shares of B Corp. No other shares have been issued. A Corp and B Corp wish to amalgamate. On the surface, it would appear to make sense to issue 100 common shares of the amalgamated corporation (AB Corp) to each shareholder on amalgamation. However, a valuation of the amalgamating corporations shows that A Corp is worth $1,000 and B Corp is worth $2,000. Therefore, on amalgamation, shareholder B should receive shares of AB Corp that are worth twice as much as the shares issued to shareholder A.

It might be appropriate for shareholder B to receive 200 common shares of AB Corp while shareholder A receives 100 common shares. However, if the two shareholders want an equal role in AB Corp, they will not accept this disparity but will expect to receive an equal number of common shares. In this case, AB Corp could issue special shares to shareholder B or to both shareholders in order to maintain the relative values of their shareholdings in A Corp and B Corp. For example, AB Corp could issue class A special shares that are redeemable and retractable at $1.00 per share. On amalgamation, shareholder A would receive 100 common shares plus 1,000 class A special shares, and shareholder B would receive 100 common shares plus 2,000 class A special shares with identical rights. Again, this method ensures that shareholder B receives shares worth twice the amount issued to shareholder A.

If stock options have been granted to shareholders of an amalgamating corporation but have not yet been exercised, these options should be taken into consideration and dealt with appropriately when considering conversion values upon amalgamation.

5. Another planning consideration, for both business and tax reasons, is the effective date of the amalgamation. The Canada Revenue Agency (CRA) takes the position that an amalgamation is effective at the beginning of the day (that is, immediately after midnight) shown on the certificate of amalgamation (discussed below). The year-end for tax purposes of each of the predecessor corporations ends immediately prior to the effective date of the amalgamation (that is, just before midnight on the day before the date on the certificate of amalgamation). In order to avoid a new year-end and the consequent cost of preparing additional year-end financial statements, it is desirable for the certificate of amalgamation to be dated the day after the year-end of the predecessor corporations (or of one of them, if they have different year-ends). For example, if the year-end of the predecessor corporations is December 31, the certificate of amalgamation should be dated January 1. Under both the CBCA and OBCA, it is possible, at the time articles of amalgamation are filed (as discussed below), to request that the amalgamation take effect on a specific future date provided that the future date is not more than 30 days after the date of filing.

Both the CBCA and the OBCA provide for two methods of amalgamation, commonly referred to as "long-form" and "short-form" amalgamations. Short-form amalgamations are either "vertical" or "horizontal." A **long-form amalgamation** is the amalgamation of two or more corporations. A **vertical short-form amalgamation**

long-form amalgamation
an amalgamation of two or more corporations, requiring an amalgamation agreement to be approved by special resolution of the shareholders

vertical short-form amalgamation
an amalgamation of a corporation and one or more of its wholly owned subsidiaries, requiring approval by resolution of the directors of each corporation but not the approval of shareholders

is the amalgamation of a holding corporation (a parent corporation) and one or more of its wholly owned subsidiaries. A **horizontal short-form amalgamation** is the amalgamation of two or more wholly owned subsidiaries of the same parent corporation.

The procedures for amalgamation vary for CBCA and OBCA corporations. These procedures and the related documentation requirements are described below and summarized in the amalgamation checklist in figure 3.1 at the end of the chapter. Figure 3.2 reproduces some of the forms and other documents that are typically used in long-form and short-form amalgamations.

Long-form amalgamations

AMALGAMATION AGREEMENT

Corporations proposing to amalgamate must enter into an amalgamation agreement. In addition to specifying the terms and means of effecting the amalgamation, the amalgamation agreement must include the following information (CBCA s. 182(1); OBCA s. 175(1)):

1. the name of the amalgamated corporation;

2. if amalgamation is under the CBCA, the province or territory in Canada where the registered office will be situated;

3. if amalgamation is under the OBCA, the street address of the registered office;

4. the classes and any maximum number of shares that the amalgamated corporation will be authorized to issue;

5. if there will be two or more classes of shares, the rights, privileges, restrictions, and conditions (if any) attaching to each class of shares;

6. if a class of shares may be issued in series, the authority given to the directors to fix the number of shares in each series, and to determine the designation of, and rights, privileges, restrictions, and conditions (if any) attaching to, the shares of each series;

7. restrictions, if any, on the issuance, transfer, or ownership of shares of the amalgamated corporation;

8. any restrictions on the businesses that the amalgamated corporation may carry on;

9. the number (or minimum and maximum number) of directors;

10. the name, address, and residency of each proposed director of the amalgamated corporation;

11. the basis on which the shares of each amalgamating corporation will be converted into shares or other securities of the amalgamated corporation;

12. if any shares of an amalgamating corporation are not to be converted into securities of the amalgamated corporation, the amount of money or securities of any body corporate that the holders of such shares will receive in addition to or instead of securities of the amalgamated corporation;

13. if shareholders are to receive money in lieu of fractional shares or other securities, the terms on which payment will be made;

14. if amalgamation is under the CBCA, whether the bylaws of the amalgamated corporation will be those of one of the amalgamating corporations and, if not, a copy of the proposed bylaws (CBCA s. 182(1)(f));

15. if amalgamation is under the OBCA, whether the bylaws of the amalgamated corporation are to be those of one of the amalgamating corporations and the address where a copy of the proposed bylaws may be examined (OBCA s. 175(1)(d)); and

16. details of any arrangements necessary to perfect the amalgamation and to provide for the subsequent management and operation of the amalgamated corporation.

Figure 3.2 at the end of the chapter includes a sample amalgamation agreement.

As indicated above, shareholders of the amalgamating corporations may receive securities of the amalgamated corporation, money, or securities of other corporations in exchange for their shares. However, if shares of one of the amalgamating corporations are held by or on behalf of one of the other amalgamating corporations, the amalgamation agreement must provide for the cancellation of such shares when the amalgamation becomes effective without any repayment of capital in respect thereof, and no provision can be made in the agreement for the conversion of such shares into shares of the amalgamated corporation (CBCA s. 182(2); OBCA s. 175(2)).

SHAREHOLDER APPROVAL

The directors of each amalgamating corporation must submit the amalgamation agreement for approval to the shareholders of that corporation. The amalgamation agreement will be adopted when it is approved by a **special resolution** of the shareholders of each amalgamating corporation (CBCA s. 183(5); OBCA s. 176(4)). The special resolution may be passed either at a meeting of shareholders, duly called for that purpose, or by a resolution in writing signed by all the shareholders of the corporation entitled to vote. If a meeting of shareholders is to be called to pass the special resolution, the notice of the meeting must:

1. include or be accompanied by a copy of the amalgamation agreement; and

2. state that a dissenting shareholder is entitled to be paid the fair value of the shareholder's shares in accordance with CBCA s. 190 or OBCA s. 185.

Figure 3.2 includes samples of the documents that may be required to obtain shareholder approval of an amalgamation.

The CBCA and the OBCA differ with respect to voting by shareholders in respect of an amalgamation. The CBCA provides that each share carries the right to vote at a meeting of shareholders in respect of an amalgamation, whether or not it otherwise carries the right to vote (CBCA s. 183(3)). If a special resolution of the shareholders is passed by written resolution, the written resolution must be signed by all the shareholders of the corporation, even the shareholders who do not have the right to vote. The OBCA requires that the amalgamation agreement be submitted to holders of shares entitled to vote thereon (OBCA s. 176(1)); therefore, non-voting shareholders do not vote on amalgamation, with one exception. If an amalgamation agreement contains a provision that, if contained in a proposed amendment to the articles, would entitle a holder to vote separately as a class or series,

special resolution

a resolution passed by a majority of not less than two-thirds of the votes cast by the shareholders who voted in respect of the resolution or signed by all the shareholders entitled to vote on the resolution

ADVANCED CORPORATE BUSINESS TRANSACTIONS

then such holder is entitled to vote separately as a class or series, whether or not the shares otherwise carry the right to vote (OBCA s. 176(3)). The CBCA also provides for a separate class vote in the event that the amalgamation agreement contains a provision that, if contained in a proposed amendment to the articles, would entitle a holder to vote separately as a class or series (CBCA s. 183(4)). For example, a class or series vote would take place if the amalgamation agreement provided for an exchange, reclassification, or cancellation of all or part of the shares of the particular class or series. Under the OBCA, the holders of shares who are not entitled to vote may not dissent.

DISSENT RIGHTS

Long-form amalgamations give rise to shareholder rights of dissent (CBCA s. 190(1); OBCA s. 185(1)(c)). A dissenting shareholder is entitled to be paid the fair value of his or her shares, determined as of the close of business on the day before the resolution to amalgamate was adopted. It is therefore advisable to include in the amalgamation agreement a provision permitting termination of the agreement by the directors of each of the amalgamating corporations at any time before endorsement of the certificate of amalgamation (CBCA s. 183(6); OBCA s. 176(5)).

Short-form amalgamations

A short-form amalgamation may involve the amalgamation of a parent corporation with one or more wholly owned subsidiaries (vertical) or the amalgamation of wholly owned subsidiaries of the same parent (horizontal). Both the CBCA and the OBCA permit a short-form amalgamation (whether horizontal or vertical) to proceed without an amalgamation agreement and without shareholder approval, provided that certain conditions are met.

DIRECTOR APPROVAL

All short-form amalgamations require the approval, by resolution, of the directors of each of the amalgamating corporations. However, the provisions that must be included in the directors' resolutions are different from vertical and horizontal amalgamations.

In the case of a vertical short-form amalgamation, the directors' resolutions of both the parent and subsidiary corporations must provide that:

1. the shares of each of the amalgamating subsidiary corporations shall be cancelled without any repayment of capital in respect of those shares;

2. except as may be prescribed, the articles of amalgamation of the amalgamated corporation shall be the same as the articles of the parent corporation;

3. for CBCA corporations, no securities shall be issued by the amalgamated corporation in connection with the amalgamation, and the stated capital of the amalgamated corporation shall be the same as the stated capital of the parent corporation;

4. for OBCA corporations, no securities shall be issued and no assets shall be distributed by the amalgamated corporation in connection with the amalgamation; and

5. for OBCA corporations, the bylaws of the amalgamated corporation shall be the same as the bylaws of the parent corporation.

Figure 3.2 includes examples of directors' resolutions for both a parent corporation and a wholly owned subsidiary intending to amalgamate.

In the case of a horizontal short-form amalgamation, the directors' resolution of each amalgamating corporation must provide that:

1. the shares of all but one of the amalgamating subsidiary corporations shall be cancelled without any repayment of capital in respect of those shares;

2. except as may be prescribed, the articles of amalgamation shall be the same as the articles of the amalgamating subsidiary corporation whose shares are not being cancelled;

3. the stated capital of the amalgamating subsidiary corporation whose shares are being cancelled shall be added to the stated capital of the amalgamating subsidiary corporation whose shares are not being cancelled; and

4. for OBCA corporations, the bylaws of the amalgamated corporation shall be the same as the bylaws of the amalgamating subsidiary corporation whose shares are not being cancelled.

Figure 3.2 provides examples of directors' resolutions for a subsidiary whose shares will be cancelled on amalgamation and a subsidiary whose shares will not be cancelled.

Shareholders do not have rights of either approval or dissent in the case of short-form amalgamations.

Filing articles of amalgamation

Once a proposed amalgamation has been approved by the shareholders and/or the directors, as the case may be, articles of amalgamation must be filed with the Director under the applicable corporate statute. Form 9 for CBCA corporations and Form 4 for OBCA corporations are included in figure 3.2 at the end of the chapter.

For OBCA long-form amalgamations, a copy of the amalgamation agreement must be attached as a schedule to the articles of amalgamation. If the amalgamation is a short-form amalgamation under the OBCA, a certified copy of the directors' resolution of each amalgamating corporation must be attached as a schedule to the articles of amalgamation.

The CBCA does not require the filing of copies of either the amalgamation agreement or the directors' resolutions. However, for both long-form and short-form amalgamations, the articles of amalgamation must be accompanied by Form 2, Information Regarding the Registered Office and the Board of Directors.

In addition, the CBCA requires a statutory declaration and the OBCA requires a statement of a director or an officer of each amalgamating corporation to be filed with the articles of amalgamation, as discussed further below.

NAME OF THE AMALGAMATED CORPORATION

Under both the CBCA and the OBCA, an amalgamated corporation is entitled to take the name of one of the amalgamating corporations provided that it is not a number name. If the amalgamated corporation is to have a new name that is not a number name, a NUANS (newly upgraded automated name search) report and any necessary consents must be obtained and filed with the Director at the time the articles of amalgamation are filed.

STATUTORY DECLARATION/STATEMENT OF A DIRECTOR OR OFFICER

For CBCA corporations, the articles of amalgamation must be accompanied by a statutory declaration of a director or officer of each amalgamating corporation (CBCA s. 185(2)). For OBCA corporations, a statement of a director or officer of each amalgamating corporation must be attached as a schedule to the articles of amalgamation (OBCA s. 178(2)).

Under both statutes, the statutory declaration or statement, as the case may be, must state that there are reasonable grounds for believing that:

1. the amalgamating corporation is, and the amalgamated corporation will be, able to pay its liabilities as they become due;

2. the realizable value of the amalgamated corporation's assets will not be less than the aggregate of its liabilities and stated capital of all classes; and

3. no creditor will be prejudiced by the amalgamation, or adequate notice has been given to all known creditors of the amalgamating corporations and no creditor objects to the amalgamation otherwise than on grounds that are frivolous or vexatious.

In addition, under the OBCA, the director's or officer's statement must state that:

4. where creditors have notified the corporation that they object to the amalgamation, setting forth with reasonable particularity the grounds for doing so, those grounds are considered to be either frivolous or vexatious; and

5. the corporation has given notice to each person who has notified the corporation of an objection to the amalgamation, in the manner specified, that:

   a. the grounds upon which the person's objection is based are considered to be frivolous or vexatious, and

   b. a creditor of a corporation who objects to an amalgamation has the status of a complainant under s. 248 of the OBCA.

A director or an officer of an amalgamating corporation may state that no creditor will be prejudiced by the amalgamation if it is reasonable to believe that the amalgamated corporation will pay each creditor on the same terms and conditions to which the creditor is entitled as a creditor of the amalgamating corporation. To obtain reasonable grounds for this belief, the director or officer may wish to examine the financial statements of each of the amalgamating corporations and any valuations that have been made of the assets and liabilities of any amalgamating corporation.

If it is decided by an amalgamating corporation that notice should be given to a creditor, "adequate notice" is given if:

1. notice in writing is sent to each known creditor with a claim against the corporation that exceeds $1,000 (CBCA s. 185(3)) or $2,500 (OBCA s. 178(3));

2. a notice is published once in a newspaper published or distributed in the place where the corporation has its registered office (and, under the CBCA, reasonable notice thereof is given in each province where the corporation carries on business); and

3. each notice states that the corporation intends to amalgamate with one or more specified corporations in accordance with the applicable Act and that a creditor of the corporation may object to the amalgamation within 30 days of the date of the notice.

Figure 3.2 at the end of the chapter includes a statutory declaration under the CBCA, an OBCA officer's statement, and a notice to creditors.

Certificate of amalgamation

On receipt of articles of amalgamation, the Director under the applicable corporate statute issues a certificate of amalgamation. The date of the certificate is the date the articles are received by the Director unless a future date that is not more than 30 days after the date of filing is requested.

On the date shown on the certificate of amalgamation:

1. the amalgamating corporations cease to be separate entities and continue as one corporation;

2. the property of each amalgamating corporation becomes and continues to be the property of the amalgamated corporation;

3. the amalgamated corporation becomes and continues to be liable for the obligations of each amalgamating corporation;

4. an existing cause of action, claim, or liability to prosecution is unaffected;

5. a civil, criminal, or administrative action or proceeding pending by or against an amalgamating corporation may continue to be prosecuted by or against the amalgamated corporation;

6. a conviction against, or a ruling, order, or judgment in favour of or against, an amalgamating corporation may be enforced by or against the amalgamated corporation; and

7. the articles of amalgamation are deemed to be the articles of incorporation of the amalgamated corporation and the certificate of amalgamation is deemed to be the certificate of incorporation of the amalgamated corporation.

Post-amalgamation matters

Once the certificate of amalgamation has been issued, various post-amalgamation proceedings are necessary, including the adoption of new bylaws (if necessary), the passing of directors' resolutions to appoint officers, approval of banking arrangements, approval of the form of share certificates, approval of the issuance of share certificates (if necessary), approval of the form of corporate seal (if any), preservation of pre-existing divisions and divisional names, and authorization of any provincial registrations or licensing applications required in jurisdictions where the amalgamated corporation will carry on business. Figure 3.2 at the end of the chapter includes samples of directors' and shareholders' resolutions and a director's certificate and consent that may be required following an amalgamation.

All share certificates that were to be cancelled as a result of the amalgamation should be obtained from all shareholders and marked "cancelled," and new share certificates should be issued where applicable.

Although the property of each amalgamating corporation becomes the property of the amalgamated corporation, it is prudent practice for the amalgamated corporation to send notice of the amalgamation to other corporations in which the amalgamating corporation held securities and to request that the other corporation update its records accordingly. In addition, if on amalgamation a new corporate name was adopted, the amalgamated corporation may request the issuance of a replacement share certificate.

If any of the amalgamating corporations has a registered interest in land, a copy of the articles of amalgamation should be registered with the appropriate Land Registry Office.

Management of the amalgamated corporation should notify suppliers, customers, insurance agents, bankers, and other interested parties. In the case where the amalgamated corporation adopts a new corporate name, management should ensure that the proper name appears on telephone listings, new stationery, and supplies, and on all business premises.

If any of the amalgamating corporations were registered to carry on business in a jurisdiction outside the province of incorporation, and the amalgamated corporation intends to continue to carry on business in that jurisdiction, the applicable extra-provincial legislation and regulations should be checked to determine what documentation is required to be filed.

DISSOLUTION OR WINDUP

Introduction

A corporation ceases to exist if it is voluntarily dissolved, if it is wound up, or if the Director cancels its certificate of incorporation. The principal distinction between a dissolution and a windup, as the terms are used in this chapter, is the assignment of responsibility for carrying out the steps required to terminate a corporation's existence: a dissolution is handled by the existing management of the corporation; a windup is managed by another person appointed solely for that purpose (a **liquidator**).

Under the CBCA and the OBCA, one of four methods may be used to terminate a corporation's existence:

1. voluntary dissolution,
2. voluntary liquidation and dissolution (CBCA) or voluntary windup (OBCA),
3. dissolution or windup by court order, or
4. dissolution by order of the Director under the applicable Act.

Voluntary dissolution is the method most frequently used.

The following discussion describes the procedures for each method under the provisions of each statute — first the CBCA and then the OBCA — and concludes with a brief look at other considerations common to both statutes.

liquidator
a person appointed by the court to supervise and carry out the liquidation and dissolution of a corporation, including paying or making adequate provision for claims against the corporation and distributing any remaining property to the shareholders

Voluntary dissolution: CBCA

The CBCA dissolution provisions apply only to financially solvent corporations. An insolvent or bankrupt corporation must be dissolved pursuant to the *Winding-up and Restructuring Act* (Canada). Discussion of that statute is beyond the scope of this chapter.

DISSOLUTION BY DIRECTORS' RESOLUTION (CBCA S. 210(1))

If the corporation has not commenced business and has not issued any shares since its incorporation, it may be dissolved at any time by resolution of the directors. In some circumstances, a corporation may have never been active following the granting of a certificate of incorporation. Perhaps the corporation expected some financial backing that never materialized or the business environment changed. If the directors think it unlikely that the corporation will ever be operational, they may decide to dissolve the corporation.

Figure 3.3 at the end of the chapter includes a sample directors' resolution approving dissolution of a corporation under CBCA s. 210(1).

DISSOLUTION BY SPECIAL RESOLUTION (CBCA SS. 210(2), (3))

A corporation that has no property or liabilities may be dissolved by special resolution of all shareholders of all classes, whether or not they otherwise have the right to vote.

A corporation that has property or liabilities or both may be dissolved by special resolution of all shareholders of all classes, whether or not they otherwise have the right to vote, if:

1. the special resolution authorizes the directors to cause the corporation to distribute any property and discharge any liabilities; and

2. the corporation has distributed any property and discharged any liabilities before it sends articles of dissolution to the Director under the CBCA.

Figure 3.3 at the end of the chapter includes sample special resolutions for voluntary dissolution of a corporation under CBCA ss. 210(2) and (3).

ARTICLES OF DISSOLUTION (CBCA S. 210(4))

Once the directors' resolution or the special resolution, as the case may be, authorizing the dissolution has been passed, articles of dissolution (CBCA Form 17) are filed with the Director. Form 17 is included in figure 3.3.

CERTIFICATE OF DISSOLUTION (CBCA SS. 210(5), (6))

On receipt of articles of dissolution, the Director issues a certificate of dissolution and the corporation ceases to exist on the date shown on the certificate.

CONSENT OF CANADA REVENUE AGENCY

Although the consent of the CRA is not specifically required prior to the dissolution of a federal corporation, it is prudent practice to obtain it. The CRA will issue a clearance certificate under s. 159 of the ITA once all federal corporate tax returns have been filed and any outstanding taxes have been paid. If the CRA's consent is not obtained, the directors and officers of the corporation may be held personally liable for the payment of amounts owing by the corporation under the ITA to the extent of the value of property distributed by the corporation by virtue of the dissolution.

It is advisable to request the clearance certificate from the CRA well in advance of the dissolution, if possible, as it may take some time to process. The person attending to the filing of the final tax return for the corporation is the most appropriate person to request the clearance certificate. For example, if the corporation has decided to dissolve and the accountants are filing the final return, the accountants could advise the CRA that the corporation wishes to dissolve, confirm that they are filing the final tax return, and request a clearance certificate.

ALL FILINGS UP TO DATE

Before articles of dissolution are filed, it is recommended (though not required) that all outstanding annual returns be filed with Industry Canada.

PAYMENT OF DEBTS AND DISTRIBUTION TO SHAREHOLDERS BEFORE DISSOLUTION (CBCA S. 210(3))

A CBCA corporation that has property or liabilities or both must pay off or settle its debts, obligations, or liabilities before voluntarily dissolving. After such debts, obligations, or liabilities have been paid and before articles of dissolution are filed, any remaining property should be distributed to the shareholders of the corporation in accordance with their rights set out in the share conditions of the articles of the corporation and any unanimous shareholder agreement. For example, preferred shareholders are usually entitled to receive payment on dissolution in priority to any payment to the holders of common shares.

Voluntary liquidation and dissolution: CBCA

The directors or any shareholder entitled to vote may propose voluntary liquidation and dissolution of a corporation under s. 211 of the CBCA. This method is considerably more involved than a voluntary dissolution under s. 210 and is therefore seldom used.

NOTICE OF MEETING (CBCA S. 211(2))

The directors or shareholders who are proposing the voluntary liquidation and dissolution of the corporation must call a special meeting of shareholders for that purpose. Notice of the meeting must set out the terms of the proposed liquidation and dissolution. An example is included in figure 3.3 at the end of the chapter.

SPECIAL RESOLUTION (CBCA S. 211(3))

The liquidation and dissolution is approved by special resolution of the shareholders of all classes whether or not they otherwise have the right to vote. An example of a special resolution is included in figure 3.3.

STATEMENT OF INTENT TO DISSOLVE (CBCA S. 211(4))

After the special resolution has been passed, a statement of intent to dissolve (CBCA Form 19) is sent to the Director. The form is reproduced in figure 3.3. On receipt, the Director issues a certificate of intent to dissolve. On issuance of the certificate, the corporation ceases to carry on business except to the extent necessary for the liquidation. The corporation continues to exist until the Director issues a certificate of dissolution.

NOTICE OF LIQUIDATION (CBCA S. 211(7))

On issuance of the Director's certificate, the corporation must immediately notify each known creditor of the corporation of the intention to dissolve. The corporation must also, without delay, take reasonable steps to give notice of the intended dissolution in each province in Canada where the corporation carried on business at the time it sent Form 19 to the Director. This would usually be accomplished by publication of the notice in a daily newspaper in each city where the corporation was carrying on business.

Figure 3.3 includes a sample notice of liquidation under s. 211 of the CBCA.

ASSETS AND OBLIGATIONS (CBCA S. 211(7)(c))

The corporation then proceeds to collect its property, to dispose of assets that are not to be distributed to its shareholders, to discharge all its obligations, and to complete all other tasks required to liquidate its business.

DISTRIBUTION (CBCA S. 211(7)(d))

After giving the required notices and adequately providing for the payment or discharge of all its obligations, the corporation distributes its remaining property, either in money or in kind, among its shareholders according to their respective rights.

SUPERVISION BY A COURT (CBCA SS. 211(8), 215)

Director
the director appointed under s. 260 of the CBCA or under s. 278 of the OBCA, as the case may be

The **Director** or any interested person may, at any time during the liquidation, apply to a court for an order that the liquidation be continued under the supervision of the court. On such application, the court may so order and make any further order that it sees fit. The application to a court to supervise a voluntary liquidation and dissolution must state the reasons, verified by an affidavit of the applicant, why the court should supervise the liquidation and dissolution. If the court issues the order, the liquidation and dissolution of the corporation continues under the supervision of the court in accordance with the CBCA.

Notice to the Director (CBCA s. 211(9))

An applicant, who applies to the court for an order that the liquidation be continued under the supervision of the court, shall give notice to the Director of such application. The Director is entitled to appear before the court and be heard in person or by counsel.

REVOCATION OF INTENT TO DISSOLVE (CBCA S. 211(10))

At any time after the issuance of a certificate of intent to dissolve and before the issuance of a certificate of dissolution, the shareholders may, by special resolution, revoke the intention to dissolve. A statement of revocation of intent to dissolve (CBCA Form 19, referred to above) is sent to the Director. On receipt, the Director issues a certificate of revocation of intent to dissolve. The revocation is effective on the date shown on the certificate, and the corporation may continue to carry on its business.

RIGHT TO DISSOLVE (CBCA S. 211(13))

If a certificate of intent to dissolve has not been revoked and the corporation has complied with the other provisions of the liquidation, the corporation prepares articles of dissolution (Form 17) and sends them to the Director.

CERTIFICATE OF DISSOLUTION (CBCA S. 211(15))

On receipt of articles of dissolution, the Director issues a certificate of dissolution, and the corporation ceases to exist on the date shown on the certificate.

Involuntary dissolution or windup by court order: CBCA

GROUNDS FOR ORDER

Contravention of the Act (CBCA s. 213)

The Director or any interested person may apply to a court for an order dissolving the corporation if the corporation:

1. has failed for two or more consecutive years to comply with the requirements of the CBCA s. 133(1) with respect to the holding of annual meetings of its shareholders; or

2. has contravened
   a. s. 16(2) of the CBCA by exercising powers contrary to the corporation's articles, or s. 21 relating to access to corporate records, or
   b. s. 157 as to financial statements, or
   c. s. 159 with regard to the submission of copies of financial statements to shareholders; or

3. has procured any certificate under the CBCA by misrepresentation.

An interested party applying for a court order must give the Director notice of the application, and the Director is entitled to appear before the court and be heard in person or be represented by counsel. The court may order that it be dissolved or that the corporation be liquidated and dissolved under the supervision of the court, and the court may issue any other order as it sees fit.

On receipt of a court order to dissolve the corporation, the Director must issue a certificate of dissolution. If the order is to liquidate and dissolve the corporation under the supervision of the court, the Director must issue a certificate of intent to dissolve and publish notice of the order in a publication generally available to the public. The corporation ceases to exist on the date shown on the certificate of dissolution.

Other grounds (CBCA s. 214)

A court may order the liquidation and dissolution of a corporation on the application of a shareholder. The order may be made if any of the following conditions are met:

1. The court is satisfied that:
   a. the corporation has acted, or has omitted to act, or
   b. the business and affairs of the corporation have been carried on or conducted, or

c. the powers of the directors have been exercised

in a manner that is oppressive or unfairly prejudicial to, or that unfairly disregards the interests of, any security holder, creditor, director, or officer.

2. The court is satisfied that a unanimous shareholder agreement entitles a complaining shareholder to demand dissolution of the corporation after the occurrence of a specified event and that event has occurred.

3. The court is satisfied that there are just and equitable reasons for the corporation to be liquidated and dissolved.

APPLICATION FOR COURT ORDER (CBCA S. 216)

The application for an order under s. 214 must state the reasons, verified by an affidavit of the applicant, why the corporation should be liquidated and dissolved. The court may make an order requiring the corporation and any person having an interest in the corporation or a claim against it to show cause, at a time and place specified, not less than four weeks after the date of the order, why the corporation should not be liquidated and dissolved. The court has the power to order the directors and officers to provide the court with all material information known to or reasonably ascertainable by them, including financial statements, the name and address of each shareholder, and the name and address of each known creditor or claimant and any person with whom the corporation has a contract.

A copy of the order to show cause why the corporation should not be liquidated and dissolved must be published as directed in the order, at least once in each week before the time appointed for the hearing, in a newspaper published or distributed in the place where the corporation's registered office is located, and must be served on the Director and each person named in the order.

Publication and service of the order must be made by the corporation or by such other persons and in such manner as the court may order.

POWERS OF THE COURT (CBCA S. 217)

In connection with the dissolution or the liquidation and dissolution of a corporation, the court may make any order as it sees fit, including, but not limited to:

1. an order to liquidate;

2. an order to appoint a liquidator;

3. after the liquidator has rendered a final account to the court, an order dissolving the corporation; and

4. orders for other items set out in s. 217 of the CBCA.

EFFECT OF A LIQUIDATION ORDER (CBCA S. 218)

The liquidation of a corporation commences when the court issues an order to that effect. The corporation continues in existence but must cease to carry on business, except the business that is, in the opinion of the liquidator, required for an orderly liquidation.

APPOINTMENT, DUTIES, AND POWERS OF THE LIQUIDATOR (CBCA SS. 218, 220-223)

The court may appoint any person, including a director, officer, or shareholder of the corporation or any other body corporate, as liquidator. The duties and powers of the liquidator are set out in ss. 221 and 222 of the CBCA.

Generally, the liquidator is authorized to dispose of the assets of the corporation and settle its liabilities. Under the order to liquidate, the powers of the directors and shareholders cease and vest in the liquidator, except as otherwise authorized by the court. However, the liquidator may delegate any such powers to the directors or shareholders.

FINAL ACCOUNT OF THE LIQUIDATOR (CBCA S. 223(2))

Within one year after appointment and after paying or making adequate provision for all claims against the corporation, the liquidator applies to the court for approval of the final accounts and for an order permitting the liquidator to distribute in money or in kind the remaining property of the corporation to its shareholders according to their respective rights, or for an extension of time setting out the reasons therefor.

NOTICE OF APPLICATION REGARDING FINAL ACCOUNTS (CBCA S. 223(4))

A liquidator must give notice of the intention to make an application regarding the final accounts to the Director, each appointed inspector, each shareholder, and any person who provided a security or fidelity bond for the liquidator. Notice must be published in a newspaper published or distributed in the place where the corporation has its registered office, or as otherwise directed by court.

FINAL ORDER AND CERTIFICATE OF DISSOLUTION (CBCA S. 223(5))

On approval of the final accounts rendered by the liquidator, the court issues an order:

1. directing the Director to issue a certificate of dissolution;
2. directing the custody or disposal of the documents and records of the corporation; and
3. discharging the liquidator.

The liquidator must forthwith send a certified copy of the order to the Director. On receipt, the Director issues a certificate of dissolution. The corporation ceases to exist on the date shown on the certificate.

Dissolution by order of the Director: CBCA

Section 212 of the CBCA provides that the Director may dissolve the corporation where a corporation:

1. has not commenced business within three years after the date shown on the certificate of incorporation;
2. has not carried on its business for three consecutive years; or

3. is in default for a period of one year in sending to the Director any fee, notice, or document required by the CBCA.

The Director may either dissolve the corporation by issuing a certificate of dissolution or apply to a court for an order dissolving the corporation. The Director is required to give the corporation and each known director of the corporation 120 days' notice of the decision to dissolve and must publish notice of that decision in a publication generally available to the public.

Unless cause to the contrary has been shown, or the court has issued an order under s. 246 of the CBCA, the Director may, after the expiration of the 120-day period, issue a certificate of dissolution. The corporation ceases to exist on the date shown on the certificate.

Other CBCA dissolution provisions

UNKNOWN CREDITORS OR SHAREHOLDERS (CBCA S. 227)

On the dissolution of a corporation, if any of its creditors or shareholders cannot be found, the portion of the property that would otherwise be distributed to that creditor or shareholder upon dissolution must be converted into money and paid to the receiver general for Canada. If at any time a creditor or shareholder establishes that he or she is entitled to any moneys paid to the receiver general, the receiver general shall pay an equivalent amount to that creditor or shareholder.

FORFEITURE OF PROPERTY TO THE CROWN (CBCA S. 228)

On dissolution, any remaining property of the corporation that has not otherwise been disposed of is immediately forfeit to and vests in Her Majesty in right of Canada (that is, the Crown).

RETENTION OF RECORDS OF THE DISSOLVED CORPORATION (CBCA S. 225)

The documents and records of a dissolved corporation must be retained for six years following the date of dissolution. The name, address, and occupation of the person who has been granted custody of the documents and records must be set out in the articles of dissolution.

Voluntary dissolution: OBCA

DISSOLUTION BEFORE COMMENCING BUSINESS (OBCA SS. 237(c), 238(2))

If the corporation has not commenced business within two years after the date of incorporation and has not issued any shares, it may be dissolved upon authorization of its incorporators or their personal representatives.

Once the incorporators have authorized the dissolution, articles of dissolution (OBCA Form 11), together with the consent of the Corporations Tax Branch of the Ministry of Finance (discussed below) and the required filing fee, are filed with the Ontario Ministry of Government Services. Form 11 and sample consent letters are reproduced in figure 3.4 at the end of the chapter.

DISSOLUTION OF AN ACTIVE CORPORATION (OBCA SS. 237(a), (b), 238(1))

A voluntary dissolution must be authorized by special resolution passed at a meeting of shareholders called for that purpose, or in the case of a non-offering corporation by such other proportion of votes cast as the articles provide. Such other proportion must not be less than 50 percent of the votes of all the shareholders entitled to vote at the meeting. Shareholder approval may also be granted by the written consent of all the shareholders entitled to vote at such meeting. Figure 3.4 includes a sample special resolution for dissolution.

Once the special resolution approving the dissolution has been passed, articles of dissolution (OBCA Form 10) are filed with the Ontario Ministry of Government Services, together with the consent from the Corporations Tax Branch of the Ministry of Finance and the filing fee. Form 10 is reproduced in figure 3.4.

CONSENT OF CORPORATIONS TAX BRANCH, MINISTRY OF FINANCE

As indicated above, before dissolving, an Ontario corporation must obtain the consent of the Corporations Tax Branch of the Ministry of Finance and file the letter of consent with the articles of dissolution. In order to obtain the consent, the corporation must file all outstanding Ontario corporate tax returns and pay any taxes owing. The consent of the Corporations Tax Branch is in the form of a letter and usually states that the consent is null and void if the articles of dissolution are not filed within 21 days after the date of the consent.

It is advisable to request consent from the Corporations Tax Branch well in advance of the dissolution, if possible, as it may take some time to process. Generally, if the corporation is up to date in filing its tax returns and has paid all taxes owing, the consent of the Corporations Tax Branch can be obtained within a few days.

CONSENT OF CANADA REVENUE AGENCY

As in the case of dissolution of a CBCA corporation, although the consent of the CRA is not specifically required prior to the dissolution of an Ontario corporation, it is prudent practice to obtain it.

ALL FILINGS UP TO DATE

One of the statements contained in the articles of dissolution is that the corporation has filed all notices required under the *Corporations Information Act* (Ontario) (CIA). Therefore, before articles of dissolution are filed with the Ministry of Government Services, all filings under the CIA must be up to date, including the filing of all outstanding annual returns.

CERTIFICATE OF DISSOLUTION (OBCA S. 239)

On receipt of articles of dissolution (Form 10 or Form 11), the Director issues a certificate of dissolution, and the corporation ceases to exist on the date shown on the certificate.

PROVIDING FOR DEBTS (OBCA S. 238(1)(c))

On filing articles of dissolution, an active corporation must confirm that it has no debts, obligations, or liabilities, or that its debts, obligations, and liabilities have been duly provided for, or that its creditors or other persons with interests in its debts, obligations, or liabilities have consented to the dissolution.

DISTRIBUTION OF PROPERTY TO SHAREHOLDERS (OBCA S. 238(1)(d))

If the corporation is an active corporation, after the discharge of its debts, obligations, or liabilities, the corporation must distribute any remaining property ratably among its shareholders according to their rights and interests in the corporation. These rights and interests are determined by reviewing the share conditions set out in the articles of incorporation and any shareholder agreement. Although the authorization to dissolve is sufficient authority for the corporation to distribute its property ratably among its shareholders, in some circumstances it may be prudent for the corporation to enter into a distribution agreement with its shareholders. The distribution agreement would provide for a general assignment and conveyance of all the assets of the corporation to the shareholders. An example of when a distribution agreement may be entered into would be if a corporation wishes to distribute its assets to the shareholders on a specific date, but the actual dissolution will not be completed until a later date.

Voluntary windup: OBCA

A corporation's business may be so extensive that discontinuing the business requires the involvement of a liquidator. The shareholders may pass a special resolution requiring the corporation to be wound up voluntarily and appointing a liquidator to manage the process. The voluntary windup commences at the time the special resolution is passed or at such later time as may be specified in the special resolution. The provisions for a voluntary windup under the OBCA are found in ss. 193-205.

A corporation being wound up voluntarily shall cease to carry on business from the date of commencement of the windup, except as may be beneficial for the windup. After the special resolution has been passed, any subsequent transfer of shares is void unless it is approved by the liquidator. The existence of the corporation and all its corporate powers continue until the affairs of the corporation are wound up. After the commencement of the windup, no action or proceeding may be commenced against the corporation, and no proceedings to attach or otherwise levy execution against its assets may be brought without leave of the court.

SPECIAL RESOLUTION

A special meeting of shareholders is called to pass a special resolution requiring the corporation to be wound up and appointing one or more persons to act as liquidator. Alternatively, the shareholders may appoint a committee of inspectors, who may be shareholders, **contributories**, or creditors, to appoint and oversee the activities of the liquidator. Figure 3.4 at the end of the chapter includes a sample special resolution authorizing a voluntary windup.

contributory
a person who is liable to contribute to the property of the corporation in the event of the corporation's being wound up under the OBCA

APPOINTMENT OF A LIQUIDATOR (OBCA S. 193(2))

If the shareholders decide to appoint a liquidator, they may appoint a director, officer, or employee of the corporation as a liquidator or they may delegate the appointment of the liquidator to a committee of shareholders, contributories, or creditors. The liquidator attends to the winding up of the business of the corporation and the distribution of its property. All powers of the directors cease upon the appointment of a liquidator, except insofar as the liquidator may sanction the continuation of such powers. The shareholders may also enter into an arrangement with creditors of the corporation with respect to the powers to be executed by the liquidator and the manner in which the powers are to be exercised.

NOTICE OF WINDUP (OBCA S. 193(4))

Notice of the special resolution requiring the corporation to be wound up (OBCA Form 16) must be filed with the Director under the OBCA within 10 days after the resolution has been passed. Form 16 is reproduced in figure 3.4 at the end of the chapter. Notice must also be published in the *Ontario Gazette* within 20 days after the resolution has been passed.

It is also recommended that notice of the windup be published in a daily newspaper in the city or community where the corporation's registered office is located.

DUTIES OF THE LIQUIDATOR (OBCA SS. 200-205)

The liquidator must dispose of the corporation's assets and settle its liabilities. During the period of the windup, the liquidator may call a meeting of the shareholders for any purpose as the liquidator sees fit. If the voluntary windup continues for more than one year, the liquidator must call a meeting of shareholders at the end of the first year and of each succeeding year from the commencement of the windup, to report on the liquidator's actions and dealings and the status of the windup.

FINAL MEETING OF SHAREHOLDERS (OBCA S. 205(2))

The liquidator must call a final meeting of shareholders once all assets have been distributed and all liabilities have been settled. The liquidator shall present to the meeting an account of the winding up. Within 10 days of the meeting, the liquidator must file notice with the Director (Form 16), stating that the meeting has been held and setting out the date of the meeting. Notice must also be published forthwith in the *Ontario Gazette*.

EFFECTIVE DATE OF DISSOLUTION (OBCA S. 205(3))

Three months after the filing date of the Form 16 notice regarding the final meeting of shareholders, the corporation is dissolved, unless the dissolution is deferred or accelerated by a court order obtained at the request of the liquidator or any other interested person. In such event, the effective date of the dissolution is the date fixed in the court order.

If a court order is made to defer or accelerate the dissolution, the person who applied for such order must file a certified copy of the order with the Director within 10 days after the order was made, and must publish notice of the order in the *Ontario Gazette*.

Windup by court order: OBCA

A court may order that a corporation be wound up, in which case the windup is compulsory. The applicable provisions are found in ss. 207-218 of the OBCA.

WHO MAY APPLY (OBCA S. 208)

An application for a court order to wind up a corporation may be made by the corporation, by a shareholder, or, where the corporation is being wound up voluntarily, by the liquidator, a contributory, or a creditor with a claim of $2,500 or more.

GROUNDS FOR COURT ORDER (OBCA S. 207)

A court order may be made if any of the following conditions are met:

1. The court is satisfied that

    a. the corporation has acted, or has omitted to act, or

    b. the business and affairs of the corporation have been carried on or conducted, or

    c. the powers of the directors have been exercised

    in a manner that is oppressive or unfairly prejudicial to, or that unfairly disregards the interests of, any security holder, creditor, director, or officer.

2. The court is satisfied that a unanimous shareholder agreement entitles a complaining shareholder to demand dissolution of the corporation after the occurrence of a specified event, and that event has occurred.

3. The court is satisfied that it is in the interests of contributors and creditors that the proceedings by a liquidator under a voluntary windup be supervised by a court.

4. The court is satisfied that although the corporation may not be insolvent, it cannot carry on its business because of its liabilities, and it is advisable that it be wound up.

5. The court is satisfied that there are just and equitable reasons, other than bankruptcy or insolvency, for winding up the corporation.

6. The shareholders of the corporation, by special resolution, authorize an application to be made to the court to wind up the corporation.

PROCEDURE (OBCA SS. 209-217)

The procedure for winding up by court order is much the same as the procedure for voluntary winding up, except that all proceedings in the winding up are subject to the order and direction of the court.

ORDER FOR DISSOLUTION (OBCA S. 218)

At any time after the corporation's business and affairs have been fully wound up, the court may, upon the application of the liquidator or any other interested person, issue an order dissolving the corporation. The corporation ceases to exist on the date fixed in the order.

The person who applied for such order must file a certified copy of the order with the Director, within 10 days after it was made, and must forthwith publish notice of the order in the *Ontario Gazette*.

Dissolution by order of the Director: OBCA

Section 240 of the OBCA gives the Director the power to cancel the certificate of incorporation or any other certificate issued or endorsed under the OBCA if the Director is shown sufficient cause. Cancellation can take place only after the corporation has been given an opportunity to be heard. Sufficient cause includes any of the following:

1. The corporation has failed to comply with the requirements for the board of directors to consist of at least one director in the case of a non-offering corporation and not fewer than three directors in the case of an offering corporation (OBCA s. 115(2)).

2. The corporation does not have a majority of directors who are resident Canadians (OBCA s. 118(3)).

3. The corporation has been convicted of a criminal offence under the *Criminal Code* (Canada) or any other federal statute, or an offence as defined in the *Provincial Offences Act*, and dissolution is deemed to be in the public interest.

4. a. The corporation has acted, omitted to act, or threatened that it will act, or

   b. the corporation has carried on its business or affairs or threatened that it will carry on its business or affairs, or

   c. the powers of the directors have been or are threatened to be exercised

   in a manner that is oppressive or unfairly prejudicial to, or that unfairly disregards the interests of, any security holder, creditor, director, or officer of the corporation (OBCA s. 248(2)).

In the case of the cancellation of a certificate of incorporation, the corporation is dissolved on the date fixed in the order. In the case of the cancellation of any other certificate, the matter that became effective upon the issuance of the certificate ceases to be in effect from the date fixed in the order.

Section 241 of the OBCA provides that if a corporation is in default in complying with the provisions of the *Corporations Tax Act* and the minister of finance has notified the Director of such default, or the corporation is in default of complying with ss. 77 and 78 of the *Securities Act* and the Ontario Securities Commission has notified the Director of such default, the Director may give notice by registered mail to the corporation or publish once in the *Ontario Gazette* that an order dissolving the corporation will be issued unless the corporation remedies its default within 90 days after the date of the notice.

Section 241 also provides that where a corporation fails to comply with the filing requirements under the CIA or fails to pay a fee required under the OBCA, the Director may give notice to the corporation or publish once in the *Ontario Gazette* that an order dissolving the corporation will be issued unless the corporation complies with the requirements or pays the fee within 90 days after the date of the notice.

If the corporation does not remedy its defaults or comply with the requirements or pay the fee within the 90-day period, the Director may, by order, cancel the certificate of incorporation. The corporation is then dissolved on the date fixed in the order.

Other OBCA dissolution/windup provisions

UNKNOWN CREDITOR (OBCA SS. 234(1), 238(3))

If a creditor or the location of a creditor is unknown, the corporation (or the liquidator in the case of voluntary or court-ordered windup) may, by agreement with the public trustee, pay to the public trustee an amount equal to the amount of the debt due to the creditor to be held in trust for the creditor.

UNKNOWN WHEREABOUTS (OBCA SS. 235(1), 238(4))

In some cases, it may be difficult to make a complete distribution of the corporation's assets among the shareholders because some shareholders cannot be located. As in the case of an unknown creditor, if a shareholder is unknown or cannot be located, the corporation (or the liquidator in the case of voluntary or court-ordered windup) may, by agreement with the public trustee, deliver or convey the shareholder's share of the property to the public trustee, to be held in trust for the shareholder.

CLAIM BY A PERSON ENTITLED TO PAYMENT (OBCA S. 238(6))

A creditor or a shareholder who was entitled to receive payment and who could not be located at the time of dissolution has 10 years within which to apply to the public trustee to receive such payment. If the amount has not been claimed within that period, it vests with the public trustee for the use of Ontario. Thereafter, if the person beneficially entitled to receive payment establishes his or her right to receive payment to the satisfaction of the lieutenant governor in council, an amount equal to the amount so vested in the public trustee shall be paid to the person.

FORFEITURE OF PROPERTY TO THE CROWN (OBCA S. 244)

On dissolution, any remaining property of the corporation that has not otherwise been disposed of is immediately forfeit to and vests in Her Majesty in right of the province of Ontario.

Tax and legal consequences of dissolution: ITA, CBCA, and OBCA

TAX CONSEQUENCES

A windup or dissolution involves two levels of disposition for tax purposes:

1. The corporation disposes of its assets to its shareholders and the shareholders acquire the assets.

2. The shareholders dispose of their shares in the corporation.

The tax consequences under the ITA to the dissolving corporation and the shareholders depend upon whether the dissolving corporation is a taxable Canadian corporation that is a wholly owned (90 percent or more) subsidiary of another taxable Canadian corporation (the parent), as provided for in s. 88(1) of the ITA, in which case a tax-free rollover is available. Section 88(1) of the ITA applies when the following conditions are met:

1. The subsidiary and the parent are both taxable Canadian corporations.

2. The parent owns at least 90 percent of the shares of each class of the subsidiary.

3. All shares of the subsidiary not owned by the parent are owned by persons with whom the parent was dealing at arm's length.

In all other cases, tax consequences under the ITA arise for one or other of the corporation and the shareholder and are beyond the scope of this chapter.

LEGAL ACTION OR PROCEEDING (CBCA S. 226(2); OBCA S. 242(1))

Despite dissolution of a corporation, a civil, a criminal, or an administrative action or proceeding commenced by or against the corporation before dissolution may continue as if the corporation had not been dissolved. In addition, a civil, a criminal, or an administrative action or proceeding may be brought against the corporation after dissolution as if the corporation had not been dissolved.

LIABILITY OF SHAREHOLDERS TO CREDITORS (CBCA S. 226(4); OBCA S. 243(1))

In connection with any action commenced by a creditor before or after dissolution, under the CBCA, each shareholder of a dissolved corporation who received property on dissolution remains liable for two years after the dissolution to the extent of the amount received by the shareholder on distribution. Under the OBCA, the shareholder remains liable for five years after dissolution.

ROLLOVER REORGANIZATION

Introduction

The term "rollover" is commonly used to describe a disposition of property that does not result in any immediate tax consequences that would ordinarily result from the disposition. The ITA contains provisions that permit a transfer of assets (s. 85) or reorganization of a corporation's share capital (s. 86) on a tax-deferred, or rollover, basis. The rules in the ITA are very complex and change often; therefore, only the general principles of ss. 85 and 86 and some practical aspects of their application in a typical situation will be reviewed here. Generally speaking, a rollover transaction should not be undertaken without a review of the particular facts by a lawyer who practises in the income tax area.

Section 85 rollover

Probably the most common corporate rollover is a transfer of property by a shareholder to a corporation contemplated by s. 85 of the ITA. Ordinarily, a transfer of property by a person ("the transferor") to a corporation ("the transferee") involves a disposition of property and can give rise to gains that are taxable to the transferor if the property's value has increased since the time it was acquired. A s. 85 rollover can be used to transfer the property in such a manner that the gain, capital or otherwise, is not realized and subject to tax until the corporation/transferee subsequently disposes of the property. Other situations in which a s. 85 rollover is common include the incorporation of a sole proprietor to take advantage of the benefits associated with a corporation and the implementation of an estate freeze. Here we will focus on the first situation, the transfer of property by a shareholder to a corporation.

For a transaction to be governed by s. 85 of the ITA, all of the following conditions must be met (s. 85(1)):

1. A transferor must be a taxpayer. (There is no requirement that the transferor be a resident of Canada.)

2. The transferee must be a "taxable Canadian corporation" within the meaning of the ITA (see below).

3. The property that is transferred must be "eligible property" within the meaning of the ITA.

4. The transferor must receive at least one share of the transferee corporation in exchange for the property transferred.

5. The transferor and the transferee must jointly elect in prescribed form and within the prescribed time to have the provisions of s. 85(1) apply.

It is important to understand that s. 85 provides for only a deferral or postponement of tax. Any appreciation in the value of the property (assets) transferred that is not recognized at the time of the transfer will be taxed at the time the assets are sold or otherwise disposed of by the transferee. The deferred gain may also be taxed when the transferor disposes of the share(s) received from the transferee corporation in exchange for the transferred assets. If the asset transferred has declined in value, losses created at the time of the rollover cannot be utilized until 30 days after the transferee has disposed of the asset.

ELIGIBLE PERSONS

In order to use the s. 85 rollover in the purchase and sale of corporate shares or assets, both the purchasing corporation and the vendor must be eligible for the rollover.

The purchasing corporation (the transferee) must be a **taxable Canadian corporation** as defined in s. 89(1) of the ITA.

The vendor (the transferor) may be any taxpayer. This includes any individual, corporation, or trust, whether or not resident in Canada. A partnership is not a taxpayer and therefore is not eligible to use the rollover in s. 85(1); however, a similar rollover is available to a partnership under s. 85(2).

ELIGIBLE PROPERTY

Section 85(1.1) lists the types of assets that are eligible for a transfer under s. 85(1). They include:

1. any capital property, including depreciable property but excluding real property owned by a non-resident except as noted in item (5) below;

2. Canadian and foreign resource properties;

3. eligible capital property (that is, goodwill);

4. inventory (other than real property, an interest in real property, or an option in respect of real property); and

taxable Canadian corporation
a Canadian corporation (that is, a corporation either incorporated in Canada or resident in Canada continuously since June 18, 1971) that is not exempt from tax under the *Income Tax Act* (Canada)

5. real property, an interest in real property, or an option in respect of real property owned by a non-resident and used in a business carried on in Canada by the non-resident.

CONSIDERATION RECEIVED

Consideration, simply defined, is payment. More formally, it is the value that flows from the purchaser to the vendor in a purchase and sale transaction. The form of payment may be monetary, non-monetary, or a combination of the two, as agreed between the parties. In an asset or share purchase transaction, the purchaser typically gives monetary or a combination of monetary and non-monetary consideration in exchange for the assets or shares.

In a s. 85 rollover, the vendor must receive consideration from the purchaser with a value equal to the full fair market value of the assets transferred. The consideration must also include at least a fraction of a share for each property transferred.

The vendor may also receive non-share consideration for the transfer. The non-share consideration may include cash, promissory notes, the assumption of liabilities (such as mortgages), or any other property. The combined fair market value of the share consideration and the non-share consideration must be equal to the fair market value of the assets transferred.

If the consideration paid to the vendor is less than the fair market value of the assets transferred, the vendor may be considered to have made a gift to another shareholder and will then be taxed on the value of that gift. Therefore, the valuation of the assets to be transferred is critical.

If there are other common shareholders of the corporation, it is suggested that the vendor receive another class of shares (for example, special shares) of the corporation, not common shares. The special shares should be designed to have and to maintain a value equal to the value of the assets transferred. The mechanism used for this is to make the shares redeemable by the corporation and retractable by the shareholder at an amount equal to the value of the assets transferred. For example, if the fair market value of the assets transferred is $2,000, the corporation could issue to the vendor 2,000 special shares redeemable and retractable at $1.00 per share.

The following are typical rights and conditions attached to a class of shares issued on a s. 85 rollover:

- non-voting;
- discretionary, non-cumulative dividends;
- redeemable at the option of the corporation at an amount of $1 per share;
- retractable at the option of the shareholder at an amount of $1 per share;
- price adjustment clause; and
- priority over common shares to receive the redemption amount on dissolution.

Figure 3.5 at the end of the chapter includes an example of rights and conditions attached to special shares issued in a s. 85 rollover.

consideration
payment; the value that flows from the purchaser to the vendor in a purchase and sale transaction; in an asset or share purchase, usually takes the form of monetary or a combination of monetary and non-monetary payment in exchange for the assets or shares

ELECTED AMOUNT

Section 85 provides that the amount that the transferor and the corporation have agreed upon in their election (the "elected amount" or sometimes referred to as the "agreed amount") in respect of the property shall be deemed to be the transferor's proceeds of disposition of the property and the corporation's cost of the property. Where the transferor has received only common shares as consideration for the property transferred, the elected amount is also deemed to be the transferor's adjusted cost base for the shares.

For example, assume that an individual owns capital property with a cost of $100 and a fair market value of $200 and wishes to transfer the property to a corporation using the rollover provisions of s. 85. The corporation pays consideration in the form of common shares. If the elected amount is $100, the transferor's proceeds of disposition will be $100; therefore, the transferor will not realize a capital gain. The common shares received on the transfer will have an adjusted cost base of $100. The corporation's cost of the transferred property will also be $100. However, the property has an accrued but unrealized gain of $100 that will be realized and will be taxable to the corporation when it disposes of the property.

Section 85 contains several rules that place upper and lower limits on the elected amount that the parties can choose, depending on the type of asset transferred. Basically, the elected amount cannot be less than the fair market value of any non-share consideration received (the lower limit) and cannot exceed the fair market value of the assets transferred to the corporation (the upper limit).

ELECTION

In order to claim the rollover, the vendor and the purchasing corporation must jointly execute and file an election form (Form T2057) with the CRA. Form T2057 is reproduced in figure 3.5 at the end of the chapter. In the election form, the parties must set out the elected amount for each asset transferred. The following information is required to complete the T2057:

- the name, address, and taxation account number or social insurance number of the transferor/vendor (that is, the shareholder);
- the taxation year of the transferor in which the transfer occurred;
- the district taxation office of the transferor;
- the name, address, and taxation account number of the transferee/ purchaser (that is, the corporation);
- the taxation year of the transferee in which the transfer occurred;
- the district taxation office of the transferee;
- if shares of a private corporation are included in the property disposed of, the name of the corporation, the taxation account number, and the paid-up capital of the shares transferred;
- with respect to the shares received, the number and class of shares received, the redemption value per share (if any), the paid-up capital, and whether the shares are voting or retractable;
- the date of the transfer;

- a description of the property transferred;
- classification of the property transferred (that is, capital property, depreciable property, inventory, etc.);
- elected amount limits;
- the fair market value of the property transferred; and
- a description of the consideration received by the transferor and its fair market value.

In addition, there are several questions to be answered on page 2 of T2057.

The T2057 must be filed on or before the day by which either the vendor or the purchasing corporation is required to file its tax return for the taxation year in which the transfer took place, whichever is the earlier date. For example:

> Mary transfers assets to Johnco in exchange for common shares of Johnco. The year-end of Johnco is June 30. The transfer of assets occurs on September 1, 2000. Mary, as an individual taxpayer, is required to file a tax return by April 30, 2001. Johnco is required to file a tax return by December 31, 2001 (six months after its taxation year-end). The election form must therefore be filed on or before April 30, 2001, because that is the earlier of the two dates by which the respective returns must be filed.

One party to the transaction files the executed election in duplicate and the other files a copy. In order to avoid any misunderstanding, it is very important for the parties involved to establish who will take responsibility for the preparation and filing of the T2057 with CRA. Even though the T2057 may not have to be filed immediately after the closing of a section 85 rollover transaction, it is prudent practice to have the parties execute the form at the closing of the transaction if possible.

Late filing of the T2057 election form is permitted up to three years after the filing deadline, but is subject to a late filing penalty. After three years, a T2057 election form may be filed only if, in the opinion of the federal minister of revenue, it is just and equitable to allow the late filing, in which case it will be subject to the late filing penalty.

VALUATIONS OF FAIR MARKET VALUE AND USE OF PRICE ADJUSTMENT CLAUSES

The concept of fair market value is crucial to a rollover under s. 85; however, valuation of the fair market value of an asset is not always easy. In recognition of this, the CRA permits a price adjustment clause to be used in the valuation of the shares issued on a s. 85 rollover. It is recommended that the price adjustment clause be included in the rollover agreement between the vendor and the purchaser. It is preferable for the price adjustment clause to permit the parties and the CRA to agree on the valuation, and to send the question to court or to arbitration if they cannot agree. This not only gives protection to the corporation and the shareholder, but it makes it more likely that a court would enforce the price adjustment clause in the first place. It should be emphasized that the use of a price adjustment clause cannot replace an actual valuation. The courts will be reluctant to enforce a price adjustment clause if the original price was "pulled out of a hat," rather than being the result of a bona fide attempt to reach a value.

As indicated above, a price adjustment clause is also very often included in the rights and conditions of the shares issued to the shareholder on the rollover.

PAID-UP CAPITAL AND STATED CAPITAL

In order to understand any tax transactions, it is necessary to understand the concepts of paid-up capital and stated capital.

Stated capital is a corporate concept found in the CBCA and the OBCA. Basically, stated capital is the sum of all consideration received by the corporation when it issues shares, subject to certain adjustments. Both the CBCA (s. 26) and the OBCA (s. 24) provide that a corporation must maintain a separate stated capital account for each class and series of shares issued, and the corporation must add to the appropriate stated capital account the full amount of any consideration received for any shares issued.

The relevance of stated capital in the CBCA or the OBCA is that it limits the amount of dividends that can be paid by the corporation and prevents the redemption of shares in some instances. Because stated capital is the amount contributed to the corporation by its shareholders, and dividends and other payments to shareholders are intended to be made out of the profit of the corporation, the corporation is prohibited from paying dividends or repurchasing shares if this would result in the corporation being unable to pay its debts and maintain its stated capital intact (CBCA ss. 34, 42; OBCA ss. 30, 38).

Paid-up capital is a tax concept found in the ITA. Paid-up capital also represents the amount of capital contributed to the corporation by its shareholders. However, adjustments are made to paid-up capital in many transactions, such as s. 85 rollovers.

From a tax point of view, the relevance of paid-up capital is that it represents, generally, the amount of money that a shareholder can receive from the corporation tax-free in certain circumstances (for example, upon a redemption of shares). This is money that was contributed to the corporation by the shareholder in the first place, and was paid out of after-tax income; therefore, the theory is that it is fair to permit its repayment without tax.

Stated capital only applies to a class or series of shares, whereas paid-up capital can be determined for a class of shares, for one particular share, or for all the issued shares of a corporation. Paid-up capital is most often determined for a particular share. In this case, the paid-up capital of the particular share is the paid-up capital for the particular class of shares divided by the number of issued shares in the class.

CALCULATION OF STATED CAPITAL AND PAID-UP CAPITAL

A corporation is not free to choose the amount of its stated capital and paid-up capital accounts. These amounts must be determined by applying specific rules set out in the CBCA or OBCA and the ITA, respectively.

As discussed above, the CBCA and the OBCA state that, except in very limited circumstances, a corporation must add to its stated capital account for each class of shares the full amount of the consideration paid to the corporation for those shares. The stated capital per share is the aggregate stated capital for the class of shares divided by the number of shares of that class outstanding at that time. If the shares of that class were issued for differing amounts, the stated capital per share

stated capital
a corporate law concept; essentially, the sum of all amounts received by a corporation as consideration for a class or series of shares issued by the corporation; subject to restrictions on distribution to shareholders

paid-up capital
a tax law concept; essentially, the amount or sum of amounts received by a corporation as consideration for a particular share, a particular class of shares, or all shares issued by the corporation; may be distributed to shareholders tax-free in certain circumstances

will not be exactly the same as the amount the shareholder actually paid. This has little relevance to the shareholder for corporate law purposes.

The starting point for calculating paid-up capital under the ITA is the stated capital. The paid-up capital of a share may also be different from the amount paid by the shareholder, because of the way stated capital is calculated. This does have significance for the shareholder for income tax purposes.

Consider the following example:

> Mary purchases 100 common shares from Johnco for $1.00 per share. Under the CBCA, the directors of Johnco are required to add $100 to the stated capital account for the common shares. Sometime later, the value of the common shares of Johnco increases and Susan purchases 100 common shares for $2.00 per share. The directors are then required to add $200 to the stated capital account for the common shares. The aggregate amount in the stated capital account is therefore $300. The stated capital per share is calculated as follows: $300 ÷ 200 = $1.50 per share.
>
> Under the ITA, the paid-up capital of each common share is also $1.50, since it is based on the stated capital. However, this represents the amount that the shareholder can, in certain transactions, receive from the corporation free of tax.

Using the same facts, suppose Johnco decides to redeem its common shares for $2.00 per share. Both Mary and Susan will receive $200 each for their 100 common shares; however, the amounts they will receive free of tax will be different.

> Mary:
> Paid-up capital of 100 shares = $150
> Adjusted cost base of 100 shares = $100
> Redemption proceeds = $200

Section 84(3) of the ITA provides that proceeds on shares redeemed, acquired, or cancelled, minus the paid-up capital, constitute a deemed dividend; therefore, Mary will have a $50 deemed dividend. In addition, since the shares have been acquired by the corporation, a disposition of the shares has occurred, which Mary must report on her personal tax return. To do so, she must determine the proceeds of disposition. It might appear that the proceeds would be $200; however, the definition of "proceeds of disposition" in the ITA specifically excludes a s. 84(3) deemed dividend from the proceeds received for the shares (ITA s. 54, paragraph (j) of the definition). Mary's proceeds are therefore $150 ($200 – $50 deemed dividend). Since Mary's adjusted cost base is $100, she will report a **capital gain** of $50, which will be included in her taxable income for the year.

capital gain
in tax law, the portion of the proceeds from the sale of an asset in excess of the initial tax cost of the asset, to be included in the calculation of the recipient's taxable income for the year

capital loss
in tax law, the shortfall that results where the proceeds from the sale of an asset are less than the initial tax cost of the asset, deductible in the calculation of the recipient's taxable income for the year

> Susan:
> Paid-up capital of 100 shares = $150
> Adjusted cost base of 100 shares = $200
> Redemption proceeds = $200

Susan will also have a disposition and a deemed dividend of $50. However, because her adjusted cost base is $200 and the net proceeds are only $150, she will report a **capital loss** of $50 on her personal tax return. Therefore, Susan will pay no tax on the redemption proceeds.

This is an example of the distortion that can occur for different taxpayers as a result of the fact that s. 89(1) of the ITA spreads the paid-up capital of shares over the number of outstanding shares in that class.

SITUATIONS WHERE PAID-UP CAPITAL DIFFERS FROM STATED CAPITAL

There are a number of situations in which paid-up capital for tax purposes will be different from stated capital. One of the most common examples is a transaction where property is transferred to a corporation in return for shares pursuant to a s. 85 election. In this case, the paid-up capital of the shares received as consideration for the transferred assets generally cannot exceed the aggregate elected amount in respect of the asset less any non-share consideration.

Another example is a transaction where, under s. 84.1 of the ITA, an individual transfers shares of a corporation to a corporation with which the individual deals not at arm's length and, after the transfer, the two corporations are "connected" within the meaning of s. 186(4) of the ITA. In this case, the paid-up capital of the shares received is reduced to equal the greater of the paid-up capital of the transferred shares and the actual adjusted cost base. The adjusted cost base represents the shareholder's purchase price for the shares.

Where shares are to be issued on a s. 85 rollover and the paid-up capital of the shares for tax purposes is affected by one of these provisions, it is usually desirable (if possible) to have the directors select a stated capital amount that equals the reduced or limited paid-up capital. This reduces the circumstances in which the stated capital and paid-up capital are different. It is common practice in this situation to specify the selected stated capital amount in the directors' resolution approving the s. 85 rollover.

DIFFERENCES BETWEEN PAID-UP CAPITAL AND ADJUSTED COST BASE

Paid-up capital generally represents the average issue price for a particular class of shares. The adjusted cost base represents the shareholder's purchase price for the shares. For example:

> ABC Co. Ltd. issues 2 common shares to Joseph for $100 each. Joseph subsequently sells 1 common share to Jack for $150. The aggregate paid-up capital of the common shares is $200 (2 × $100). The adjusted cost base of the share to Joseph is $100 and the adjusted cost base to Jack is $150.

EXAMPLE OF A S. 85 ROLLOVER TRANSACTION

Applying the concepts discussed in this chapter, let's look at an example of a transfer of an asset by a shareholder to a corporation using s. 85.

> Cathy owns an asset that she purchased personally for $2,000. The asset is 100,000 common shares of Opco Inc., an Ontario corporation. The asset is currently worth $4,000 and Cathy wishes to transfer it to Holdco Limited, a Canadian corporation incorporated by Cathy to purchase the shares of Opco. Using the s. 85 rollover provisions, Cathy could transfer the asset to Holdco in exchange for 4,000 special shares. The special

shares must have a value of $4,000, being the same value as the asset. The special shares will therefore be redeemable and retractable at $1.00 per share $(4,000 \times \$1.00 = \$4,000)$. However, if the transfer takes place at $4,000, Cathy will have a capital gain of $2,000, which will be taxable. In order to defer the tax payable, Cathy and Holdco can elect that the transfer will take place at $2,000. The adjusted cost base of the asset to Holdco will be $2,000, so that when Holdco sells the asset — for example, for $4,000 — Holdco will pay tax on the gain. The adjusted cost base of the special shares received by Cathy will also be $2,000, so that the gain will not be taxable until Cathy eventually sells the shares. The paid-up capital will be set at the same amount as the adjusted cost base of $2,000.

If Cathy wanted to extract actual cash from Holdco for the transfer of the asset, Holdco could issue a promissory note for up to $2,000 and shares for the remainder of the value, without triggering tax. In this case, the elected amount for the shares will be nominal, since the full $2,000 of cost base is allocated to the promissory note. If the elected amount for the shares were more than a nominal amount, a capital gain would be triggered, because the total of the non-share consideration and the adjusted cost base of the shares would be more than the original adjusted cost base of the asset. The paid-up capital of the shares in this case will also be nominal.

This example is exactly the situation contemplated by s. 84.1 of the ITA. To avoid a deemed dividend or a reduction in paid-up capital, the capital gains exemption must not be claimed and the non-share consideration should not exceed the adjusted cost base of the shares transferred.

DOCUMENTS USED IN A TYPICAL S. 85 TRANSACTION

The following is a list of typical documents prepared in a s. 85 rollover transaction:

1. Rollover agreement between the transferor and the transferee. The rollover agreement should include the following:

   a. Identity and description of the parties

   b. Description of the asset to be transferred and the fair market value

   c. Effective date of the transfer

   d. Purchase price

   e. Number and class of shares to be issued to the transferor in consideration of purchase price

   f. Cost amount

   g. Elected amount

   h. Statement that the parties intend that s. 85(1) of the ITA shall apply to the transfer of the assets

   i. Statement that the parties agree to jointly elect in the form prescribed pursuant to s. 85(1) of the ITA

   j. Price adjustment clause

2. Resolution of the directors of the transferee approving the purchase of the asset, authorizing the transferee to enter into and execute the rollover agreement, issuing shares to the transferor, specifying additions to the stated capital account, and authorizing the transferee to elect jointly with the transferor under s. 85(1) of the ITA

3. Share certificate of the transferee issued to the transferor

4. T2057 election form

5. Updating of shareholders' ledgers and registers of the transferee to record issuance of shares to transferor

Figure 3.5 at the end of the chapter includes a document list for Cathy's rollover transaction in the example above; a sample rollover agreement and directors' resolution; and the s. 85 election form, T2057.

Section 86 reorganization of capital

Generally speaking, a s. 86 rollover involves an exchange of old shares of a corporation for new shares of the same corporation in the course of a reorganization of capital without recognition of any gain or loss. Section 86 does not apply to a disposition of securities other than shares. A capital gain will occur only where the fair market value of any non-share consideration received exceeds the adjusted cost base of the shares exchanged.

For a transaction to qualify under s. 86, all of the following conditions must be met (s. 86(1)):

1. An exchange of shares by a shareholder (the taxpayer) must occur "in the course of a reorganization of the capital of a corporation." (There is no Canadian residency requirement for either the shareholder or the corporation.)

2. The exchanged shares disposed of by the taxpayer must be capital property.

3. The exchanged shares must be *all* of the shares of a particular class of capital stock of the corporation that were owned by the taxpayer at the particular time.

4. The consideration received from the corporation must include other shares of the corporation. (If non-share consideration is received, a rollover is not available unless the value of the non-share consideration is equal to or less than the adjusted cost base of the exchanged shares.)

Section 86 is not available if s. 85 applies (s. 86(3)). Note that s. 86 does not require an election form to be filed with the CRA.

If the exchange of shares meets the conditions set out above, the following rules apply:

1. The adjusted cost base to the taxpayer of any non-share consideration received for the old shares is deemed to be its fair market value.

2. The adjusted cost base to the taxpayer of the new shares of the corporation received for the old shares is deemed to be the difference between the aggregate of the adjusted cost base of the taxpayer's old shares and the fair market value of the non-share consideration.

3. The taxpayer is deemed to have disposed of the old shares of the corporation in return for proceeds of disposition equal to the adjusted cost base of the non-share consideration and the new shares received by the taxpayer.

The issue that must be considered in determining whether a transaction qualifies for the s. 86 rollover is whether there is a "reorganization of capital." This is not a defined term under the ITA. It is generally accepted, however, that an amendment to a corporation's articles of incorporation will constitute a reorganization of capital sufficient to meet the requirements of s. 86.

A typical s. 86 reorganization is effected by filing articles of amendment that create a new class of shares, usually with rights identical to the rights of the shares used for s. 85 rollovers. The articles of amendment also provide that all of the shares to be exchanged (the old shares) will be exchanged for the new shares at the time the articles of amendment come into effect (that is, at the time of filing).

Sometimes a s. 86 reorganization will be effected by authorizing the new shares in the articles of amendment, or by using an existing class of shares if they have the required rights and have not yet been issued, and then having the shareholder enter into a share exchange agreement with the corporation to exchange the original shares for the new shares. There is a concern that such an arrangement may not be interpreted as a "reorganization of capital." Therefore, if this method is to be used, care should be taken to ensure that the corporation can rely on other facts in order to meet the "reorganization of capital" requirement. Generally, it is considered prudent to provide for the exchange to take place at the time the articles of amendment are filed.

In a s. 86 reorganization involving an exchange of common shares for new shares, the shareholder usually subscribes for additional common shares for a nominal subscription price. This ensures that the shareholder remains entitled to shares that are voting equity shares. It may be prudent to ensure that the additional common shares that are being issued to the shareholder have slightly different rights than the old common shares. This will ensure that there is no uncertainty as to whether the shareholder has actually disposed of his old shares. For example, the articles of amendment creating the new shares and approving the exchange of existing common shares into new shares may also include the creation of a new class of common shares that have two votes per share instead of the one vote per share of the existing common shares. Although it may seem strange for the shareholder to exchange all of his common shares for new shares and then subscribe for more common shares, this is not unusual. For example, this method is often used in an estate freeze where the shareholder wishes to freeze only part of his or her assets in the corporation or where the common shares are ultimately intended to be held by married children. In the latter case, the shareholder can subscribe for common shares and gift them to the married children. This ensures that the shares will not fall into net family property of a married child in the event of breakdown of the marriage.

COMPUTATION OF PAID-UP CAPITAL

Section 86 contains specific provisions that reduce the addition to the paid-up capital of the new shares, if necessary, to prevent such addition, together with the fair market value of any non-share consideration received on the exchange, from exceeding the paid-up capital of the old shares. Usually, the paid-up capital of the new shares is ground down to the paid-up capital of the old shares.

DEEMED DIVIDEND

The reduction in the paid-up capital ensures that a shareholder does not recognize a deemed dividend as a result of the exchange of shares where no non-share consideration is received. However, where non-share consideration is received as part of an exchange under s. 86, it is important to ensure that the fair market value of the non-share consideration does not exceed the paid-up capital of the old shares, because the amount of the excess will be treated as a deemed dividend under s. 84(3) of the ITA.

DOCUMENTS USED IN A TYPICAL S. 86 REORGANIZATION

The following is a list of typical documents used in a section 86 "freeze" reorganization:

1. Articles of amendment
    a. to create special shares
    b. to create a new class of common shares
    c. provide for the exchange of all existing common shares into special shares
    d. to cancel the existing common shares (if they are no longer needed)
    as the case may be
2. Special resolution authorizing the articles of amendment
3. Cancellation of old common share certificates
4. Directors' resolution adopting the form of share certificate for the special shares and the new class of common shares and issuing the new class of common shares to the shareholder for a nominal amount
5. New share certificate of the corporation issued to the shareholder, representing the special shares
6. New share certificate of the corporation issued to the shareholder representing the new common shares
7. Updating of shareholders' ledgers and registers

KEY TERMS

capital gain

capital loss

consideration

continuance

contributory

horizontal short-form amalgamation

liquidator

long-form amalgamation

paid-up capital

stated capital

taxable Canadian corporation

vertical short-form amalgamation

REFERENCES

Statutes and regulations

Canada Business Corporations Act (CBCA), RSC 1985, c. C-44, as amended, and regulations.

Business Corporations Act (Ontario) (OBCA), RSO 1990, c. B.16, as amended, and regulations.

Income Tax Act (Canada)(ITA), RSC 1985, c. 1 (5th Supp.), as amended.

Other sources

Campbell, John, and Steven Adams, *Selected Tax Aspects of Corporate Reorganizations*, Miller Thomson LLP, Toronto, March 26, 1996.

Grover, Warren M.H., *Canada Corporation Manual* (Toronto: Carswell, looseleaf): "Amalgamation," 11-101 to 11-131; "Liquidation-Dissolution," 12-11 to 12-824.

Kingston, Robert A., *Ontario Corporation Manual* (Toronto: Carswell, 2005), "Dissolution," 11-11 to 11-77.

Law Society of Upper Canada, Bar Admission course material: chapter 3, "Taxation of Corporations and Their Shareholders"; chapter 8, "Corporate Capital Structure: Share Capitalization"; chapter 9, "Corporate Changes" (Toronto: LSUC, April 2001).

Welch, Jillian M., McCarthy Tétrault, "When Tax Drives the Deal: Advanced Corporate and Basic Securities Law for Law Clerks," Law Society of Upper Canada, Continuing Legal Education seminar, June 16, 1994.

FORMS AND PRECEDENTS

Figure 3.1: Amalgamation Checklist

Figure 3.2: Forms and sample documents for long-form and short-form amalgamations, including amalgamation agreement, directors' resolution approving amalgamation agreement, notice of special meeting of shareholders, special resolution of shareholders approving amalgamation agreement, directors' resolutions approving vertical short-form amalgamation (parent and subsidiary), directors' resolutions approving horizontal short-form amalgamation, articles of amalgamation (CBCA Form 9, OBCA Form 4), statutory declaration (CBCA corporations), officer's statement (OBCA corporations), notice to creditors, and post-amalgamation resolutions and director's consent

Figure 3.3: Forms and sample documents for dissolution of a CBCA corporation, including directors' resolution approving dissolution under s. 210(1), special resolution approving dissolution under s. 210(2) or (3), articles of dissolution (CBCA Form 17), notice of special meeting of shareholders to approve liquidation and dissolution under s. 211, special resolution approving liquidation and dissolution under s. 211, statement of intent to dissolve (CBCA Form 19), and notice of liquidation under s. 211

Figure 3.4: Forms and sample documents for dissolution of an OBCA corporation, including articles of dissolution (OBCA Form 11), letter to Corporations Tax Branch, Ministry of Finance requesting consent to dissolution, consent of Corporations Tax Branch, special resolution approving dissolution, articles of dissolution (OBCA Form 10), special Resolution requiring the corporation to be wound up and appointing liquidator, and notice of the special resolution requiring the corporation to be wound up (OBCA Form 16)

Figure 3.5: Example of a s. 85 rollover, including document list, rollover agreement, resolutions, share rights, and s. 85 election form (T2057)

NOTES

1. See *R v. Black and Decker Manufacturing Company Limited* (1974), 43 DLR (3d) 393 (SCC).

REVIEW QUESTIONS

Amalgamation

1. An Ontario corporation and a federal corporation wish to amalgamate and be governed by the CBCA. Explain the first step in the process of amalgamating these two corporations.

2. Briefly explain the differences between a long-form amalgamation and a short-form amalgamation under the CBCA.

3. When a special meeting of shareholders is called for the purpose of approving an amalgamation, what documents, if any, must accompany the notice of the meeting?

4. Is it possible to approve a long-form amalgamation without calling a meeting of shareholders?

5. In addition to articles of amalgamation, list the other documents that must be filed with Industry Canada to complete an application for amalgamation.

Dissolution

1. Name the four methods of dissolution under the CBCA.

2. List the documents that must be prepared in order to dissolve a CBCA corporation that has never actively carried on business.

3. Would your answer to question 2 be different if the corporation was dissolving under s. 210(2) of the CBCA? If yes, explain your answer.

4. List the steps required to voluntarily liquidate and dissolve under s. 211 of the CBCA.

5. Name the grounds for a court order dissolving a CBCA corporation.

6. List the documents that must be obtained and/or prepared in order for an OBCA corporation to dissolve under s. 237(a).

7. List the steps required to wind up voluntarily under the OBCA.

8. Who may apply for a court order to dissolve an OBCA corporation?

9. A CBCA corporation was dissolved on September 30, 2002 and the sole shareholder of the corporation received $20,000, which was the remaining property of the corporation after the payment of its debts and liabilities. Is it possible for an individual to commence an action against the corporation on June 30, 2005, and is there any consequence to the shareholder?

Rollover

1. Give two examples of non-share consideration that could be received by a vendor on a rollover under s. 85 of the ITA.

2. Explain paid-up capital and stated capital and the relevance of each.

3. What are the conditions that must be met in order for a transaction to be governed by s. 85(1) of the ITA?

4. A client wishes to transfer an asset that he owns personally to a corporation incorporated in Delaware. Is it possible for the transaction to be governed by s. 85 of the ITA? Provide an explanation for your answer.

5. A transaction under s. 85 of the ITA closed on September 1, 2004. The transaction involved the transfer of shares from Joseph to Holdco. In exchange, Joseph received shares in Holdco and a promissory note. The year-end of Holdco is June 30. What must be filed with the CRA, and what is the filing deadline?

6. Would your answer be different if the transaction was governed by s. 86 of the ITA?

7. A shareholder owns 150 common shares of ABC Co. She wishes to exchange 100 common shares for 100 special shares of ABC Co. Is it possible for her to take advantage of s. 86 of the ITA?

FIGURE 3.1   AMALGAMATION CHECKLIST

THINGS TO CONSIDER PRIOR TO AMALGAMATION

- Are all of the amalgamating corporations governed by the same act? If not, determine which act the amalgamated corporation should be governed by.
- Are the amalgamating corporations equal in value?
- Determine if corporation is a long-form or short-form amalgamation.
- Determine the name of the amalgamated corporation. If the name is not the name of one of the amalgamating corporations, order a NUANS name search report.

CBCA CORPORATIONS

Long-form amalgamation

1. Amalgamation agreement
2. Directors' resolution of each amalgamating corporation approving the amalgamation agreement
3. Notice of meeting of shareholders to be sent to shareholders of each amalgamating corporation entitled to vote (not required if a special resolution is to be passed by all shareholders by written resolution)
4. Special resolution of shareholders of each amalgamating corporation, passed either at a meeting of shareholders or by written resolution
5. Notice to creditors (if statement that no creditor will be prejudiced cannot be made)
6. Statutory declaration of an officer or director of each amalgamating corporation
7. Form 9, Articles of Amalgamation
8. Form 2, Information Regarding the Registered Office and the Board of Directors
9. NUANS name search report (if the name of the amalgamated corporation is not the name of one of the amalgamating corporations)
10. Filing fee

Short-form amalgamation

1. Directors' resolution of each amalgamating corporation approving amalgamation
2. Notice to creditors (if the statement that no creditor will be prejudiced cannot be made)
3. Statutory declaration of an officer or director of each amalgamating corporation
4. Form 9, Articles of Amalgamation
5. Form 2, Information Regarding the Registered Office and the Board of Directors
6. NUANS name search report (if the name of the amalgamated corporation is not the name of one of the amalgamating corporations)
7. Filing fee

FIGURE 3.1 CONTINUED

OBCA CORPORATIONS
Long-form amalgamation

1. Amalgamation agreement
2. Directors' resolution of each amalgamating corporation approving the amalgamation agreement
3. Notice of meeting of shareholders to be sent to shareholders of each amalgamating corporation entitled to vote (not required if a special resolution is to be passed by all shareholders by written resolution)
4. Special resolution of shareholders of each amalgamating corporation, passed either at a meeting of shareholders or by written resolution
5. Notice to creditors (if the statement that no creditor will be prejudiced cannot be made)
6. Statement of an officer or director of each amalgamating corporation
7. Articles of Amalgamation, including attachment of a copy of the amalgamation agreement as a schedule.
8. NUANS name search report (if the name of the amalgamated corporation is not the name of one of the amalgamating corporations)
9. Filing fee

Short-form amalgamation

1. Directors' resolution of each amalgamating corporation approving the amalgamation
2. Notice to creditors (if the statement that no creditor will be prejudiced cannot be made)
3. Statement of an officer or director of each amalgamating corporation
4. Form 4, Articles of Amalgamation, including attachment of a certified copy of directors' resolutions of each amalgamating corporation as schedules
5. NUANS name search report (if the name of the amalgamated corporation is not the name of one of the amalgamating corporations)
6. Filing fee

FOLLOWING ISSUANCE OF A CERTIFICATE OF AMALGAMATION

1. Post-amalgamation resolutions of directors to:
   a. enact bylaw (if necessary)
   b. appoint officers
   c. approve banking arrangements
   d. approve forms of share certificates
   e. adopt corporate seal (if any)
   f. confirm year-end
   g. authorize issuance of share certificates (if applicable)
   h. preserve pre-existing divisions and divisional names
   i. authorize any provincial registrations or licensing applications required

FIGURE 3.1 CONCLUDED

2. Post-amalgamation resolutions of shareholders to:

   a. enact bylaw (if necessary)

   b. appoint auditors or consent to exemption from audit requirements

   c. fix the number of directors (if the articles of amalgamation provide for a minimum and maximum number of directors) (required for OBCA corporations only)

3. Consents of directors to act as directors

4. Banking documents

5. Cancellation of share certificates of amalgamating corporations

6. Issuance of new share certificates of amalgamated corporation (if applicable)

7. Initial Return, Form 1 under the *Corporations Information Act* for the amalgamated corporation (OBCA corporations)

8. Initial Return, Form 2 under the *Corporations Information Act* for the amalgamated corporation (for CBCA corporations if the registered office is in Ontario) to be filed with Ontario Ministry of Government Services, together with a copy of the articles of amalgamation

9. Notice of Change, Form 2 under the *Corporations Information Act* for each amalgamating corporation, indicating that the corporation ceased to carry on business in Ontario on the date of amalgamation (for CBCA corporations if the registered office is in Ontario)

10. Notice of the amalgamation to all other corporations in which the amalgamating corporations hold securities and request for issuance of replacement share certificates if necessary

11. Filing of a copy of articles of amalgamation with the applicable Land Registry Office, if one of the amalgamating corporations had a registered interest in land

12. Notice to various parties such as suppliers, customers, insurance agents, bankers

13. If any of the amalgamating corporations were extra-provincially registered and the amalgamated corporation intends to continue to carry on business in that province or territory, completion and filing of all documents in the particular province or territory

14. Following amalgamation, the amalgamated corporation can either get a new business number (BN) issued to it or retain the BN of one of the existing corporations (the dominant corporation). The CRA will automatically issue a new BN (which usually takes about 6 weeks to 3 months) if it has not received a request to the contrary. If the amalgamated corporation wishes to keep the BN of one of the amalgamating corporations, the amalgamated corporation should advise the CRA of the amalgamation and request that the BN be retained.

15. If any of the amalgamating corporations previously registered a business name and the amalgamated corporation wishes to continue to use the business name, file an "Amendment" under the *Business Names Act* indicating the new corporate name and new corporate number. If the amalgamated corporation does not wish to continue to use any of the business names previously registered by any of the amalgamating corporations, the business names should be cancelled.

SAMPLE AMALGAMATION AGREEMENT

THIS AGREEMENT is made as of the _____ day of _____, 200__.

BETWEEN:

_____,

a corporation incorporated under the laws of [Canada/Ontario]

(hereinafter referred to as "Corp 1")

AND:

_____,

a corporation incorporated under the laws of [Canada/Ontario]

(hereinafter referred to as "Corp 2")

WHEREAS:

A.   Corp 1 was incorporated under the [*Canada Business Corporations Act*/*Business Corporations Act* (Ontario)] by Certificate of Incorporation dated _____.

B.   Corp 2 was incorporated under the [*Canada Business Corporations Act*/*Business Corporations Act* (Ontario)] by Certificate of Incorporation dated _____.

C.   The authorized capital of Corp 1 consists of _____ shares of which the following are issued and outstanding and held as follows:

Shareholder	Number and Class of Shares Held

D.   The authorized capital of Corp 2 consists of _____ shares of which the following are issued and outstanding and held as follows:

Shareholder	Number and Class of Shares Held

FIGURE 3.2   CONTINUED

E.   Corp 1 and Corp 2 have each made full disclosure to the other of all their respective assets and liabilities;

F.   Corp 1 and Corp 2 have agreed to amalgamate pursuant to the provisions of the *Canada Business Corporations Act*/[*Business Corporations Act* (Ontario)];

NOW THEREFORE in consideration of the premises and the mutual covenants herein and other good and valuable consideration (the receipt and sufficiency of which is hereby acknowledged by each of the parties) the parties hereto covenant and agree as follows:

1.   **DEFINITIONS**

In this Agreement:

1.1.   "Act" means the [*Canada Business Corporations Act*/*Business Corporations Act* (Ontario)];

1.2.   "Agreement" means this Amalgamation Agreement;

1.3.   "Amalgamated Corporation" means the corporation continuing from the amalgamation of the Amalgamating Corporations;

1.4.   "Amalgamating Corporations" means Corp 1 and Corp 2;

1.5.   "Amalgamation" means the amalgamation of the Amalgamating Corporations as contemplated in the Agreement;

1.6.   "Effective Date" means the date of the Amalgamation as set forth in the Certificate of Amalgamation issued to the Amalgamated Corporation.

1.7.   Words and phrases used herein and defined in the Act shall have the same meaning herein as in the Act unless the context otherwise requires.

2.   **AMALGAMATION**

The Amalgamating Corporations agree to amalgamate as of the Effective Date and to continue as one corporation on the terms and conditions herein described.

3.   **NAME**

The name of the Amalgamated Corporation shall be _____.

4.   **BUSINESS**

There shall be no restriction on the type of business which the Amalgamated Corporation is authorized to carry on.

5.   **REGISTERED OFFICE**

The registered office of the Amalgamated Corporation shall be in the Province of Ontario [or, *or an OBCA corporation*: The registered office of the Amalgamated Corporation shall be in the City of _____, in the Province of Ontario].

FIGURE 3.2   CONTINUED

6. ## AUTHORIZED CAPITAL

The authorized capital of the Amalgamated Corporation shall consist of _____ shares which shall have attached thereto the rights, privileges, restrictions and conditions set out in Schedule "A" annexed hereto.

7. ## RESTRICTIONS ON TRANSFER

No shares of the Amalgamated Corporation may be transferred without either:

7.1.   the previous consent of the directors of the Amalgamated Corporation expressed by a resolution passed by the board of directors or by an instrument or instruments in writing signed by all the directors; or

7.2.   the previous consent of the holders of at least fifty-one percent (51%) of the voting shares for the time being outstanding expressed by a resolution passed by the shareholders or by an instrument or instruments in writing signed by such shareholders.

8. ## OTHER PROVISIONS

8.1.   Without in any way restricting the powers of the Amalgamated Corporation, the board of directors may from time to time and without authorization of the shareholders:

8.1.1.   borrow money on the credit of the Amalgamated Corporation;

8.1.2.   issue, reissue, sell, pledge or hypothecate debt obligations of the Amalgamated Corporation;

8.1.3.   give a guarantee on behalf of the Amalgamated Corporation to secure performance of an obligation of any person; and

8.1.4.   mortgage, hypothecate, pledge or otherwise create a security interest in all or any property of the Amalgamated Corporation, owned or subsequently acquired, to secure any obligation of the Amalgamated Corporation.

8.2.   The board of directors may from time to time delegate any or all of the foregoing powers to such officers or directors of the Amalgamated Corporation to such extent and in such manner as the board of directors may from time to time determine.

8.3.   The Corporation shall be entitled to a lien on any share registered in the name of a shareholder or the shareholder's personal representative for a debt of that shareholder to the Corporation.

FIGURE 3.2 CONTINUED

9. **BOARD OF DIRECTORS**

9.1. The board of directors of the Amalgamated Corporation shall, until otherwise changed in accordance with the Act, consist of a minimum number of [*e.g.*: 1] and a maximum number of [*e.g.*: 10] directors.

9.2. The first directors of the Amalgamated Corporation shall be as follows:

Name	Address	Resident Canadian

9.3. The first directors of the Amalgamated Corporation shall hold office until the first annual meeting of the shareholders of the Amalgamated Corporation or until their successors are duly elected or appointed.

10. **BY-LAWS**

The by-laws of the Amalgamated Corporation until repealed, amended or altered, shall be the by-laws of _____ [*name of amalgamating corporations whose by-laws are being adopted*]. [*Insert the following for OBCA corporations*: The address where the proposed by-laws may be examined is _____.]

OR

The by-laws of the Amalgamated Corporation will not be the same as those of any of the Amalgamating Corporations. A copy of the proposed by-laws of the Amalgamated Corporation [*for a CBCA corporation*: are annexed hereto as Schedule "B"] / *for an OBCA corporation*: may be examined at the registered office of the _____ _____ [*name and address of one of the amalgamating corporations*] at any time during normal business hours prior to the Effective Date].

11. **CONVERSION OF SHARES**

11.1. On the Effective Date:

11.1.1. the [*e.g.*: 100 common] shares of Corp 1 shall be converted into [*e.g.*: 100 common] shares of the Amalgamated Corporation;

11.1.2. the [*e.g.*: 200 special] shares of Corp 2 shall be converted into [*e.g.*: 200 special] shares of the Amalgamated Corporation; and

[*Note: insert the next paragraph only if applicable*]

provided, however, that any fractional _____ share of the Amalgamated Corporation to which any holder of _____ shares of [Corp 1] would otherwise be entitled to receive in accordance with paragraph 11.1.1 shall be disregarded and, in lieu thereof, such holder shall be entitled to receive a cash

FIGURE 3.2 CONTINUED

payment from the Amalgamated Corporation in an amount equal to the relevant fraction multiplied by the fair market value of a _____ share of the Amalgamated Corporation immediately following the Amalgamation, as determined by the board of directors of the Amalgamated Corporation in its sole discretion, such payment to be made upon presentation and surrender by such holder to the Amalgamated Corporation of the certificates representing such holder's _____ shares of [Corp 1] so converted as provided in paragraph 11.4.

11.2.　After the conversion of shares the shareholders of the Amalgamated Corporation shall be as follows:

Name of Shareholder	Common Shares	Special Shares

11.3.　All of the shares of the Amalgamated Corporation to be issued in accordance with the foregoing shall be deemed to have been issued as fully paid and non-assessable, and the Amalgamated Corporation shall be deemed to have received the full consideration for the issue thereof.

11.4.　On or after the Effective Date, the shareholders of the Amalgamating Corporations shall surrender to the Amalgamated Corporation for cancellation all share certificates held by them representing the shares of the Amalgamating Corporations held by them immediately prior to the Amalgamation in exchange for certificates representing the shares of the Amalgamated Corporation into which such shares were converted.

12.　**STATED CAPITAL**

12.1.　The stated capital of the [*e.g.*: common] shares of the Amalgamated Corporation shall be equal to $_____;

12.2.　the stated capital of the [*e.g.*: special] shares of the Amalgamated Corporation shall be equal to $_____.

13.　**ARTICLES OF AMALGAMATION**

If the shareholders of the Amalgamating Corporations approve and adopt this Agreement in accordance with the Act, the Amalgamating Corporations shall jointly file with the Director under the Act articles of amalgamation and such other documents as may be required in order that the Amalgamation become effective.

FIGURE 3.2   CONTINUED

14.   **SHAREHOLDER APPROVAL**

Each of the Amalgamating Corporations will submit this Agreement to its shareholders for approval as provided by the Act.

[*Note: include the following paragraph only if applicable*]

15.   **TERMINATION**

At any time before the endorsement of a certificate of amalgamation in respect of the Amalgamation, this Agreement may be terminated by the directors of each of the Amalgamating Corporations in their sole discretion, regardless of whether this Agreement has been approved by the shareholders of any or all of the Amalgamating Corporations.

16.   **GOVERNING LAW**

This Agreement shall be governed by and construed in accordance with the laws of the Province of Ontario and the laws of Canada applicable therein.

17.   **COUNTERPARTS**

This Agreement may be executed in several counterparts of like form, which when executed by each of the parties hereto shall be deemed to be an original and such counterparts shall together constitute one and the same instrument.

18.   **FURTHER ASSURANCES**

The parties hereto shall do all further acts and things and execute all further documents reasonably required in the circumstances to effect the provisions and intent of this Agreement.

19.   **HEADINGS**

The headings appearing throughout this Agreement are inserted for convenience only and form no part of the Agreement.

20.   **ENTIRE AGREEMENT**

This Agreement together with the schedules attached hereto constitutes the entire agreement between the parties and supersedes all prior and contemporaneous agreements, understandings and discussions, whether oral or written, and there are no other warranties, agreements or representations between the parties except as expressly set forth herein.

21.   **AGREEMENT BINDING**

This Agreement shall enure to the benefit of and be binding upon the parties hereto and their respective successors and permitted assigns.

22.   **WAIVERS**

No amendment, waiver or termination of this Agreement will be binding unless executed in writing by the parties to be bound hereby. No waiver of any provision of

FIGURE 3.2 CONTINUED

this Agreement will be deemed or will constitute a waiver of any other provision, nor will any such waiver constitute a continuing waiver unless expressly provided.

23. **SEVERABILITY**

The invalidity or unenforceability of any provision of this Agreement will not affect the validity or enforceability of any other provision hereof and any such invalid or unenforceable provision will be deemed to be severable.

24. **AMENDMENT OF AGREEMENT**

This Agreement may be altered, amended or annulled at any time by the mutual consent in writing of the parties hereto.

IN WITNESS WHEREOF this Agreement has been executed by the parties hereto.

SIGNED, SEALED AND DELIVERED

Corp 1

Per: _____
     Name:
     Title:

Corp 2

Per: _____
     Name:
     Title:

FIGURE 3.2   CONTINUED

SCHEDULE "A"
SHARE RIGHTS
OF
AMALGAMATED CORPORATION

FIGURE 3.2   CONTINUED

SCHEDULE "B"
[PROPOSED BY-LAWS]

FIGURE 3.2   CONTINUED

LONG-FORM AMALGAMATION: DIRECTORS' RESOLUTION
APPROVING AMALGAMATION AGREEMENT

RESOLUTION OF THE DIRECTORS
OF

_____

AMALGAMATION WITH _____

WHEREAS the Corporation wishes to amalgamate with _____
_____ (" _____ ") pursuant to [section 183 of the *Canada Business Corporations Act*/section 174 of the *Business Corporations Act* (the "Act") (Ontario)] substantially on the terms set out in the draft amalgamation agreement annexed hereto as Schedule "A" (the "Draft Amalgamation Agreement");

NOW THEREFORE BE IT RESOLVED that:

1.   the Corporation is hereby authorized to amalgamate with _____
_____ and to enter into an amalgamation agreement substantially in the form of the Draft Amalgamation Agreement attached hereto as Schedule "A";

2.   any officer of the Corporation is hereby authorized for and on behalf of the Corporation to execute, under the corporate seal of the Corporation or otherwise, and deliver an agreement (the "Amalgamation Agreement"), substantially in the form and on the terms of the Draft Amalgamation Agreement presented to the directors with such additions, deletions and changes thereto as such officer may approve and execution in such manner shall be conclusive evidence of such approval and that the Amalgamation Agreement and any amending instrument relating thereto, when so executed and delivered are instruments authorized by this resolution and shall be valid and binding on the Corporation; and

3.   any officer is hereby authorized and directed from time to time to execute or cause to be executed under the corporate seal of the Corporation or otherwise all such other documents and to do all such other acts as in his discretion may be necessary or desirable to give effect to this resolution and to perform the obligations of the Corporation under the Amalgamation Agreement.

The undersigned, being all the directors of the Corporation, hereby consent, by their signatures, to the foregoing resolution, pursuant to the provisions of the [*Canada Business Corporations Act*/*Business Corporations Act* (Ontario)].

DATED _____

_____

_____

FIGURE 3.2   CONTINUED

LONG-FORM AMALGAMATION:
NOTICE OF SPECIAL SHAREHOLDERS' MEETING

NOTICE OF SPECIAL MEETING OF SHAREHOLDERS
OF

_____

NOTICE IS HEREBY GIVEN that a special meeting of the shareholders of _____ (the "Corporation") will be held at [*address*] on [*date*] at [*time*] for the following purposes:

1.   to consider and, if thought advisable, pass a special resolution (the "Special Resolution") approving the amalgamation agreement between the Corporation and _____ _____ [*name of other amalgamating corporations*] (the "Amalgamation Agreement") providing for the amalgamation of the Corporation and _____ [name of other amalgamating corporations] pursuant to the [*Canada Business Corporations Act/Business Corporations Act* (Ontario)] on the terms set out in the Amalgamation Agreement; and

2.   to transact such other business as may properly come before the meeting or any adjournments thereof.

A copy of the Amalgamation Agreement and the text of the Special Resolution are annexed hereto as Schedules A and B, respectively.

TAKE NOTICE that pursuant to the [*Canada Business Corporations Act/Business Corporations Act* (Ontario)] you may, at or before the meeting, give the Corporation a written notice of dissent with respect to the Special Resolution. As a result of giving a notice of dissent, you may require the Corporation to purchase all of your shares at their fair value.

DATED _____

BY ORDER OF THE BOARD OF DIRECTORS

_____
Secretary

FIGURE 3.2   CONTINUED

LONG-FORM AMALGAMATION: SPECIAL SHAREHOLDERS' RESOLUTION APPROVING AMALGAMATION

SPECIAL RESOLUTION OF THE SHAREHOLDERS
OF

_____

<u>**AMALGAMATION WITH**</u> _____

WHEREAS the Corporation wishes to amalgamate with _____ _____ ("_____") pursuant to [section 183 of the *Canada Business Corporations Act*/section 174 of the *Business Corporations Act* (Ontario) (the "Act") substantially on the terms set out in the draft amalgamation agreement annexed hereto as Schedule "A" (the "Draft Amalgamation Agreement");

NOW THEREFORE BE IT RESOLVED as a special resolution that the Corporation is hereby authorized to amalgamate with _____ and to enter into an amalgamation agreement (the "Amalgamation Agreement"), substantially in the form and on the terms and subject to the conditions of the Draft Amalgamation Agreement annexed hereto as Schedule "A", with such changes thereto as any director or officer of the Corporation may approve (such approval to be evidenced conclusively by the execution and delivery by such director or officer of the Amalgamation Agreement).

The undersigned, being all the shareholders of the Corporation, hereby consent, by their signatures, to the foregoing special resolution pursuant to the provisions of the [*Canada Business Corporations Act*/*Business Corporations Act* (Ontario).

DATED _____

_____

_____

FIGURE 3.2 CONTINUED

VERTICAL SHORT-FORM AMALGAMATION:
RESOLUTION OF DIRECTORS OF PARENT COMPANY

RESOLUTION OF THE DIRECTORS
OF

_____

ARTICLES OF AMALGAMATION

WHEREAS the Corporation has agreed to amalgamate with its wholly owned subsidiary _____ pursuant to [section 184(1) of the *Canada Business Corporations Act*/section 177(1) of the *Business Corporations Act* (Ontario)] (the "Act");

NOW THEREFORE BE IT RESOLVED that:

1. the amalgamation of the Corporation and _____ pursuant to section [184(1)/177(1)] of the Act is hereby approved;

2. upon the issuance of a Certificate of Amalgamation pursuant to section [185(4)/178(4)] of the Act, all shares of _____ [*name of subsidiary corporation*], including all shares which have been issued and are outstanding at the date hereof, are hereby cancelled without any repayment of capital in respect thereof;

[*Note: the following paragraph is only required for an OBCA corporation*]

3. the by-laws of the amalgamated corporation shall be the same as the by-laws of the Corporation;

4. except as may be prescribed, the articles of amalgamation of the amalgamated corporation shall be the same as the articles of the Corporation;

5. no securities shall be issued [for an OBCA corporation, add: and no assets shall be distributed] by the amalgamated corporation in connection with the amalgamation;

[*Note: the following paragraph is only required for a CBCA corporation*]

6. the stated capital of the amalgamated corporation shall be the same as the stated capital of the Corporation; and

7. the proper officers of the Corporation are hereby authorized to do all things and execute all instruments and documents necessary or desirable to carry out and give effect to the foregoing.

FIGURE 3.2   CONTINUED

The undersigned, being all the directors of the Corporation, hereby consent, by their signatures, to the foregoing resolutions pursuant to the provisions of the [*Canada Business Corporations Act*/*Business Corporations Act* (Ontario)].

DATED _____

_____

_____

FIGURE 3.2 CONTINUED

VERTICAL SHORT-FORM AMALGAMATION:
RESOLUTION OF DIRECTORS OF SUBSIDIARY

RESOLUTION OF THE DIRECTORS
OF

_____

ARTICLES OF AMALGAMATION

WHEREAS the Corporation is a wholly owned subsidiary of, and has agreed to amalgamate with _____, pursuant to [section 184(1) of the *Canada Business Corporations Act*/section 177(1) of the *Business Corporations Act* (Ontario)] (the "Act");

NOW THEREFORE BE IT RESOLVED that:

1. the amalgamation of the Corporation and _____ pursuant to section [184(1)/177(1)] of the Act is hereby approved;

2. upon the issuance of a Certificate of Amalgamation pursuant to section [185(4)/178(4)] of the Act, all shares of the Corporation, including all shares which have been issued and are outstanding at the date hereof, are hereby cancelled without any repayment of capital in respect thereof;

[*Note: the following paragraph is only required for BCA corporations*]

3. the by-laws of the amalgamated corporation shall be the same as the by-laws of _____ [name of amalgamating parent corporation];

4. except as may be prescribed, the articles of amalgamation of the amalgamated corporation shall be the same as the articles of _____ [name of amalgamating parent corporation];

5. no securities shall be issued [for an OBCA corporation, add: and no assets shall be distributed] by the amalgamated corporation in connection with the amalgamation;

[*Note: the following paragraph is only required for CBCA corporations*]

6. the stated capital of the amalgamated corporation shall be the same as the stated capital of _____ [*name of amalgamating parent corporation*]; and

7. the proper officers of the Corporation are hereby authorized to do all things and execute all instruments and documents necessary or desirable to carry out and give effect to the foregoing.

FIGURE 3.2 CONTINUED

The undersigned, being all the directors of the Corporation, hereby consent, by their signatures, to the foregoing resolutions pursuant to the provisions of the [*Canada Business Corporations Act/Business Corporations Act* (Ontario)].

DATED _____

_____

_____

FIGURE 3.2 CONTINUED

HORIZONTAL SHORT-FORM AMALGAMATION: RESOLUTION OF DIRECTORS OF A COMPANY WHOSE SHARES ARE BEING CANCELLED

RESOLUTION OF THE DIRECTORS
OF

_____

ARTICLES OF AMALGAMATION

WHEREAS the Corporation and _____ are both wholly owned subsidiaries of _____ and have decided to amalgamate pursuant to [section 184(2) of *Canada Business Corporations Act*/section 177(2) of the *Business Corporations Act* (Ontario)] (the "Act");

NOW THEREFORE BE IT RESOLVED that:

1. the amalgamation of the Corporation and _____ pursuant to section [184(2)/177(2)] of the Act, is hereby approved;

2. upon the issuance of a Certificate of Amalgamation pursuant to section [185(4)/178(4)] of the Act, all shares of _____ [name of subsidiary corporation whose shares are being cancelled], including all shares which have been issued and are outstanding at the date of this resolution, are hereby cancelled without any repayment of capital in respect thereof;

[*Note: the following paragraph is only required for OBCA corporations*]

3. the by-laws of the amalgamated corporation shall be the same as the by-laws of the Corporation; [*Note: the by-laws must be the same as the by-laws of the subsidiary corporation whose shares are NOT being cancelled*]

4. except as may be prescribed, the articles of amalgamation of the amalgamated corporation shall be the same as the articles of the Corporation; [*Note: the articles of amalgamation must be the same as the articles of the subsidiary corporation whose shares are NOT being cancelled*]

5. the stated capital of _____ [name of subsidiary corporation whose shares are being cancelled] shall be added to the stated capital of the Corporation; and

6. the proper officers of the Corporation are hereby authorized to do all things and execute all instruments and documents necessary or desirable to carry out and give effect to the foregoing.

The undersigned, being all the directors of the Corporation, hereby consent, by their signatures, to the foregoing resolutions pursuant to the provisions of the [*Canada Business Corporations Act/Business Corporations Act* (Ontario)].

DATED _____

_____

_____

FIGURE 3.2   CONTINUED

HORIZONTAL SHORT-FORM AMALGAMATION: RESOLUTION OF DIRECTORS OF A COMPANY WHOSE SHARES ARE NOT BEING CANCELLED

RESOLUTION OF THE DIRECTORS
OF

_____

ARTICLES OF AMALGAMATION

      WHEREAS the Corporation and _____ are both wholly owned subsidiaries of _____ and have decided to amalgamate pursuant to [section 184(2) of *Canada Business Corporations Act*/section 177(2) of the *Business Corporations Act* (Ontario)] (the "Act");

      NOW THEREFORE BE IT RESOLVED that:

1.   the amalgamation (the "Amalgamation") of the Corporation and _____ _____ pursuant to section [184(2)/177(2)] of the Act is hereby approved;

2.   upon the Amalgamation becoming effective, all shares of the Corporation (whether issued or unissued) shall be cancelled without any repayment of capital in respect thereof;

3.   except as may be prescribed, the articles of amalgamation of the corporation (the "Amalgamated Corporation") continuing from the Amalgamation shall be the same as the articles of _____ [*name of subsidiary corporation whose shares are NOT being cancelled*]; [*Note: the articles of amalgamation must be the same as the articles of the subsidiary corporation whose shares are NOT being cancelled*]

[*Note: the following paragraph is only required for OBCA corporations*]

4.   upon the Amalgamation becoming effective, the by-laws of _____ [*name of subsidiary corporation whose shares are NOT being cancelled*] as in effect immediately prior to the Amalgamation shall be the by-laws of the Amalgamated Corporation; [*Note: the by-laws must be the same as the by-laws of the subsidiary corporation whose shares are NOT being cancelled*]

5.   upon the Amalgamation becoming effective, the stated capital of the Corporation shall be added to the stated capital of _____ [*name of subsidiary corporation whose shares are NOT being cancelled*]; and

6.   any officer of the Corporation is hereby authorized to do all things and execute all instruments and documents necessary or desirable to carry out and give effect to the foregoing.

      The undersigned, being all the directors of the Corporation, hereby consent, by their signatures, to the foregoing resolution pursuant to the provisions of the *Canada Business Corporations Act*/*Business Corporations Act* (Ontario)].

DATED _____

_____

_____

FIGURE 3.2   CONTINUED

CBCA FORM 9, ARTICLES OF AMALGAMATION

I✶I Industry Canada	Industrie Canada	**FORM 9** **ARTICLES OF AMALGAMATION** **(SECTION 185)**	**FORMULAIRE 9** **STATUTS DE FUSION** **(ARTICLE 185)**
Canada Business Corporations Act	Loi canadienne sur les sociétés par actions		

1 -- Name of the Amalgamated Corporation   Dénomination sociale de la société issue de la fusion

2 -- The province or territory in Canada where the registered office is to be situated   La province ou le territoire au Canada où se situera le siège social

3 -- The classes and any maximum number of shares that the corporation is authorized to issue   Catégories et tout nombre maximal d'actions que la société est autorisée à émettre

4 -- Restrictions, if any, on share transfers   Restrictions sur le transfert des actions, s'il y a lieu

5 -- Number (or minimum and maximum number) of directors   Nombre (ou nombre minimal et maximal) d'administrateurs

6 -- Restrictions, if any, on business the corporation may carry on   Limites imposées à l'activité commerciale de la société, s'il y a lieu

7 -- Other provisions, if any   Autres dispositions, s'il y a lieu

8 -- The amalgamation has been approved pursuant to that section or subsection of the Act which is indicated as follows: La fusion a été approuvée en accord avec l'article ou le paragraphe de la Loi indiqué ci-après

☐ 183

☐ 184(1)

☐ 184(2)

9 -- Name of the amalgamating corporations Dénomination sociale des sociétés fusionnantes	Corporation No. N° de la société	Signature	Date	Title Titre	Tel. No. N° de tél.

FOR DEPARTMENTAL USE ONLY · À L'USAGE DU MINISTÈRE SEULEMENT

IC 3190 (2004/12)

FIGURE 3.2 CONTINUED

Canada Business Corporations Act

Articles of Amalgamation
FORM 9
INSTRUCTIONS

General
If you require more information in order to complete Form 9, you may wish to consult the Name Granting Compendium or the Name Granting Guidelines and the Amalgamation Kit.

You must file Form 9 by sending or faxing the completed documents to the address provided below.

Prescribed Fees
By mail or fax: $200

Item 1
Set out the proposed name for the amalgamated corporation that complies with sections 10 and 12 of the Act. If this name is not the same as one of the amalgamating corporations, articles of amalgamation must be accompanied by a Canada-biased NUANS search report dated not more than ninety (90) days prior to the receipt of the articles by the Director. On request, a number name may be assigned under subsection 11(2) of the Act, without a search.

Item 2
Set out the name of the province or territory within Canada where the registered office is to be situated.

Item 3
Set out the details required by paragraph 6(1)(c) of the Act, including details of the rights, privileges, restrictions and conditions attached to each class or series of shares. All shares must be without nominal or par value and must comply with the provisions of Part V of the Act.

Item 4
If restrictions are to be placed on the right to transfer shares of the corporation, set out a statement to this effect and the nature of such restrictions.

Item 5
Set out the number of directors. If cumulative voting is permitted, the number of directors must be invariable; otherwise it is permissible to specify a minimum and maximum number of directors.

Item 6
If restrictions are to be placed on the business the corporation may carry on, set out the restrictions.

Item 7
Set out any provisions, permitted by the Act or Regulations to be set out in the by-laws of the corporation, that are to form part of the articles, including any pre-emptive rights or cumulative voting provisions.

Item 8
Indicate whether the amalgamation is under section 183 or subsection 184(1) or (2) of the Act.

Other Notices and Documents
(1) The Articles must be accompanied by Form 2 *'Information Regarding the Registered Office and the Board of Directors'* and a statutory declaration of a director or authorized officer of each amalgamating corporation in accordance with subsection 185(2) of the Act.
(2) All amalgamating corporations should ensure that all filing requirements contained in the Act have been met.

The completed document and fees payable to the Receiver General for Canada are to be sent to:

The Director, Canada Business Corporations Act
Jean Edmonds Tower, South
9th Floor
365 Laurier Ave. West
Ottawa, Ontario
K1A 0C8
or by facsimile at: (613) 941-0999
Inquiries: 1-866-333-5556

IC 3190 (2004/12) p.2

Loi canadienne sur les sociétés par actions

Statuts de fusion
FORMULAIRE 9
INSTRUCTIONS

Généralités
Si vous désirez obtenir de plus amples informations afin de compléter le formulaire 9, veuillez consulter l'Énoncé d'octroi des dénominations ou les lignes directrices pour l'octroi des dénominations ainsi que le Recueil d'information sur les fusions.

Vous devez déposer le formulaire 9 en envoyant ou en télécopiant le document complété à l'adresse indiquée au bas de cette page.

Droits payables
Par la poste ou télécopieur : 200 $

Rubrique 1
Indiquer la dénomination sociale de la société issue de la fusion, laquelle doit satisfaire aux exigences des articles 10 et 12 de la Loi. Si cette dénomination diffère de celle de l'une des sociétés fusionnantes, les statuts de fusion doivent être accompagnés d'un rapport de recherche NUANS couvrant le Canada, dont la date remonte à quatre-vingt-dix (90) jours ou moins avant la date de réception des statuts par le directeur. Si un numéro matricule est demandé en guise de dénomination sociale, il peut être assigné, sans recherche préalable, en vertu du paragraphe 11(2) de la Loi.

Rubrique 2
Indiquer le nom de la province ou du territoire au Canada où le siège social se situera.

Rubrique 3
Indiquer les détails requis par l'alinéa 6(1)c) de la Loi, y compris les détails des droits, privilèges, restrictions et conditions assortis à chaque catégorie ou série d'actions. Toutes les actions doivent être sans valeur nominale ou sans valeur au pair et doivent être conformes aux dispositions de la partie V de la Loi.

Rubrique 4
Si le droit de transfert des actions de la société doit être restreint, inclure une déclaration à cet effet et indiquer la nature de ces restrictions.

Rubrique 5
Indiquer le nombre d'administrateurs. Si un vote cumulatif est prévu, ce nombre doit être fixe; autrement, il est permis de spécifier un nombre minimal et maximal d'administrateurs.

Rubrique 6
Si des limites doivent être imposées à l'activité commerciale de la société, les indiquer.

Rubrique 7
Indiquer les dispositions que la Loi ou le règlement permet d'énoncer dans les règlements administratifs de la société et qui doivent faire partie des statuts, y compris les dispositions relatives au vote cumulatif ou aux droits de préemption.

Rubrique 8
Indiquer si la fusion est faite en vertu de l'article 183 ou du paragraphe 184(1) ou (2) de la Loi.

Autres avis et documents
(1) Les status doivent être accompagnés du formulaire 2 *'Information concernant le siège social et le conseil d'administration'* et d'une déclaration solennelle d'un administrateur ou d'un dirigeant autorisé de chaque société fusionnante conformément au paragraphe 185(2) de la Loi.
(2) Les sociétés fusionnantes doivent s'assurer que toutes les exigences de dépôt contenues dans la Loi ont été remplies.

Le document complété et les droits payables au Receveur général du Canada doivent être envoyés au :

Directeur, Loi canadienne sur les sociétés par actions
Tour Jean Edmonds, sud
9ième étage
365, av. Laurier ouest
Ottawa (Ontario)
K1A 0C8
ou par télécopieur : (613) 941-0999
Renseignements : 1-866-333-5556

FIGURE 3.2 CONTINUED

OBCA FORM 4, ARTICLES OF AMALGAMATION

 **Ontario**
Ministry of
Consumer and
Business Services

Companies and Personal
Property Security Branch

393 University Ave Suite 200
Toronto ON M5G 2M2

Articles of Amalgamation
Form 4
Business Corporations Act

INSTRUCTIONS FOR COMPLETING

Articles in duplicate may be mailed to the Toronto address listed above. For over-the-counter service, they may also be filed in person at the Toronto office or at one of the following Land Registry Offices: Hamilton, Kingston, Kitchener, London, Whitby, Sudbury, Barrie, Sarnia, Ottawa, Peterborough, Sault Ste. Marie, Thunder Bay, Windsor or Welland.

FEE
$330.00 (10 or fewer amalgamating corporations)
$500.00 (11 or more amalgamating corporations)

BY MAIL- cheque or money order payable to the Minister of Finance.
IN PERSON (at the Toronto office) - cash, cheque or money order payable to the Minister of Finance, Visa, MasterCard, American Express or debit card. (If you are filing the documents at a Land Registry Office, call first to confirm whether credit or debit cards are acceptable).

There will be a service charge payable for any cheque returned as non-negotiable by a bank or financial institution.

EFFECTIVE DATE
Articles are effective on the date set out in the certificate endorsed on the Articles by the Branch. The certificate is dated the day the Director receives the duplicate originals of the articles together with all other required documents executed in accordance with the Act and the required fee, if they are acceptable as per the Branch's endorsement as of right review policy. An effective date of up to 30 days later than the earliest date the Articles can be endorsed may be requested **in writing, in the covering letter, using bold or highlighted letters,** upon submission of the Articles to the Branch. If you are presenting your documents in person you must also verbally bring this request to the attention of the counter clerk.

SUPORTING DOCUMENTS

NAME SEARCH
The name of a corporation formed by the amalgamation of two or more corporations may be identical to the name of one of its amalgamating corporations, if it is **not a number name.** In this case a name search is not required.

If you are amalgamating under a new name, you must obtain an Ontario biased NUANS name search report. NUANS stands for Newly Upgraded Automated Name Search. It is a five-page computer-printed search report consisting of corporate names, business names and trademarks that have already been incorporated/registered and are similar to the proposed corporate name. This search must be submitted together with the duplicate Articles of Amalgamation. The NUANS report cannot be dated more than ninety days prior to the submission of the Articles. For example, articles submitted on November 28th could be accompanied by a NUANS name search report dated as early as August 30th, but not dated earlier.

The NUANS name search must be obtained from a private name search company. These companies are listed in the Yellow Pages under the heading "Searchers of Records". The Ministry does not provide this search. It is the applicant's responsibility to check the search for similar/identical names and to obtain any consent that may be required.

The Ministry will not grant a name that is identical to the current name or former name of another corporation operating in Ontario whether active or not, unless it has been more than ten years since the other corporation dissolved or changed its name. The only exception to this rule is when the corporation meets the requirements of Subsection 6(2) of Regulation 62, under the *Business Corporations Act.* In this case, Companies and Personal Property Security Branch policy requires that a legal opinion accompany the articles being filed. The legal opinion must be on legal letterhead and must be signed by an individual lawyer (not a law clerk). It must also clearly indicate that the corporations involved comply with Subsection 6(2) of Regulation 62 by referring to each clause specifically.

07121 (03/3003)

FIGURE 3.2 CONTINUED

BILINGUAL NAMES

When amalgamating a corporation under a new name with an English and French version of the name (where the versions can be used separately), a name search is required for each version of the name (English and French). There should be a forward slash (/) separating the two versions of the name.

NUMBER NAMES

You do not require a name search for a number name. In Article one on the form, leave nine empty boxes, then type or print in block capital letters the word "ONTARIO" followed by one of the legal elements…LIMITED, LIMITÉE, INCORPORATED, INCORPOREE, CORPORATION or the corresponding abbreviation LTD., LTEE.,INC., or CORP. The Director of the Companies and Personal Property Security Branch will assign a number to the corporation.

The amalgamated corporation cannot retain the number name of an amalgamating company. When two or more corporations amalgamate a new corporation is formed. The Director assigns a new corporation number and in the case of a number name, this new number becomes the number part of the name.

SCHEDULES

SCHEDULE A A statement of a director or an officer of each of the amalgamating corporations as required by subsection 178(2) of the *Business Corporations Act* must be attached to both copies of the articles.

SCHEDULE B A copy of the amalgamation agreement under subsection 176(4) of the *Business Corporations Act*

or

       The directors' resolutions required under Section 177 of the Act must be attached to both copies of the articles.

APPEARANCE OF DOCUMENTS

The Articles of Amalgamation must be completed in duplicate on a Form 4 as approved by the Minister. All documents must be legible and compatible with the microfilming process, with the information typed or hand printed in block capital letters, on one side of good quality, white bond paper 8 ½" X 11".

The article headings are numbered 1 to 12 and should remain in that order. Do not leave out any of the headings. If a section does not apply, type "nil" or "not applicable". When additional pages are required, due to lack of space, they should be the same size as all the other pages and should be inserted after the applicable heading with the same number as the heading page, but with the addition of alphabet characters to indicate sequence. For example, pages inserted after page 4 would be numbered 4A, 4B, etc.

FIGURE 3.2 CONTINUED

ARTICLE 1 Set out the name of the <u>amalgamated</u> corporation in block capital letters starting from the first box of the first line on the left with one letter per box and one empty box for a space. Punctuation marks are entered in separate boxes. Complete one line before starting in the first box of the next line. The name entered must be exactly the same as that on the name search report. Where a "number name" is to be used, leave the first nine boxes blank and complete as follows: "........Ontario Inc." (see "number names")

E	A	S	T		S	I	D	E		I	N	V	E	S	T	M	E	N	T		A	N	D		M	A	N	A	G
E	M	E	N	T		L	T	D	.																				

ARTICLE 2 The address (if multi-office building, include room or suite number) of the registered office of the corporation must be set out in full, including the street name, street number, suite, municipality, province, country and postal code. A post office box is not an acceptable address. If there is no street and number, set out the Lot and Concession numbers. The registered office must be in Ontario.

ARTICLE 3 Set out the number of directors. This must be either a fixed number of directors (i.e. "1") or a minimum and maximum number, (i.e., minimum 1, maximum 10.) <u>Do not complete both</u>.

ARTICLE 4 The name(s), (including first name, middle name and surname) and the address for service for each of the directors must be set out. The address should include the street name, street number, suite, municipality, province, country and postal code. State if the director(s) is/are resident Canadian(s). A majority of the directors must be resident Canadians. Where a corporation has only one or two directors, one shall be resident Canadian. See the definition of "resident Canadian" in s. 1(1) of the *Business Corporations Act.*

ARTICLE 5 Check the appropriate box **(A)** or **(B)**:

Check box (A) if the amalgamation agreement has been adopted by the shareholders under Subsection 176(4) of the Business Corporations Act. In this case Schedule "B" referred to in Article 12 on the form must be a copy of that amalgamation agreement.

OR

Check box (B) if the amalgamation has been approved by director's resolution under Section 177 of the Act. In this case schedule "B" referred to in Article 12 on the form should be a copy of the director's resolution for each of the amalgamating corporations. If (B) is checked, on the line provided, set out the name of the amalgamating corporation containing the same provisions in substance as the Articles of Amalgamation now being submitted.

Under the corresponding headings, set out the name of the corporation, the corporation number and the date of the adoption/approval for each of the amalgamating corporations.

ARTICLE 6 Set out restrictons, if any, on the business the corporation may carry on or on the powers that the corporation may exercise. If none, state so.

ARTICLE 7 Set out the classes and any maximum number or shares that the corporation is authorized to issue. This item must be completed (e.g., unlimited common shares).

ARTICLE 8 Set out rights, privileges, restrictions, and conditions etc. (if any) attached to each class of shares, and directors' authority with respect to any class of shares which may be issued in series.

ARTICLE 9 Set out restrictions on issue, transfer of ownership of shares (if any).

07121 (03/3003)

FIGURE 3.2 CONTINUED

ARTICLE 10   Set out any other provisions (if any).

ARTICLE 11   The statements required by Subsection 178(2) of the _Business Corporations Act_ are attached as Schedule "A". **_This statement must be included in the Articles and the required schedule must be attached._**

ARTICLE 12   A copy of the amalgamation agreement or directors' resolutions (as the case may be) is/are attached as Schedule "B". **_This statement must be included in the Articles and the required schedule must be attached._**

EXECUTION   Both copies of the Articles must have original signatures of an officer or director of each of the amalgamating corporations. Also set out the office of each person who signs (e.g., President, Director, Secretary). The name of each of the amalgamating corporations should be set out above the appropriate signature. If the corporation has a seal it should be affixed to the Articles next to the signature.

Articles with schedules "A" and "B" (in duplicate),
original Ontario-biased NUANS name search report (if applicable),
covering letter and filing fee should be
mailed or delivered to:
COMPANIES AND PERSONAL PROPERTY SECURITY BRANCH
MINISTRY OF CONSUMER AND BUSINESS SERVICES
393 UNIVERSITY AVENUE, SUITE 200
TORONTO ONTARIO M5G 2M2

FIGURE 3.2 CONTINUED

For Ministry Use Only
À l'usage exclusif du ministère

Ontario Corporation Number
Numéro de la société en Ontario

1

ARTICLES OF AMALGAMATION
STATUTS DE FUSION

Form 4
*Business
Corporations
Act*

*Formule 4
Loi sur les
sociétés par
actions*

1. The name of the amalgamated corporation is: (Set out in BLOCK CAPITAL LETTERS)
Dénomination sociale de la société issue de la fusion (écrire en LETTRES MAJUSCULES SEULEMENT) :

2. The address of the registered office is:
Adresse du siège social :

(Street & Number or R.R. Number & if Multi-Office Building give Room No.)
(Rue et numéro, ou numéro de la R.R. et, s'il s'agit d'un édifice à bureaux, numéro du bureau)

Ontario

(Name of Municipality or Post Office)
(Nom de la municipalité ou du bureau de poste)

(Postal Code /
Code postal)

3. Number of directors is/are: **or**   minimum and maximum number of directors is/are:
Nombre d'administrateurs :   **ou**   *nombres minimum et maximum d'administrateurs :*

Number   **or**   minimum   and   maximum
Nombre   **ou**   *minimum*   *et*   *maximum*

4. The director(s) is/are:
Administrateur(s) :

First name, middle names and surname *Prénom, autres prénoms et nom de famille*	Address for service, giving Street & No. or R.R. No., Municipality, Province, Country and Postal Code *Domicile élu, y compris la rue et le numéro ou le numéro de la R.R., le nom de la municipalité, la province, le pays et le code postal*	Resident Canadian State 'Yes' or' No' *Résident canadien Oui/Non*

07121 (03/3003)

FIGURE 3.2 CONTINUED

2

5. **Check A or B**
   Cocher A ou B

   ☐ A) The amalgamation agreement has been duly adopted by the shareholders of each of the amalgamating corporations as required by subsection 176 (4) of the *Business Corporations Act* on the date set out below.

   A) Les actionnaires de chaque société qui fusionnne ont dûment adopté la convention de fusion conformément au paragraphe 176(4) de la Loi sur les sociétés par actions *à la date mentionnée ci-dessous.*

   or
   ou

   ☐ B) The amalgamation has been approved by the directors of each amalgamating corporation by a resolution as required by section 177 of the *Business Corporations Act* on the date set out below.

   B) Les administrateurs de chaque société qui fusionne ont approuvé la fusion par voie de résolution conformément à l'article 177 de la Loi sur les sociétés par actions *à la date mentionnée ci-dessous.*

   The articles of amalgamation in substance contain the provisions of the articles of incorporation of
   Les statuts de fusion reprennent essentiellement les dispositions des statuts constitutifs de

   _____

   and are more particularly set out in these articles.
   et sont énoncés textuellement aux présents statuts.

Names of amalgamating corporations *Dénomination sociale des sociétés qui fusionnent*	Ontario Corporation Number *Numéro de la société en Ontario*	Date of Adoption/Approval *Date d'adoption ou d'approbation* Year / *année* Month / *mois* Day / *jour*

07121 (03/3003)

FIGURE 3.2   CONTINUED

3

6.   Restrictions, if any, on business the corporation may carry on or on powers the corporation may exercise.
Limites, s'il y a lieu, imposées aux activités commerciales ou aux pouvoirs de la société.

7.   The classes and any maximum number of shares that the corporation is authorized to issue:
Catégories et nombre maximal, s'il y a lieu, d'actions que la société est autorisée à émettre :

07121 (03/3003)

FIGURE 3.2   CONTINUED

4

8. Rights, privileges, restrictions and conditions (if any) attaching to each class of shares and directors authority with respect to any class of shares which may be issued in series:
    Droits, privilèges, restrictions et conditions, s'il y a lieu, rattachés à chaque catégorie d'actions et pouvoirs des administrateurs relatifs à chaque catégorie d'actions qui peut être émise en série :

07121 (03/3003)

FIGURE 3.2   CONTINUED

5

9. The issue, transfer or ownership of shares is/is not restricted and the restrictions (if any) are as follows:
    L'émission, le transfert ou la propriété d'actions est/n'est pas restreint. Les restrictions, s'il y a lieu, sont les suivantes :

10. Other provisions, (if any):
    Autres dispositions, s'il y a lieu :

11. The statements required by subsection 178(2) of the *Business Corporations Act* are attached as Schedule "A".
    Les déclarations exigées aux termes du paragraphe 178(2) de la Loi sur les sociétés par actions *constituent l'annexe A.*

12. A copy of the amalgamation agreement or directors' resolutions (as the case may be) is/are attached as Schedule "B".
    Une copie de la convention de fusion ou les résolutions des administrateurs (selon le cas) constitue(nt) l'annexe B.

07121 (03/3003)

FIGURE 3.2 CONTINUED

6

These articles are signed in duplicate.
Les présents statuts sont signés en double exemplaire.

Names of the amalgamating corporations and signatures and descriptions of office of their proper officers.
Dénomination sociale des sociétés qui fusionnent, signature et fonction de leurs dirigeants régulièrement désignés.

07121 (03/3003)

FIGURE 3.2   CONTINUED

STATUTORY DECLARATION (CBCA CORPORATION)

IN THE MATTER OF THE *CANADA BUSINESS CORPORATIONS ACT*
AND
IN THE MATTER OF THE ARTICLES OF AMALGAMATION FILED PURSUANT TO SECTION 185 IN THE NAME

_____

STATUTORY DECLARATION

I, _____, of the City of _____, in the Province of Ontario, DO SOLEMNLY DECLARE THAT:

1.   I am a director or officer of _____, one of the amalgamating corporations (hereinafter called the "Corporation"), and I have personal knowledge of the matters herein deposed to.

2.   I am satisfied that there are reasonable grounds for believing that:

    (a)   the Corporation is and the amalgamated corporation will be able to pay its liabilities as they become due; and

    (b)   the realizable value of the assets of the amalgamated corporation will not be less than the aggregate of its liabilities and stated capital of all classes.

3.   There are reasonable grounds for believing that no creditor will be prejudiced by the amalgamation.

[*Note: if the declarant is unable to say that no creditor will be prejudiced by the amalgamation, then substitute the following*]

Adequate notice has been given by the Corporation to all known creditors of the Corporation in accordance with the provisions of section 185(3) of the *Canada Business Corporations Act* and no creditor has notified the Corporation of an objection to the amalgamation.

AND I MAKE THIS SOLEMN DECLARATION conscientiously believing it to be true and knowing that it is of the same force and effect as if made under oath and by virtue of the *Canada Evidence Act*.

DECLARED BEFORE ME at the   )
City of _____,   )
Province of Ontario this _____ day   )
of _____, 200__.   )   _____
)

A Commissioner, etc.

FIGURE 3.2 CONTINUED

OFFICER'S STATEMENT (OBCA CORPORATION)

SCHEDULE "A"

STATEMENT OF DIRECTOR OR OFFICER
PURSUANT TO SUBSECTION 178(2) OF
THE BUSINESS CORPORATIONS ACT (ONTARIO)

I, _____, of the City of _____, Province of Ontario, hereby certify and state as follows:

1.   This Statement is made pursuant to subsection 178(2) of the *Business Corporations Act*.

2.   I am the _____ of _____, one of the amalgamating corporations (hereinafter called the "Corporation"), and as such have knowledge of its affairs.

3.   I have conducted such examination of the books and records of the Corporation as are necessary to enable me to make the statements hereinafter set forth.

4.   There are reasonable grounds for believing that:

   4.1.   the Corporation is and the amalgamated corporation will be able to pay its liabilities as they become due; and

   4.2.   the realizable value of the assets of the amalgamated corporation will not be less than the aggregate of its liabilities and stated capital of all classes.

5.   There are reasonable grounds for believing that no creditor of the Corporation will be prejudiced by the amalgamation.

   [*Note: if the person executing this statement is unable to say that no creditor will be prejudiced by the amalgamation, then substitute the following*]

   Adequate notice has been given by the Corporation to all known creditors of the Corporations in accordance with the provisions of section 178(2)(b) of the *Business Corporations Act* and no creditor has notified the Corporation of an objection to the proposed amalgamation.

   DATED this _____ day of _____, 200__.

   _____

FIGURE 3.2 CONTINUED

NOTICE OF PROPOSED AMALGAMATION TO CREDITORS

NOTICE TO CREDITORS
OF

_____
[*name of amalgamating corporation*]

TAKE NOTICE that _____ [*name of amalgamating corporation*] intends to amalgamate with _____ [*name of other amalgamating corporations*] in accordance with the [*Canada Business Corporations Act/Business Corporations Act* (Ontario)] unless any creditor of _____ [*name of amalgamating corporation*] objects to the amalgamation within 30 days from the date of this Notice.

On the effective date of the amalgamation, all of the properties and assets of _____ [*name of amalgamating corporation*] and _____ [*name of other amalgamating corporations*] will continue to be the properties and assets of the amalgamated corporation, which in turn will continue to be liable for the obligations of _____ [*name of amalgamating corporation*] and _____ [*name of other amalgamating corporations*] including the liabilities of _____ [*name of amalgamating corporation*] to its creditors.

This Notice is given pursuant to [section 185(3) of the *Canada Business Corporations Act/section 178(2) of the Business Corporations Act* (Ontario)].

DATED _____

_____
[*name of amalgamating corporation*]

Per: _____
Name:
Title:

FIGURE 3.2 CONTINUED

POST-AMALGAMATION RESOLUTIONS:
DIRECTORS

RESOLUTIONS OF THE DIRECTORS
OF

_____

WHEREAS the Corporation is the amalgamated corporation continuing from the amalgamation of _____ and _____ _____, which amalgamation became effective on _____, 200__ (the "Amalgamation");

[Note: the following paragraph is necessary only if the amalgamation agreement provided for enactment of a new by-law]

ENACT NEW GENERAL BY-LAW NO. 1

BE IT RESOLVED that By-law No. 1 of the Corporation's by-laws is hereby enacted and the President and Secretary of the Corporation are hereby authorized and directed to sign By-law No. 1 of the by-laws of the Corporation.

[Note: use the following paragraph for a short-form amalgamation of CBCA corporations]

ADOPTION OF BY-LAWS

BE IT RESOLVED that the by-laws of _____ *[name of amalgamating corporation whose by-laws are to be adopted]*, one of the predecessor corporations of the Corporation, as in effect immediately prior to the Amalgamation, copies of which by-laws are annexed hereto as Schedule "A", are hereby confirmed as the by-laws of the Corporation.

FORM OF SHARE CERTIFICATES

BE IT RESOLVED that the form of share certificate for the common shares of the Corporation, a specimen of which is attached hereto as Schedule "A", is hereby adopted and approved as the form of share certificate for the common shares of the Corporation.

[Note: use the following paragraph if shares were converted on amalgamation or if the name changed on amalgamation]

ISSUANCE OF SHARE CERTIFICATES

WHEREAS on Amalgamation the common shares of _____ _____ were converted into common shares of the amalgamated corporation;

NOW THEREFORE BE IT RESOLVED that the upon the cancellation of share certificates of _____ *[name of amalgamating corporations whose shares are to be cancelled]* the proper officers of the Corporation are hereby authorized and directed to issue share certificates to the following shareholders:

FIGURE 3.2 CONTINUED

Shareholder	Number of Common Shares

APPOINTMENT OF OFFICERS

BE IT RESOLVED that the following persons are hereby appointed officers of the Corporation to hold the office referred to opposite their respective names:

PRESIDENT   _____

VICE-PRESIDENT   _____

SECRETARY   _____

CORPORATE SEAL [*no longer required but corporation may choose to adopt*]

BE IT RESOLVED that until changed by resolution of the board, the corporate seal of the Corporation shall be in the form impressed hereon.

[*Note: use the following paragraph if by-laws allow the board of directors to determine signing authority*]

EXECUTION OF DOCUMENTS

BE IT RESOLVED that deeds, transfers, assignments, contracts, obligations, certificates and other instruments may be signed on behalf of the Corporation by _____ [*e.g.*: any director or officer/any two (2) directors or officers] of the Corporation. In addition, the directors may from time to time direct the manner in which and the person or persons by whom any particular instrument or class of instruments may or shall be signed.

BANKING RESOLUTION

BE IT RESOLVED that the banking resolution, in the form required by the _____, [*name of bank*] a copy of which is annexed hereto as Schedule "B", is hereby approved.

FINANCIAL YEAR

BE IT RESOLVED that the directors hereby ratify and confirm that the financial year of the Corporation terminates on the _____ day of _____ in each year or on such other date as the directors may from time to time determine.

DIVISIONS

BE IT RESOLVED that the various divisions of the predecessor corporations of the Corporation and the officers thereof, as they were immediately prior to the amalgamation, are hereby continued as divisions of the Corporation and officers thereof respectively, and all resolutions in effect with respect to such divisions and officers shall, until changed by resolution of the board, remain in full force and effect.

FIGURE 3.2 CONTINUED

The undersigned, being all the directors of the Corporation, hereby consent, by their signatures, to the foregoing resolutions pursuant to the [*Canada Business Corporations Act/Business Corporations Act* (Ontario)].

DATED _____

_____

_____

FIGURE 3.2 CONTINUED

POST-AMALGAMATION RESOLUTIONS:
SHAREHOLDERS

RESOLUTION OF THE SHAREHOLDERS
OF

_____

WHEREAS the Corporation is the amalgamated corporation continuing from the amalgamation of _____ and _____ _____, which amalgamation became effective on _____, 200__ (the "Amalgamation");

[*Note: the following paragraph is necessary only if a new by-law is to be enacted*]

NEW GENERAL BY-LAW NO. 1

BE IT RESOLVED that By-law No. 1 previously enacted by the directors of the Corporation is hereby approved, ratified, sanctioned and confirmed.

[*Note: use the following paragraph for a short-form amalgamation of CBCA corporations*]

ADOPTION OF BY-LAWS

BE IT RESOLVED that the by-laws of _____ [*name of amalgamating corporation whose by-laws are to be adopted*], one of the predecessor corporations of the Corporation, as in effect immediately prior to the Amalgamation, copies of which by-laws are annexed hereto as Schedule "A", are hereby confirmed as the by-laws of the Corporation.

APPOINTMENT OF AUDITORS

BE IT RESOLVED that _____ are hereby appointed auditors of the Corporation until the next annual meeting of shareholders, or until a successor is appointed, at a remuneration to be fixed by the directors, the directors being hereby authorized to fix such remuneration.

[*or*]

EXEMPTION FROM APPOINTMENT OF AUDITORS

BE IT RESOLVED that:

1. pursuant to the [*Canada Business Corporations Act/Business Corporations Act* (Ontario)] an auditor of the Corporation shall not be appointed for the year ending _____; and

2. _____ be appointed the accountants of the Corporation until the next annual meeting of shareholders or until a successor is appointed, at a remuneration to be fixed by the directors, the directors being hereby authorized to fix such remuneration.

FIGURE 3.2 CONTINUED

The undersigned, being all the shareholders of the Corporation, hereby consent, by their signatures, to the foregoing resolutions pursuant to the provisions of the [*Canada Business Corporations Act/Business Corporations Act* (Ontario)] .

DATED _____

_____

_____

FIGURE 3.2 CONTINUED

POST-AMALGAMATION RESOLUTIONS:
DIRECTORS OF OBCA CORPORATION

SPECIAL RESOLUTIONS
OF

_____

NUMBER OF DIRECTORS

BE IT RESOLVED as a special resolution of the Corporation that the number of directors on the board of directors until changed in accordance with the *Business Corporations Act*, as amended from time to time, is hereby fixed at _____.

DIRECTORS AUTHORIZED TO FIX NUMBER OF DIRECTORS

BE IT RESOLVED as a special resolution of the Corporation that the directors of the Corporation are hereby authorized to fix by resolution of the directors the number of directors on the board of directors.

The undersigned, being all the shareholders of the Corporation, hereby consent, by their signatures, to the foregoing special resolutions pursuant to the provisions of the *Business Corporations Act*.

DATED _____

_____

_____

FIGURE 3.2   CONCLUDED

POST-AMALGAMATION RESOLUTIONS: DIRECTOR'S CONSENT

CERTIFICATE AND CONSENT

TO: _____ (the "Corporation")

AND TO: THE DIRECTORS AND SHAREHOLDERS THEREOF

I hereby certify that I am:

(a)   a Canadian citizen ordinarily resident in Canada; or

(b)   a permanent resident within the meaning of *The Immigration Act* (Canada), ordinarily resident in Canada and not eligible to apply for Canadian citizenship,

and acknowledge that the Corporation is relying upon this Certificate for purposes of ensuring compliance by the Corporation with the provisions of the [*Canada Business Corporations Act/Business Corporations Act* (Ontario)], and agree to advise the Corporation of any change in my citizenship, place of residence or eligibility to apply for Canadian citizenship.

I hereby consent to act as a director of the Corporation. This consent shall continue in effect from year to year so long as I am re-elected to the board by the shareholders, but if I resign or am removed from the board, the consent shall cease to have effect from the effective date of such resignation or removal.

I further consent to any one or more of the directors of the Corporation from time to time participating in meetings of the board of directors or committees of directors of the Corporation by means of such telephone, electronic or other communications facilities as permit all persons participating in the meeting to communicate with each other simultaneously and instantaneously, such consent to continue in effect unless revoked by an instrument in writing delivered to the Corporation.

I HEREBY AGREE TO ADVISE THE CORPORATION BY A NOTICE IN WRITING DELIVERED TO THE CORPORATION OF ANY CHANGE IN MY PLACE OF RESIDENCE FORTHWITH AFTER SUCH CHANGE.

DATED _____

_____
[director's name]

_____
[director's residential address]

DIRECTORS' RESOLUTION APPROVING DISSOLUTION
UNDER CBCA S. 210(1)

RESOLUTION OF THE DIRECTORS
OF

_____

ARTICLES OF DISSOLUTION

BE IT RESOLVED that:

1.   the dissolution of the Corporation is hereby authorized pursuant to subsection 210(1) of the *Canada Business Corporations Act* (the "Act");

2.   for the purpose of bringing such dissolution into effect, the Corporation shall send articles of dissolution in the prescribed form to the Director appointed under the Act; and

3.   any director or officer of the Corporation is hereby authorized and directed to execute, under the corporate seal or otherwise, and deliver all such documents and to do all such other acts and things as such director or officer may determine to be necessary or advisable in connection with such dissolution, the execution of any such document or the doing of any such other act or thing being conclusive evidence of such determination.

The undersigned, being all the directors of the Corporation, hereby consent, by their signatures, to the foregoing resolution pursuant to the provisions of the *Canada Business Corporations Act*.

DATED _____

_____

_____

FIGURE 3.3 CONTINUED

SHAREHOLDERS' RESOLUTION APPROVING DISSOLUTION
UNDER CBCA S. 210(2)

SPECIAL RESOLUTION OF THE SHAREHOLDERS
OF

_____

ARTICLES OF DISSOLUTION

BE IT RESOLVED as a special resolution that:

1.   the dissolution of the Corporation is hereby authorized pursuant to subsection 210(2) of the *Canada Business Corporations Act* (the "Act");

2.   for the purpose of bringing such dissolution into effect, the Corporation shall send articles of dissolution in the prescribed form to the Director appointed under the Act; and

3.   any director or officer of the Corporation is hereby authorized and directed to execute, under the corporate seal or otherwise, and deliver all such documents and to do all such other acts and things as such director or officer may determine to be necessary or advisable in connection with such dissolution, the execution of any such document or the doing of any such other act or thing being conclusive evidence of such determination.

The undersigned, being all the shareholders of the Corporation, hereby consent, by their signatures, to the foregoing special resolution pursuant to the provisions of the *Canada Business Corporations Act*.

DATED _____

_____

_____

FIGURE 3.3   CONTINUED

SHAREHOLDERS' RESOLUTION APPROVING DISSOLUTION
UNDER CBCA S. 210(3)

SPECIAL RESOLUTION OF THE SHAREHOLDERS
OF

_____

ARTICLES OF DISSOLUTION

BE IT RESOLVED as a special resolution that:

1.   the dissolution of the Corporation is hereby authorized pursuant to subsection 210(3) of the *Canada Business Corporations Act* (the "Act");

2.   the directors of the Corporation are hereby authorized to cause the Corporation to discharge all its debts, obligations or liabilities and thereafter to distribute its remaining property to _____ (the "Shareholder"), the sole shareholder of the Corporation;

[*Note: use next paragraph only if the corporation is going to enter into a distribution agreement with the shareholders*]

3.   the Corporation is hereby authorized to execute and deliver an agreement between the Corporation and the Shareholder, substantially in the form and on the terms and subject to the conditions set out in the draft agreement annexed hereto as Schedule "A";

4.   after the distribution of the property of the Corporation, the Corporation shall dissolve and, for the purpose of bringing such dissolution into effect, the Corporation shall send articles of dissolution in the prescribed form to the Director appointed under the Act; and

5.   any director or officer of the Corporation is hereby authorized and directed to execute, under the corporate seal or otherwise, and deliver all such documents and to do all such other acts and things as such director or officer may determine to be necessary or advisable in connection with such dissolution, the execution of any such document or the doing of any such other act or thing being conclusive evidence of such determination.

The undersigned, being all the shareholders of the Corporation, hereby consent, by their signatures, to the foregoing special resolution pursuant to the provisions of the *Canada Business Corporations Act*.

DATED _____

_____

_____

FIGURE 3.3 CONTINUED

CBCA FORM 17, ARTICLES OF DISSOLUTION

	Industry Canada	Industrie Canada	FORM 17 ARTICLES OF DISSOLUTION (SECTIONS 210 AND 211)	FORMULAIRE 17 CLAUSES DE DISSOLUTION (ARTICLES 210 ET 211)
	Canada Business Corporations Act	Loi canadienne sur les sociétés par actions		

Note: All corporations are to complete Items 1, 2, 3 and 6, and either complete Item 4 or 5.
Nota : Toutes les sociétés doivent remplir les rubriques 1, 2, 3 et 6, ainsi que la rubrique 4 ou 5.

1 -- Name of the Corporation - Dénomination sociale de la société	2 -- Corporation No. - N° de la société

3 -- Is the Corporation bankrupt or insolvent within the meaning of the *Bankruptcy and Insolvency Act*?
La société est-elle en faillite ou insolvable au sens de la *Loi sur la faillite et l'insolvabilité* ?

☐ Yes - Oui   ☐ No - Non

Complete either Item 4 or 5, but not both - Remplir la rubrique 4 ou 5, mais non les deux

4 -- Has the corporation previously filed a statement of intent to dissolve (Form 19) under subsection 211(4) of the Act?
La société a-t-elle déjà déposé une déclaration d'intention de dissolution (formulaire 19) en vertu du paragraphe 211(4) de la Loi ?

☐ Yes - Oui   If the answer is negative, please complete only Item 5 - Si la réponse est négative, veuillez remplir seulement la rubrique 5

If yes, has the corporation provided for the payment or discharge of its obligations and distributed its remaining property as required by subsection 211(7) of the Act?
Dans l'affirmative, conformément au paragraphe 211(7) de la Loi, la société a-t-elle constitué une provision pour honorer ses obligations et réparti le reliquat de l'actif ?

☐ Yes - Oui   ☐ No - Non

5 -- Is the Corporation applying for dissolution under section 210 of the Act? (To apply under section 210, the corporation cannot have previously filed a statement of intent to dissolve (Form 19) under subsection 211(7) of the Act.)

La société dépose-t-elle une demande de dissolution en vertu de l'article 210 de la Loi? (Pour être admissible en vertu de l'article 210, la société ne peut pas avoir déposé une déclaration d'intention de dissolution (formulaire 19) en vertu du paragraphe 211(7) de la Loi.)

☐ Yes - Oui   If the answer is negative, please complete only Item 4 - Si la réponse est négative, veuillez remplir seulement la rubrique 4

If yes, under what subsection of the Act is the corporation applying for dissolution? (**CHECK ONLY ONE ITEM**)
Dans l'affirmative, en vertu de quel paragraphe de la Loi la société procède-t-elle ? (**COCHER UNE RUBRIQUE SEULEMENT**)

☐ Subsection 210(1) of the Act applying to a corporation that has not issued any shares.
Paragraphe 210(1) de la Loi applicable à une société qui n'a pas émis d'actions.
or / ou

☐ Subsection 210(2) of the Act applying to a corporation that has no property and no liabilities.
Paragraphe 210(2) de la Loi applicable à une société sans biens ni dettes.
or / ou

☐ Subsection 210(3) of the Act applying to a corporation that has discharged its liabilities and distributed its property.
Paragraphe 210(3) de la Loi applicable à une société qui a réglé ses dettes et réparti ses biens.

6 -- Name, address and occupation of the person keeping the documents and records of the corporation for six years after the date of dissolution.
Nom, adresse et profession de la personne qui garde les documents et livres de la société pour une période de six ans suivant la date de dissolution.

Signature	Printed Name - Nom en lettres moulées	7 -- Capacity of - En qualité de	8 -- Tel. No. - N° de tél.

FOR DEPARTMENTAL USE ONLY - À L'USAGE DU MINISTÈRE SEULEMENT

IC 3317 (2003/06)

Canada

FIGURE 3.3   CONTINUED

Canada Business Corporations Act	Loi canadienne sur les sociétés par actions
Articles of Dissolution **FORM 17** **INSTRUCTIONS**	**Clauses de dissolution** **FORMULAIRE 17** **INSTRUCTIONS**

General

If you require more information in order to complete Form 17, you may wish to consult the Dissolution Kit.

You can file Form 17 through the Corporations Canada On-line Filing Centre at http://strategis.ic.gc.ca/corporations or you can send or fax the completed documents to the address provided below.

All corporations must complete Items 1, 2, 3 and 6. All corporations must also complete either Item 4 or 5, but not both.

Item 1

The full legal name of the corporation.

Item 2

The corporation number.

Item 3

It is not possible to dissolve an insolvent or bankrupt corporation under the provisions of the Act.

Item 4

If the corporation is applying for dissolution under Section 211 of the Act and has previously filed a statement of intent to dissolve (Form 19), indicate whether the corporation has provided for payment or discharge of its obligations and distributed its remaining property, as required by subsection 211(7) of the Act.

Item 5

If the corporation is applying for dissolution under Section 210 of the Act, check the appropriate box (check only one). To apply under Section 210, a corporation cannot have previously filed a statement of intent to dissolve (Form 19).

Item 6

The first given name, initials, family name and business address of the person who will be liable to produce the documents and records of the dissolved corporation under Section 225 of the Act.

Item 7

Indicate the capacity of the signing person. Form 17 must be signed by one of the following persons:

- a **director** of the corporation
- an **authorized officer** of the corporation

Caution

This form should not be filed at the same time as a Statement of Intent to Dissolve.

Completed document is to be sent to:

The Director, Canada Business Corporations Act
Jean Edmonds Tower, South
9th Floor
365 Laurier Ave. West
Ottawa, Ontario
K1A 0C8
or by facsimile at: (613) 941-0999
Inquiries: 1-866-333-5556

Généralités

Si vous désirez obtenir de plus amples informations afin de compléter le formulaire 17, veuillez consulter le Recueil d'information sur la dissolution.

Vous pouvez déposer le formulaire 17 par l'entremise du Centre de dépôt des formulaires en ligne de Corporations Canada au http://strategis.ic.gc.ca/corporations **ou** encore envoyer ou télécopier le document complété à l'adresse indiquée au bas de cette page.

Toutes les sociétés doivent remplir les rubriques 1, 2, 3 et 6. Toutes les sociétés doivent aussi remplir soit la rubrique 4 ou 5, mais non les deux.

Rubrique 1

La dénomination sociale complète de la société.

Rubrique 2

Le numéro de la société.

Rubrique 3

Il n'est pas possible selon les dispositions de la Loi de dissoudre une société insolvable ou en faillite.

Rubrique 4

Si la société veut faire une demande de dissolution en vertu de l'article 211 de la Loi et qu'elle a déjà déposé une déclaration d'intention de dissolution (formulaire 19), indiquer si la société a constitué une provision suffisante pour honorer ses obligations et répartir le reliquat de l'actif, conformément ou paragraphe 211(7) de la Loi.

Rubrique 5

Si la société veut faire une demande de dissolution en vertu de l'article 210 de la Loi, cochez la case appropriée (cocher une boîte seulement). Afin de faire une demande en vertu de l'article 210 de la Loi, la société ne doit pas avoir déposé une déclaration d'intention de dissolution (formulaire 19).

Rubrique 6

Le prénom, les initiales, le nom de famille et l'adresse d'affaires de la personne qui peut être tenue de produire, en vertu de l'article 225 de la Loi, les documents et livres de la société dissoute.

Rubrique 7

Veuillez indiquer la qualité du signataire. Le formulaire 17 doit être signé par une des personnes suivantes :

- un **administrateur** de la société
- un **dirigeant autorisé** de la société

Remarque

Ce formulaire ne doit pas être déposé en même temps qu'une déclaration d'intention de dissolution (formulaire 19).

Le document complété doit être envoyé au :

Directeur, Loi canadienne sur les sociétés par actions
Tour Jean-Edmonds, sud
9ième étage
365, ave Laurier ouest
Ottawa (Ontario)
K1A 0C8
ou par télécopieur : (613) 941-0999
Renseignements : 1-866-333-5556

IC 3317 (2003/06)

FIGURE 3.3   CONTINUED

CBCA S. 211 DISSOLUTION:
NOTICE OF SPECIAL SHAREHOLDERS' MEETING

NOTICE OF SPECIAL MEETING OF SHAREHOLDERS
OF

_____

NOTICE IS HEREBY GIVEN that a special meeting of the shareholders of
_____ (the "Corporation") will be held at
_____ [*address*] on _____ [*date*] at
_____ [*time*] for the following purposes:

1.   to consider and, if thought advisable, pass a special resolution, in the form annexed hereto as Schedule "A", requiring the Corporation to be liquidated and dissolved voluntarily pursuant to section 211 of the *Canada Business Corporations Act*;

2.   [*insert any terms of liquidation and dissolution*]; and

3.   to transact such other business as may properly come before the meeting or any adjournments thereof.

DATED _____

                    BY ORDER OF THE BOARD OF DIRECTORS

                    _____
                    Secretary

FIGURE 3.3   CONTINUED

CBCA S. 211 DISSOLUTION: SPECIAL SHAREHOLDERS' RESOLUTION APPROVING LIQUIDATION AND DISSOLUTION

SPECIAL RESOLUTION OF THE SHAREHOLDERS OF

_____

LIQUIDATION AND DISSOLUTION

BE IT RESOLVED as a special resolution that:

1. the Corporation is hereby required to be liquidated and dissolved pursuant to the provisions of section 211 of the *Canada Business Corporations Act* (the "Act");

2. a statement of intent to dissolve in the prescribed form shall be sent to the Director appointed under the Act;

3. after the issuance by the Director appointed under the Act of a certificate of intent to dissolve in respect of the Corporation, the Corporation shall take all steps necessary to comply with section 211(7) of the Act; and

4. any director or officer of the Corporation is hereby authorized and directed to execute, under the corporate seal or otherwise, and deliver all such documents and to do all such other acts and things as such director or officer may determine to be necessary or advisable in connection with such liquidation and dissolution, the execution of any such document or the doing of any such other act or thing being conclusive evidence of such determination.

The undersigned, being all the shareholders of the Corporation, hereby consent, by their signatures, to the foregoing special resolution pursuant to the provisions of the *Canada Business Corporations Act*.

DATED _____

_____

_____

FIGURE 3.3 CONTINUED

CBCA FORM 19, STATEMENT OF INTENT TO DISSOLVE

 Industry Canada   Industrie Canada

Canada Business   Loi canadienne sur les
Corporations Act   sociétés par actions

**FORM 19
STATEMENT OF INTENT TO
DISSOLVE
OR REVOCATION
OF INTENT TO DISSOLVE
(SECTION 211)**

**FORMULAIRE 19
DÉCLARATION D'INTENTION
DE DISSOLUTION
OU DE RENONCIATION
D'INTENTION DE DISSOLUTION
(ARTICLE 211)**

1 -- Name of the Corporation - Dénomination sociale de la société	2 -- Corporation No. - N° de la société

3 -- The Corporation intends to liquidate and dissolve   ☐   La société a l'intention de procéder à sa liquidation et à sa dissolution

4 -- The Corporation revokes its certificate of intent to dissolve   ☐   La société révoque son certificat d'intention de dissolution

Signature	Printed Name - Nom en lettres moulées	5 -- Capacity of - En qualité de	6 -- Tel. No. - N° de tél.

FOR DEPARTMENTAL USE ONLY - À L'USAGE DU MINISTÈRE SEULEMENT

IC 3344 (2003/09)

Canada

FIGURE 3.3 CONTINUED

Canada Business Corporations Act	Loi canadienne sur les sociétés par actions
Statement of Intent to Dissolve or Statement of Revocation of Intent to Dissolve **FORM 19** **INSTRUCTIONS**	**Déclaration d'Intention de dissolution ou déclaration de renonciation d'intention de dissolution** **FORMULAIRE 19** **INSTRUCTIONS**

General

If you require more information in order to complete Form 19, you may wish to consult the Dissolution Kit.

You can file Form 19 through the Corporations Canada On-line Filing Centre at http://strategis.ic.gc.ca/corporations or you can send or fax the completed documents to the address provided below.

Prescribed Fees

Statement of Intent to Dissolve: no fee
Revocation of Intent to Dissolve: $50

Item 1

The full legal name of the corporation.

Item 2

The corporation number.

Item 3

Check item 3 if the corporation intends to liquidate and dissolve under subsection 211(3) of the Act.

Item 4

Check item 4 if the corporation intends to revoke under subsection 211(10) of the Act a certificate of intent to dissolve issued to it under subsection 211(5) of the Act.

Item 5

Indicate the capacity of the signing person. Form 19 must be signed by one of the following persons:

- a **director** of the corporation
- an **authorized officer** of the corporation

Caution

This form should not be filed at the same time as the Articles of Dissolution (Form 17).

The completed document and fees, if applicable, payable to the Receiver General for Canada are to be sent to:

    The Director, Canada Business Corporations Act
    Jean Edmonds Tower, South
    9th Floor
    365 Laurier Ave. West
    Ottawa, Ontario
    K1A 0C8
    or by facsimile at: (613) 941-0999
    Inquiries: 1-866-333-5556

Généralités

Si vous désirez obtenir de plus amples informations afin de compléter le formulaire 19, veuillez consulter le Recueil d'information sur la dissolution.

Vous pouvez déposer le formulaire 19 par l'entremise du Centre de dépôt des formulaires en ligne de Corporations Canada au http://strategis.ic.gc.ca/corporations ou encore envoyer ou télécopier le document complété à l'adresse indiquée au bas de cette page.

Droits payables

Déclaration d'intention de dissolution : aucun frais
Déclaration de renonciation d'intention de dissolution : 50 $

Rubrique 1

La dénomination sociale complète de la société.

Rubrique 2

Le numéro de la société.

Rubrique 3

Cocher la rubrique 3, si la société envisage de procéder à sa liquidation et à sa dissolution en vertu du paragraphe 211(3) de la Loi.

Rubrique 4

Cocher la rubrique 4, si la société entend révoquer, en vertu du paragraphe 211(10) de la Loi, un certificat d'intention de dissolution délivré en vertu du paragraphe 211(5) de la Loi.

Rubrique 5

Veuillez indiquer la qualité du signataire. Le formulaire 19 doit être signé par une des personnes suivantes :

- un **administrateur** de la société
- un **dirigeant autorisé** de la société

Remarque

Ce formulaire ne peut être déposé en même temps que les clauses de dissolution (formulaire 17).

Le document complété et les droits payables au Receveur général du Canada, s'il y a lieu, doivent être envoyés au :

    Directeur, Loi canadienne sur les sociétés par actions
    Tour Jean Edmonds, sud
    9ième étage
    365, av. Laurier ouest
    Ottawa (Ontario)
    K1A 0C8
    ou par télécopieur : (613) 941-0999
    Renseignements : 1-866-333-5556

IC 3344 (2003/09) p.2

FIGURE 3.3 CONCLUDED

CBCA S. 211 DISSOLUTION:
NOTICE OF INTENT TO DISSOLVE

NOTICE OF ISSUANCE OF CERTIFICATE OF INTENT TO DISSOLVE
OF

_____

TAKE NOTICE that the shareholders of _____
[*name of corporation*] have passed a special resolution requiring the liquidation and dissolution of the Corporation under the *Canada Business Corporations Act* (the "Act") and a Certificate of Intent to Dissolve was issued by the Director appointed under the Act to the Corporation on _____ [*date*].

TAKE FURTHER NOTICE that if you have any claim against the Corporation, proof of such claim must be filed with the Corporation within two months of the date of this notice, after which time the property of the Corporation shall be distributed amongst the persons entitled thereto, having regard to the claims of which the Corporation has then notice.

DATED _____

_____
[*name of corporation*]

Per: _____
      Name:
      Title:

_____
Address of corporation

CBCA FORM 11, ARTICLES OF DISSOLUTION

 **Ontario**

Ministry of Consumer and Business Services	Companies and Personal Property Security Branch	393 University Ave Suite 200 Toronto ON M5G 2M2

**Articles of Dissolution
Form 11
*Business Corporations Act***

INSTRUCTIONS FOR COMPLETING

This form is to be used for voluntary dissolution of a business corporation, where a corporation has not commenced business, has not issued any shares, and the dissolution is authorized by all its incorporators or their personal representatives within two years of the date of incorporation. (Please use Articles of Dissolution, Form 10, if any of these conditions do not apply.)

Articles in duplicate may be mailed to the Toronto address listed above. For over-the-counter service, they may also be filed in person at the Toronto office or at one of the following Land Registry Offices: Hamilton, Kingston, Kitchener, London, Whitby, Sudbury, Barrie, Sarnia, Ottawa, Peterborough, Sault Ste. Marie, Thunder Bay, Windsor or Welland.

FEE

$25.00   BY MAIL - cheque or money order payable to the Minister of Finance.
IN PERSON (at the Toronto office) - cash, cheque or money order payable to the Minister of Finance, Visa, MasterCard, American Express or debit card. (If you are filing the documents at a Land Registry Office, call first to confirm whether credit or debit cards are acceptable).

There will be a service charge payable for any cheque returned as non-negotiable by a bank or financial institution.

SUPPORTING DOCUMENTS

Articles must be accompanied by written consent to the dissolution from the Corporations Tax Branch, Ministry of Finance (Ontario) submitted within 60 days of issuance. To obtain this consent, contact the Ministry of Finance at the following address:

Ministry of Finance
Corporations Tax Branch
33 King Street West, 4th Floor
PO Box 622
Oshawa ON L1H 8H5

TELEPHONE: In Toronto: (416) 920-9048 or 1-800-263-7965

07123 (03/2003)

FIGURE 3.4 CONTINUED

APPEARANCE OF DOCUMENTS

The Articles of Dissolution must be completed in duplicate on a Form 11 as approved by the Minister. All documents must be legible and compatible with the microfilming process, with the information typed or hand printed in block capital letters, on one side of good quality, white bond paper 8 ½" X 11".

ARTICLES

ARTICLE 1   Set out the **current** name of the corporation in block capital letters starting from the first box on the left-hand side of the first line, with one letter per box and one empty box for a space. Punctuation marks are entered in separate boxes. Complete one line before starting in the first box of the next line. The name entered must be exactly the same as it appeared on the original Articles of Incorporation or Articles of Amalgamation, or the most recent Articles of Amendment if there has been a name change.

E	A	S	T		S	I	D	E		I	N	V	E	S	T	M	E	N	T		A	N	D		M	A	N	A	G
E	M	E	N	T		L	T	D	.																				

ARTICLE 2   Set out the date of incorporation or amalgamation.

ARTICLE 3   The corporation has not commenced business. **This statement must be included in the Articles.**

ARTICLE 4   None of the shares of the corporation has been issued. **This statement must be included in the Articles.**

ARTICLE 5   This dissolution has been duly authorized under clause 237 (c) of the *Business Corporations Act.* **This statement must be included in the Articles.**

ARTICLE 6   The corporation has no debts, obligations or liabilities. **This statement must be included in the Articles.**

ARTICLE 7   Mark (X) in the box beside the one statement that applies.

ARTICLE 8   There are no proceedings pending in any court against the corporation. **This statement must be included in the Articles.**

ARTICLE 9   The corporation has obtained the consent of the Corporations Tax Branch of the Ministry of Finance to the dissolution and has filed all notices and returns required under the *Corporations Information Act.* **This statement must be included in the Articles.**

EXECUTION   Both copies of the Articles must be signed by all of the incorporators of the corporation or their personal representatives.

Articles (in duplicate), consent letter from the Ministry of Finance and filing fee should be mailed or delivered to:

**COMPANIES AND PERSONAL PROPERTY SECURITY BRANCH
MINISTRY OF CONSUMER AND BUSINESS SERVICES
393 UNIVERSITY AVENUE, SUITE 200
TORONTO ONTARIO M5G 2M2**

07123 (03/2003)

FIGURE 3.4 CONTINUED

For Ministry Use Only
À l'usage exclusif du ministère

Ontario Corporation Number
Numéro de la société en Ontario

1

ARTICLES OF DISSOLUTION
STATUTS DE DISSOLUTION

Form 11
Business
Corporations
Act

*Formule 11
Loi sur les
sociétés par
actions*

1. The name of the corporation is: (Set out in BLOCK CAPITAL LETTERS)
   Dénomination sociale de la société : (Écrire en LETTRES MAJUSCULES SEULEMENT) :

2. Date of incorporation/amalgamation:
   Date de la constitution ou de la fusion :

   _____

   (Year, Month, Day)
   (année, mois, jour)

3. The corporation has not commenced business.
   La société n'a pas encore commencé ses opérations.

4. None of the shares of the corporation has been issued.
   La société n'a émis aucune action.

5. The dissolution has been duly authorized under clause 237 (c) of the *Business Corporations* Act.
   La dissolution de la société a été dûment approuvée aux termes de l'alinéa 237 c) de la Loi sur les sociétés par actions.

6. The corporation has no debts, obligations or liabilities.
   La société n'a ni dettes, ni obligations, ni passif.

7. After satisfying the interests of creditors, in all its debts, obligations and liabilities, if any, the corporation: (mark (x) in the box beside **the one statement that applies**):
   Après avoir désintéressé tous ses créanciers, s'il y a lieu, la société, selon le cas (cocher la case appropriée) :

   ☐ (a) has no property to distribute; **or**
   *a) n'a plus de biens à répartir; **ou***

   ☐ (b) has distributed its remaining property to the persons entitled thereto.
   b) a réparti les biens qui lui restaient entre les personnes qui y ont droit.

8. There are no proceedings pending in any court against the corporation.
   Aucune instance n'est en cours contre la société.

9. The corporation has obtained the consent of the Corporations Tax Branch of the Ministry of Finance to the dissolution and has filed all notices and returns required under the *Corporations Information Act.*
   La Direction de l'imposition des compagnies du ministère des Finances a approuvé la dissolution de la société.
   La société a déposé tous les avis et rapports requis par la Loi sur les renseignements exigés des personnes morales.

07123 (03/2003)

FIGURE 3.4 CONTINUED

2

These articles are signed in duplicate.
Les présents statuts sont signés en double exemplaire.

Signature and names of all the incorporators or their personal representatives
Signature et nom de tous les fondateurs ou de leurs représentants

07123 (03/2003)

FIGURE 3.4   CONTINUED

LETTER TO MINISTRY OF FINANCE
REQUESTING CONSENT TO DISSOLUTION

Ministry of Finance
Corporations Tax Branch
Box 622
33 King Street West
Oshawa, ON   L1H 8H5

Dear Sirs:

Re: _____ [*name of Corporation*]

We are the solicitors for _____ [*name of corporation*]
(the "Corporation"). By special resolution dated _____ the shareholders of the
Corporation have authorized the voluntary dissolution of the Corporation pursuant to section 237
of the *Business Corporations Act*.

Please provide us with a Letter of Consent to dissolve for the purpose of filing Articles of
Dissolution as soon as possible. If you are unable to provide the consent at this time, please
advise us of the steps which must be taken to obtain your consent.

Yours truly,

FIGURE 3.4   CONTINUED

MINISTRY OF FINANCE CONSENT TO DISSOLUTION

Ministry of Finance
33 King Street West
Oshawa, ON L1H 8H5

Dissolving Corporation
1 Ontario Street
Toronto, ON

Dear Sirs:

RE: Dissolving Corporation
        Account No. _____
        Consent — Voluntary Dissolution

We are pleased to advise you that the Corporations Tax Branch, Ministry of Finance, consents to the voluntary dissolution of Dissolving Corporation on condition that this consent, together with your Articles of Dissolution, are filed within 60 days from the date of this letter with the Companies Branch, Ministry of Government Services.

We urge you to present this consent to the Companies Branch within the specified time period. Until this consent is filed with the Companies Branch, which then processes the dissolution of the corporation, the corporation will remain on our tax roll and be liable to file tax returns and remit all relevant taxes in accordance with the Corporations Tax Act.

Yours truly,

FIGURE 3.4 CONTINUED

SPECIAL SHAREHOLDERS' RESOLUTION
APPROVING DISSOLUTION UNDER OBCA S. 237(b)

SPECIAL RESOLUTION
OF

_____

ARTICLES OF DISSOLUTION

BE IT RESOLVED as a special resolution that:

1.   the dissolution of the Corporation is hereby authorized pursuant to clause 237(b) of the *Business Corporations Act* (the "Act");

2.   the directors of the Corporation are hereby authorized to cause the Corporation to discharge all its debts, obligations or liabilities and thereafter to distribute its remaining property rateably among the shareholders of the Corporation;

[*Note: use the following paragraph only if the corporation is going to enter into a distribution agreement with the shareholders*]

3.   the Corporation is hereby authorized to execute and deliver an agreement between the Corporation and the shareholders of the Corporation, substantially in the form and on the terms and subject to the conditions set out in the draft distribution agreement annexed hereto as Schedule "A" (the "Distribution Agreement");

4.   after the distribution of the property of the Corporation, the Corporation shall dissolve and, for the purpose of bringing such dissolution into effect, the Corporation shall deliver to the Director appointed under the Act, articles of dissolution in the prescribed form; and

5.   any director or officer of the Corporation is hereby authorized and directed to execute, under the corporate seal or otherwise, and deliver all such documents (including, without limitation, [the aforesaid Distribution Agreement,] articles of dissolution and any notices respecting the dissolution of the Corporation) and to do all such other acts and things as such director or officer may determine to be necessary or advisable in connection with the foregoing, the execution of any such document or the doing of any such act or thing by any director of officer of the Corporation being conclusive evidence of such determination.

The undersigned, being all the shareholders of the Corporation, hereby consent, by their signatures, to the foregoing special resolution pursuant to the provisions of the *Business Corporations Act*.

DATED _____

_____

_____

FIGURE 3.4   CONTINUED

CBCA FORM 10, ARTICLES OF DISSOLUTION

 **Ontario**

Ministry of Consumer and Business Services	Companies and Personal Property Security Branch	393 University Ave Suite 200 Toronto ON M5G 2M2

Articles of Dissolution
Form 10
Business Corporations Act

INSTRUCTIONS FOR COMPLETING

This form is to be used for voluntary dissolution of a business corporation that has commenced business and issued shares.

Articles in duplicate may be mailed to the Toronto address listed above. For over-the-counter service, they may also be filed in person at the Toronto office or at one of the following Land Registry Offices: Hamilton, Kingston, Kitchener, London, Whitby, Sudbury, Barrie, Sarnia, Ottawa, Peterborough, Sault Ste. Marie,Thunder Bay, Windsor or Welland.

FEE

$25.00   BY MAIL - cheque or money order payable to the Minister of Finance.
              IN PERSON (at the Toronto office) - cash, cheque or money order payable to the Minister of Finance, Visa, MasterCard, American Express or debit card. (If you are filing the documents at a Land Registry Office, call first to confirm whether credit or debit cards are acceptable).

There will be a service charge payable for any cheque returned as non-negotiable by a bank or financial institution.

SUPPORTING DOCUMENTS

Articles must be accompanied by written consent to the dissolution from the Corporations Tax Branch, Ministry of Finance (Ontario) submitted within 60 days of issuance. To obtain this consent, contact the Ministry of Finance at the following address:

Ministry of Finance
Corporations Tax Branch
33 King Street West, 4th Floor
PO Box 622
Oshawa ON L1H 8H5

TELEPHONE: In Toronto: (416) 920-9048 or 1-800-262-0784

07122 (08/2002)

FIGURE 3.4   CONTINUED

APPEARANCE OF DOCUMENTS

The Articles of Dissolution must be completed in duplicate on a Form 10 as prescribed by Minister's Order. All documents must be legible and compatible with the microfilming process, with the information typed or hand printed in block capital letters, on one side of good quality, white bond paper 8 1/2" X 11".

ARTICLES

ARTICLE 1   Set out the **current** name of the corporation in block capital letters starting from the first box on the left-hand side of the first line, with one letter per box and one empty box for a space. Punctuation marks are entered in separate boxes. Complete one line before starting in the first box of the next line. The name entered must be exactly the same as it appeared on the original Articles of Incorporation, Articles of Amalgamation or the most recent Articles of Amendment, if there has been a name change.

E	A	S	T		S	I	D	E		I	N	V	E	S	T	M	E	N	T		A	N	D		M	A	N	A	G
E	M	E	N	T		L	T	D	.																				

ARTICLE 2   Set out the date of incorporation or amalgamation.

ARTICLE 3   The dissolution must be authorized as required by section 237 (a) or (b) *(as applicable)* of the *Business Corporations Act*. **This statement must be included in the Articles.**

ARTICLE 4   Mark (X) in the box beside the one statement that applies.

ARTICLE 5   Mark (X) in the box beside the one statement that applies.

ARTICLE 6   There are no proceedings pending in any court against the corporation. ***This statement must be included in the Articles.***

ARTICLE 7   The corporation has obtained the consent of the Corporations Tax Branch of the Ministry of Finance to the dissolution and has filed all notices and returns required under the Corporations Information Act. ***This statement must be included in the Articles.***

EXECUTION   **The current name of the corporation should be printed above the signature in BLOCK CAPITAL LETTERS.** Both copies of the Articles must have an original signature of an officer or director of the corporation. **Beside the signature set out the office of the person who is signing i.e. President, Director, Secretary....** If the corporation has a corporate seal it should be affixed to the articles next to the signature. **An executor cannot sign Articles of Dissolution.**

Articles (in duplicate), consent letter from the Ministry of Finance and filing fee should be mailed or delivered to:

COMPANIES AND PERSONAL PROPERTY SECURITY BRANCH
MINISTRY OF CONSUMER AND BUSINESS SERVICES
393 UNIVERSITY AVENUE, SUITE 200
TORONTO ONTARIO M5G 2M2

07122 (08/2002)

FIGURE 3.4 CONTINUED

1

For Ministry Use Only
À l'usage exclusif du ministère

Ontario Corporation Number
Numéro de la société en Ontario

Form 10
Business
Corporations
Act

*Formule 10
Loi sur les
sociétés par
actions*

ARTICLES OF DISSOLUTION
STATUTS DE DISSOLUTION

1. The name of the corporation is: (Set out in BLOCK CAPITAL LETTERS)
   Dénomination sociale de la société : (Écrire en LETTRES MAJUSCULES SEULEMENT)

2. Date of incorporation/amalgamation:
   Date de la constitution ou de la fusion :

   (Year, Month, Day)
   (année, mois, jour)

3. The dissolution has been duly authorized under clause 237 (a) or (b) (as applicable) of the
   Business Corporations Act.
   *La dissolution de la société a été dûment approuvée aux termes de l'alinéa 237 a) ou b) (le cas échéant)
   de la Loi sur les sociétés par actions.*

4. The corporation has, (Mark (X) in the box beside the one statement that applies.)
   La société, selon le cas : (cocher la case appropriée)

   ☐ (A) no debts, obligations or liabilities;
       (A) n'a ni dettes, ni obligations, ni passif;

   ☐ (B) duly provided for its debts, obligations or liabilities in accordance with subsection 238 (3) of the
       Business Corporations Act;
       *(B) a pourvu à ses dettes, à ses obligations ou à son passif conformément au paragraphe 238 (3) de
       la Loi sur les sociétés par actions;*

   ☐ (C) obtained consent to its dissolution from its creditors or other persons having interests in its
       debts, obligations or liabilities.
       *(C) a obtenu de ses créanciers ou des autres intéressés à ses dettes, à ses obligations ou à son
       passif, le consentement à sa dissolution.*

5. After satisfying the interests of creditors in all its debts, obligations and liabilities, if any, the corporation has,
   (Mark (X) in the box beside the one statement that applies.)
   *Après avoir désintéressé tous ses créanciers, s'il y a lieu, la société, selon le cas :
   (cocher la case appropriée)*

   ☐ (A) no property to distribute among its shareholders; or
       (A) n'a plus de biens à répartir entre ses actionnaires;

   ☐ (B) distributed its remaining property rateably among its shareholders according to their rights and
       interests in the corporation or in accordance with subsection 238 (4) of the *Business Corporations*
       Act where applicable.
       *(B) a réparti les biens qui lui restaient entre ses actionnaires au prorata de leurs droits dans la société
       ou conformément au paragraphe 238 (4) de la Loi sur les sociétés par actions, s'il y a lieu.*

07122 (08/2002)

FIGURE 3.4 CONTINUED

2

6. There are no proceedings pending in any court against the corporation.
    Aucune instance n'est en cours contre la société.

7. The corporation has obtained the consent of the Corporations Tax Branch of the Ministry of Finance
    to the dissolution and has filed all notices and returns required under the *Corporations Information Act.*
    *La Direction de l'imposition des compagnies du ministère des Finances a approuvé la dissolution de
    la société. La société a déposé tous les avis et rapports requis par la* Loi sur les renseignements exigés
    des personnes morales.

These articles are signed in duplicate.
Les présents statuts sont signés en double exemplaire.

_____
(Name of Corporation)
(Dénomination sociale de la société)

By
Par :

_____   _____
(Signature)   (Description of Office)
(Signature)   *(Fonction)*

07122 (08/2002)

FIGURE 3.4 CONTINUED

SPECIAL SHAREHOLDERS' RESOLUTION APPROVING VOLUNTARY WINDUP UNDER OBCA S. 193 AND APPOINTMENT OF LIQUIDATOR

SPECIAL RESOLUTION OF THE SHAREHOLDERS
OF

_____

VOLUNTARY WIND UP AND APPOINTMENT OF LIQUIDATOR

BE IT RESOLVED as a special resolution that:

1. the Corporation is hereby required to be wound up voluntarily pursuant to the provisions of section 193 of the _Business Corporations Act_ (the "Act");

2. _____ [_insert name of liquidator_] is hereby appointed liquidator (the "Liquidator") of the estate and effects of the Corporation for the purpose of winding up its business and affairs and distributing its property;

3. the Corporation is hereby authorized to enter into a personal services agreement between the Corporation and the Liquidator with respect to remuneration to be paid to the Liquidator in the form annexed hereto as Schedule "A" (the "Personal Services Agreement");

4. any director or officer of the Corporation is hereby authorized and directed to execute, under the corporate seal or otherwise, and deliver the Personal Services Agreement and all such documents and to do all such other acts and things as such director or officer may determine to be necessary or advisable in connection with such liquidation and dissolution, the execution of the Personal Services Agreement and any such other document or the doing of any such other act or thing being conclusive evidence of such determination.

The undersigned, being all the shareholders of the Corporation, hereby consent, by their signatures, to the foregoing special resolution pursuant to the provisions of the _Business Corporations Act_.

DATED _____

_____

_____

FIGURE 3.4 CONCLUDED

OBCA FORM 16, NOTICE OF SHAREHOLDER APPROVAL OF VOLUNTARY WINDUP

For Ministry Use Only
À l'usage exclusif du ministère

Ontario Corporation Number
Numéro de la société en Ontario   1.

STAT
| V |

Form 16
Business
Corporations
Act

*Formule 16
Loi sur les
sociétés par
actions*

NOTICE CONCERNING WINDING UP
AVIS CONCERNANT LA LIQUIDATION

1. The name of the corporation is: *Dénomination sociale de la société:*

2. Date of incorporation/amalgamation: *Date de la constitution ou de la fusion:*

(Year, Month, Day)
(année, mois, jour)

3. Liquidator(s)   *Liquidateur(s)*

Name *Nom*	Address *Adresse*	Date Appointed *Date de la nomination*

4. This notice is filed under subsection 193 (4) of the Business Corporations Act. The special resolution requiring the corporation to be wound up voluntarily was passed/consented to by the shareholders of the corporation on

Le présent avis est déposé conformément au paragraphe 193 (4) de la Loi sur les sociétés par actions. Les actionnaires de la société ont adopté/approuvé la résolution spéciale exigeant la liquidation volontaire de la société le

(Year, Month, Day)
(année, mois, jour)

5. This notice is filed under subsection 205(2) of the Business Corporations Act. A meeting of the shareholders of the corporation pursuant to subsection 205(1) of the Act was held on

Le présent avis est déposé conformément au paragraphe 205 (2) de la Loi sur les sociétés par actions. Une assemblée des actionnaires de la société a été tenue le

(Year, Month, Day)
(année, mois, jour)

Pursuant to subsection 205(3) of the Business Corporations Act, on the expiration of three months after the date of filing of this notice, the corporation is dissolved.

conformément au paragraphe 205 (1) de la Loi sur les sociétés par actions. En vertu du paragraphe 205(3) de la Loi sur le sociétés par actions, la société est dissoute trois mois après le dépôt du présent avis.

or

6. This notice is filed under subsection 210(4) of the Business Corporations Act. The court has appointed the above named as the liquidator(s) of the corporation.

*ou
Le présent avis est déposé conformément au paragraphe 210 (4) de la Loi sur les sociétés par actions. La tribunal a nommé les personnes susmentionnées comme liquidateurs de la société.*

DSG 01/2000

By/*Par:* _____

Signature of an Officer of the Corporation or the Liquidator
Signature d'un dirigeant de la société ou du liquidateur

FIGURE 3.5 FORMS AND SAMPLE DOCUMENTS FOR AN ITA S. 85 ROLLOVER

Note: The following document list and sample documents are based on the scenario described in the text involving a transfer of assets of Opco Inc. from Cathy to Holdco Limited.

DOCUMENT LIST

1. Articles of Incorporation of Holdco Limited ("Holdco")

2. Organizational resolutions of the directors of Holdco

3. By-law No. 1 of Holdco

4. Resolution of directors of Holdco approving rollover agreement, issuing 4,000 special shares of Holdco to Cathy in exchange for 100,000 common shares of Opco Inc. ("Opco"), agreeing to elect under s. 85 of the *Income Tax Act* (Canada), and fixing the stated capital of the special shares of Holdco

5. Rollover agreement between Holdco and Cathy

6. Share certificate of Opco for 100,000 common shares in the name of Cathy endorsed for transfer

7. Resolution of the directors of Opco approving the transfer of 100,000 common shares from Cathy to Holdco

8. New share certificate of Opco for 100,000 common shares issued to Holdco

9. New share certificate of Holdco for 4,000 special shares issued to Cathy

10. T2057 election form (usually prepared and filed by accountant)

11. Organizational resolutions of shareholder of Holdco

Note: Prior to commencing the preparation of any documents, the articles of the purchasing corporation should be reviewed in order to ensure that the authorized capital of the purchasing corporation consists of the class of shares to be issued to the shareholder on the rollover (for example, special shares). If the purchasing corporation does not currently have the required class of shares or the existing class of shares does not meet the requirements for the particular circumstances, the first step in the process of the transaction would be for the purchasing corporation to apply for articles of amendment to create the necessary class of shares.

FIGURE 3.5   CONTINUED

SAMPLE AGREEMENT FOR A S. 85 ROLLOVER

ROLLOVER AGREEMENT

THIS AGREEMENT is made as of the _____ day of _____, 200__.

BETWEEN:

_____,

of the City of _____, Province of Ontario

(hereinafter referred to as the "Transferor")

AND:

_____,

a corporation incorporated under the laws of _____

(hereinafter referred to as the "Transferee")

WHEREAS:

A.   The Transferor is the owner of _____ Shares of _____
(the "Assets");

B.   The Transferor wishes to transfer and the Transferee wishes to purchase the Assets for a price that represents the current fair market value of such Assets on the terms set out herein; and

C.   The parties intend that subsection 85(1) of the *Income Tax Act* of Canada shall apply to the transfer of the Assets by the Transferor to the Transferee, as is more fully set out in this Agreement;

NOW THEREFORE in consideration of the premises and the mutual covenants herein and other good and valuable consideration (the receipt and sufficiency of which is hereby acknowledged by each of the parties) the parties hereto covenant and agree as follows:

1.   **DEFINITIONS**

In this Agreement:

1.1.   **"Act"** shall mean the *Income Tax Act* of Canada;

1.2.   **"Assets"** shall mean the _____ Shares of _____
held by the Transferor and transferred pursuant to this Agreement as set out in Schedule 2 attached hereto;

1.3.   **"Cost"** shall have the same meaning as "cost" or "cost amount" in section 85 of the Act and shall be set out in Schedule 1 attached hereto;

1.4.   **"Effective Date"** shall mean the date hereof or such other date as the parties may agree upon;

FIGURE 3.5   CONTINUED

1.5.   **"Elected Amount"** shall mean the elected amount set out in Schedule 1 attached hereto;

1.6.   **"Issued Shares"** shall mean _____ Shares of the Transferee; and

1.7.   **"Price"** shall mean the estimated fair market value of the Assets on the Effective Date, as set out in Schedule 1 attached hereto.

2.   TRANSFER

2.1.   The Transferor agrees to transfer, assign and convey the Assets to the Transferee as of and from the Effective Date.

3.   PRICE AND ELECTION

3.1.   The Transferee shall pay to the Transferor as consideration for the Assets the Price set out in Schedule 1.

3.2.   The Price shall be satisfied by the issue to the Transferor of the Issued Shares [*insert if applicable*: and the granting of a promissory note in favour of the Transferor in the amount of $_____].

3.3.   The parties shall jointly elect in the form prescribed pursuant to subsection 85(1) of the Act that the Transferor's proceeds of disposition of the Assets and the Transferee's Cost thereof shall be the Elected Amount set out in Schedule 1, or such other amount as the parties may agree upon within the time specified in subsection 85(6) of the Act.

3.4.   The parties shall cause the Secretary of the Transferee to add to the stated capital account of the Transferee for the Issued Shares, pursuant to subsection [26(3) of the *Canada Business Corporations Act*/24(3) of the *Business Corporations Act* (Ontario)], the stated capital set out in Schedule 1 attached hereto.

3.5.   For the purposes of the Act, the amount to be added to the paid up capital account of the Transferee for the Issued Shares will be the paid up capital set out in Schedule 1 attached hereto.

3.6.   Notwithstanding paragraphs 3.4 and 3.5 of this Agreement, in the event that an adjustment is made to the elected amount pursuant to paragraph 3.3 or 4.2, the parties shall make any corresponding amendments which may be required to the paid up capital and stated capital accounts of the Transferee, and such amended amounts shall be deemed to have been added to such accounts on the Effective Date.

4.   PRICE ADJUSTMENT

4.1.   It being the intention of the parties hereto that the Price shall be the fair market value on the Effective Date of the Assets being purchased and sold under this Agreement, the Transferor and Transferee agree that if a different value is determined or assumed, upon assessment or reassessment of either the Transferor or Transferee under the Act or upon agreement with officials of Canada Revenue Agency ("the CRA") or upon agreement between the Transferor and Transferee

FIGURE 3.5   CONTINUED

(with or without agreement of officials of the CRA) then the value so determined or assumed, either after objection or appeal or by agreement with officials of the CRA or by agreement between the Transferor and Transferee (with or without agreement of officials of the CRA), shall be deemed to be the value assigned to the Assets under the Agreement, and the Price shall be adjusted accordingly and retroactively, *nunc pro tunc*, to the Effective Date. The Transferor and Transferee further agree to pay such additional sum or to refund such part of the Price paid herein as the circumstances may require. The provisions of this paragraph shall also apply to the Issued Shares. For greater certainty for purposes of paragraphs 4.1 and 4.2 of this Agreement, the parties further agree that if the CRA invokes the use of paragraph 85(1)(e.2) of the Act and if as a result a different value or adjusted cost base is determined or assumed, upon assessment or reassessment, or upon agreement with officials of the CRA, then the provisions set out in paragraphs 4.1 and 4.2 of this Agreement shall apply as the circumstances may require.

4.2.   The parties further agree that if a different Cost than the amount set out in Schedule 1 of this Agreement is determined or assumed upon assessment or reassessment of either the Transferor or Transferee under the Act, or upon agreement with officials of the CRA, or upon agreement between the Transferor and Transferee (with or without agreement of officials of the CRA), then the Cost so determined or assumed, either after objection or appeal or by agreement with officials of the CRA or by agreement between the Transferor and Transferee (with or without agreement of officials of the CRA), shall be deemed to be the Cost assigned to the Assets under this Agreement, and the allocation of the consideration given for the Assets shall be adjusted accordingly and retroactively, *nunc pro tunc*, to the Effective Date. The Transferor and Transferee further agree to pay such additional sum or refund such part of the consideration paid herein as the circumstances may require.

5.   **REPRESENTATIONS**

5.1.   The Transferor represents and warrants that:

5.1.1.   the Transferor owns the Assets both legally and beneficially and has good and marketable title to the Assets; and

5.1.2.   on the Effective Date, the Transferor will be a resident of Canada, or shall supply adequate evidence before the Effective Date that the provisions of the Act regarding payment to non-residents shall be complied with at or before the Effective Date.

5.2.   The Transferee represents and warrants that the Transferee is a "taxable Canadian corporation" within the meaning of the Act.

6.   **SCHEDULE**

6.1.   Schedule 1 attached hereto forms an integral part of this Agreement.

6.2.   Schedule 2 attached hereto forms an integral part of this Agreement.

FIGURE 3.5   CONTINUED

7.   **CURRENCY**

    7.1.   All sums of money referred to in this Agreement are expressed in Canadian Dollars unless otherwise stated.

8.   **TIME OF ESSENCE**

    8.1.   Time shall be of the essence of this Agreement.

9.   **FURTHER ASSURANCES**

    9.1.   The parties hereto shall do all further acts and things and execute all further documents reasonably required in the circumstances to give effect to the provisions and intent of this Agreement.

10.   **ENUREMENT**

    10.1.   This Agreement shall enure to the benefit of and be binding upon the parties hereto and their respective personal representatives, heirs, executors, administrators, successors and assigns.

11.   **PROPER LAW**

    11.1.   This Agreement shall be governed by and interpreted in accordance with the laws of the Province of Ontario, and the laws of Canada applicable therein.

    IN WITNESS WHEREOF this Agreement has been executed by the parties hereto.

SIGNED, SEALED AND DELIVERED

_____

Witness

                      Per: _____

                                    Name:
                                    Title:

FIGURE 3.5 CONTINUED

SCHEDULE 1

ROLLOVER AGREEMENT BETWEEN

_____

AND

_____

Cost	$_____
Price:	$_____
Elected Amount:	$_____
Non-Share Consideration	$_____
Share Consideration:	_____ Shares of the Transferee
Stated Capital:	$_____
Paid up Capital:	$_____

FIGURE 3.5 CONTINUED

SCHEDULE 2

ROLLOVER AGREEMENT BETWEEN

_____

AND

_____

[*list assets being transferred*]
Assets: _____ Shares of_____

FIGURE 3.5 CONTINUED

DIRECTORS' RESOLUTION APPROVING THE ROLLOVER

RESOLUTION OF THE DIRECTORS
OF

_____

APPROVAL OF ROLLOVER AGREEMENT AND ISSUE OF _____ SHARES [*insert if applicable*: AND ISSUANCE OF PROMISSORY NOTE]

WHEREAS the Corporation wishes to enter into a rollover agreement (the "Rollover Agreement") with _____ (the "Transferor") wherein the Transferor agrees to transfer and the Corporation agrees to purchase _____ shares of _____ (the "Subject Shares") in consideration of the issue by the Corporation of _____ Shares of the Corporation to the Transferor [*insert the following if applicable*: and the granting by the Corporation to the Transferor of a non-interest bearing demand promissory note in favour of the Transferor in the amount of $_____ on the conditions and in the form presented to the directors at the date of this resolution (the "Note")];

NOW THEREFORE BE IT RESOLVED that:

1. the entry of the Corporation into the Rollover Agreement on substantially the terms and conditions and in the form presented to the directors is hereby authorized and approved, and any officer of the Corporation is hereby authorized to execute the Rollover Agreement on behalf of the Corporation, under corporate seal or otherwise, and to do all acts and things necessary to give effect to the foregoing;

2. _____ Shares of the Corporation be hereby allotted to the Transferor in consideration of the transfer to the Corporation of the Subject Shares;

3. upon the transfer of the Subject Shares to the name of the Corporation, the _____ Shares of the Corporation be issued as fully paid and non-assessable and a certificate representing the said _____ Shares be issued to the Transferor;

   [*Note: include the following paragraph if a promissory note is issued*]

4. upon the transfer of the Subject Shares to the name of the Corporation, any officer of the Corporation is hereby authorized to execute the Note on substantially the terms and conditions and in the form presented to the directors at the time of execution of this resolution;

5. pursuant to [subsection 26(3) of the *Canada Business Corporations Act*/subsection 24(3) of the *Business Corporations Act* (Ontario)], the Stated Capital set out in Schedule 1 of the Rollover Agreement be added to the stated capital account of the Corporation for the _____ Shares; and

6. the Corporation elect jointly with the Transferor pursuant to the provisions of subsection 85(1) of the *Income Tax Act* that the proceeds of disposition of the Subject Shares by the Transferor and the cost of acquisition of the Subject Shares by the Corporation shall be the Elected Amount set out in Schedule 1 to the Rollover Agreement.

FIGURE 3.5   CONTINUED

The undersigned, being all the directors of the Corporation, hereby consent, by their signatures, to the foregoing resolution, pursuant to the provisions of the [*Canada Business Corporations Act/Business Corporations Act* (Ontario)].

DATED: _____

_____

_____

FIGURE 3.5   CONTINUED

TYPICAL SHARE RIGHTS IN A
S. 85 ROLLOVER

SPECIAL SHARES

(a)   the Special Shares shall have attached thereto the following rights, privileges, restrictions and conditions:

1.   Voting

Except as provided by the *Canada Business Corporations Act* (the "Act"), as amended from time to time, the holders of the Special Shares shall not be entitled to receive notice of or to attend any meeting of the shareholders of the Corporation and shall not be entitled to vote at any meetings of the shareholders of the Corporation but shall be entitled to notice of meetings of shareholders called for the purpose of authorizing the dissolution of the Corporation or the sale, lease or exchange of all or substantially all the property of the Corporation other than in the ordinary course of business of the Corporation.

2.   Dividends

The holders of the Special Shares shall be entitled to receive non-cumulative dividends if, as and when declared by the directors of the Corporation out of the moneys of the Corporation properly applicable to the payment of dividends, the amount of which the directors, in their absolute discretion, may from time to time or at any time determine. The directors may declare and pay dividends on the Special Shares to the exclusion of any other class or classes of shares.

3.   Redemption

The Corporation may, upon giving notice as hereinafter provided in paragraph (a)5, redeem at any time the whole or from time to time any part of the then outstanding Special Shares on payment for each share to be redeemed of the Redemption Price as set out in paragraph (a)7 hereof, together with all declared and unpaid non-cumulative dividends thereon.

4.   Retraction

A holder of Special Shares may, upon giving notice as hereinafter provided in paragraph (a)6, require the Corporation to redeem the whole or from time to time any part of the Special Shares held by such holder at the Redemption Price as set out in paragraph (a)7 hereof, together with all declared and unpaid non-cumulative dividends thereon.

5.   Manner of Redemption by Corporation

In the case of redemption of Special Shares under the provisions of paragraph (a)3 herein, unless waived in writing by a registered holder of Special Shares, the Corporation shall at least ten (10) days before the date specified for redemption, mail, to each person who at the date of mailing is a registered holder of Special Shares to be redeemed, a notice in writing of the intention of the Corporation to redeem such Special Shares. Such notice shall be mailed, postage prepaid, addressed to each such holder at the address of such holder as it appears on the books of the Corporation or in the event of the address of any

FIGURE 3.5 CONTINUED

such shareholder not so appearing, then to the last known address of such shareholder; provided, however, that accidental failure to give any such notice to one or more of such shareholders shall not affect the validity of such redemption. Such notice shall set out the Redemption Price and the date on which redemption is to take place, and if only part of the shares held by the person to whom it is addressed is to be redeemed, the number thereof so to be redeemed. On or after the date so specified for redemption, the Corporation shall pay or cause to be paid to or to the order of the registered holders of the Special Shares to be redeemed the amount payable in accordance with paragraph (a)3 on presentation and surrender, at the registered office of the Corporation or any other place designated in such notice, of the certificate representing the Special Shares called for redemption. If only a part of the shares represented by any certificate be redeemed, a new certificate for the balance shall be issued at the expense of the Corporation. From and after the dates specified in any such notice, the Special Shares called for redemption shall cease to be entitled to dividends and the holders thereof shall not be entitled to exercise any of the rights of shareholders in respect thereof unless payment of the amount payable in accordance with paragraph (a)3 shall not be made upon presentation of certificates in accordance with the foregoing provisions, in which case the rights of the shareholders shall remain unaffected. The Corporation shall have the right, at any time after the mailing of notice of its intention to redeem any Special Shares, to deposit the amount payable in accordance with paragraph (a)3 in respect of the shares so called for redemption, or of such of the said shares represented by certificates which have not at the date of such deposit been surrendered by the holders thereof in connection with such redemption, to a special account at any chartered bank or trust company in Canada named in such notice. Such amount shall be paid without interest to or to the order of the respective holders of such Special Shares called for redemption, upon presentation and surrender to such bank or trust company of the certificates representing the shares and, upon such deposit being made or upon the date specified for redemption in the notice, whichever is the later, the Special Shares in respect whereof such deposit shall have been made shall be redeemed, and the rights of the holders thereof after such deposit or such redemption date, as the case may be, shall be limited to receiving without interest their proportionate part of the total amount so deposited against presentation and surrender of the said certificates.

6.   Manner of Redemption by Holder

In the case of a redemption pursuant to paragraph (a)4 herein, a holder of Special Shares shall be entitled to require the Corporation to redeem, at any time or times, all or any of the Special Shares registered in the name of such holder on the books of the Corporation, by tendering to the Corporation at its registered office a share certificate or certificates representing the Special Shares which the registered holder desires to have the Corporation redeem, together with, unless waived by the Corporation, a request in writing specifying

6.1   that the registered holder desires to have the Special Shares represented by such certificate or certificates redeemed by the Corporation; and

6.2   the business day (in this paragraph referred to as the "Redemption Date") on which the holder desires to have the Corporation redeem such Special Shares.

Requests in writing shall specify a Redemption Date which shall not be less than ten (10) days after the day on which the request in writing is given to the Corporation. Upon receipt of a share certificate or certificates representing the Special Shares which the registered holder desires to have the Corporation redeem, together with such a request,

FIGURE 3.5 CONTINUED

the Corporation shall on or before the Redemption Date redeem such Special Shares by paying to such registered holder for each such share an amount equal to the Redemption Price as set out in paragraph (a)7 plus all declared and unpaid non-cumulative dividends thereon. Such payment shall be made by cheque payable at par at any branch of the Corporation's bankers in Canada. The said Special Shares shall be redeemed on the Redemption Date and from and after the Redemption Date such shares shall cease to be entitled to dividends, and the holders thereof shall not be entitled to exercise any of the rights of the holders of Special Shares in respect thereof unless payment of the amount payable as aforesaid is not made on the Redemption Date, in which event the rights of the holders of the said shares shall remain unaffected.

7.   **Redemption Price**

7.1   Subject to paragraph (a)7.3 hereof, the price (the "Redemption Price") payable by the Corporation in respect of each Special Share upon the liquidation, dissolution or winding-up of the Corporation, or for each Special Share purchased for cancellation or redeemed by the Corporation (at its option or at the option of the holder of Special Shares) shall be $1.00 per share;

7.2   provided that if at any time the Canada Revenue Agency or any other taxing authority shall assert by assessment, reassessment or otherwise, that the fair market value of the assets transferred to the Corporation in exchange for the Special Shares minus the value of any other consideration received therefor divided by the number of shares issued in exchange for such consideration was other than $1.00 per share (the "Share Consideration") then with respect to all redemptions or purchases for cancellation or payments as aforesaid, the fair market value of the Share Consideration shall be increased or decreased, *nunc pro tunc*, to an amount equal to:

7.2.1   such amount as may be agreed by the taxing authority, the Corporation and the holders of all of the Special Shares to have been the fair market value of the Share Consideration on the date of issue of the Special Shares; or

7.2.2   in the absence of such agreement, such amount as may be determined by a court having jurisdiction in the matter, if any, (after all appeal rights have been exhausted or all time for appeal has expired without appeal having been taken) to be the fair market value of the Share Consideration on the date of issuance of the Special Shares.

7.3   In the event that an adjustment to the fair market value of the Share Consideration is made pursuant to paragraph (a)7.2 hereof, the Redemption Price shall be adjusted to an amount equal to the fair market value of the Share Consideration as so determined, and all necessary transfers, cancellations, issuances or payments shall be made to effect such adjustment.

7.4   In the event that the Redemption Price is increased pursuant to subparagraph (a)7.3 hereof following a redemption or purchase for cancellation or otherwise of a Special Share or following the payment of a dividend on a Special Share, the Corporation shall pay to the holder of

FIGURE 3.5 CONTINUED

such share that was so previously redeemed or purchased for cancellation or on which a dividend was so previously paid, to reflect an increase in the Redemption Price or to reflect an additional dividend, as the case may be, an amount equal to the aggregate of:

7.4.1 such amount as is required to ensure that such holder will have received the amount which such holder would have been entitled to receive if the said increase had been made prior to such redemption or purchase for cancellation or otherwise or such payment of dividend, as the case may be, and

7.4.2 interest at the prescribed rate as defined in Regulation 4301(c) to the *Income Tax Act* (Canada) on the amount described in subparagraph (a)7.4.1 hereof computed from the date of the redemption or purchase for cancellation or otherwise or the date of payment of such previous dividend, as the case may be, up to and including the date of such payment by the Corporation.

7.5 In the event that the Redemption Price is decreased pursuant to subparagraph (a)7.3 hereof following a redemption or purchase for cancellation or otherwise of a Special Share or following the payment of a dividend on a Special Share, the holder of such share that was so previously redeemed or purchased for cancellation or on which a dividend was so previously paid shall be liable to pay to the Corporation, to reflect a reduction of the Redemption Price or dividend previously paid per such Special Share, as the case may be, an amount equal to the aggregate of:

7.5.1 such amount as is necessary to reduce the amount which such holder has theretofore so received to the amount which such holder would have been entitled to receive if the said reduction had been made prior to such redemption or purchase for cancellation or otherwise or such payment of dividend, as the case may be, and

7.5.2 interest at the prescribed rate as defined in Regulation 4301(c) to the *Income Tax Act* (Canada) on the amount described in subparagraph (a)7.5.1 hereof, computed from the date of the redemption or purchase for cancellation or otherwise or the date of payment of such dividend, as the case may be, up to and including the date of such payment by such holder.

7.6 Notwithstanding the redemption or purchase for cancellation of the Special Shares, the rights and obligations of the shareholders tendering for redemption and of the Corporation shall continue, with respect only to the adjustment of the Redemption Price and for no other purpose whatsoever.

8. Dissolution

In the event of the liquidation, dissolution or winding-up of the Corporation, whether voluntary or involuntary, or other distribution of assets of the Corporation among its shareholders for the purpose of winding up its affairs, the holders of the Special Shares shall be entitled to receive from the property and assets of the Corporation an amount per share equal to the Redemption Price as set out in paragraph (a)7 herein, together with all declared and unpaid non-cumulative dividends thereon, before any amount shall be paid or any property or assets of the Corporation shall be distributed to the holders of the

FIGURE 3.5   CONTINUED

Common Shares or any other class ranking junior to the Special Shares. After payment to the holders of the Special Shares of the amounts so payable to them as provided above, they shall not be entitled to share in any further distribution of the property or assets of the Corporation.

COMMON SHARES

(b)   the Common Shares shall have attached thereto the following rights, privileges, restrictions and conditions:

1.   Voting

The holders of the Common Shares shall be entitled to receive notice of and to attend and shall be entitled to one (1) vote at any meeting of the shareholders of the Corporation for each Common Share held, except meetings at which only holders of a specified class of shares are entitled to vote.

2.   Dividends

Subject to paragraph (b)4, the holders of the Common Shares shall be entitled to receive non-cumulative dividends if, as and when the directors shall in their discretion declare dividends on the Common Shares and pay the same. The directors may declare and pay dividends on the Common Shares to the exclusion of any other class or classes of shares.

3.   Dissolution

Subject to the rights of the holders of shares ranking prior to or on a parity with the Common Shares, the holders of the Common Shares shall be entitled to receive the remaining property of the Corporation in the event of any liquidation, dissolution or winding-up of the Corporation, whether voluntary or involuntary, or other distribution of assets of the Corporation among its shareholders for the purpose of winding up its affairs.

4.   Non-Impairment

The Corporation shall not declare or pay any dividends on the Common Shares of the Corporation nor purchase, including by way of redemption, any of the Common Shares if such dividend or purchase would result in the Corporation having insufficient net assets to redeem any issued and outstanding Special Shares or to pay the redemption price upon dissolution in respect of any issued and outstanding Special Shares.

FIGURE 3.5 CONTINUED

ITA S. 85 ELECTION FORM T2057

Canada Customs and Revenue Agency **Agence des douanes et du revenu du Canada**

ELECTION ON DISPOSITION OF PROPERTY BY A TAXPAYER TO A TAXABLE CANADIAN CORPORATION

- For use by a taxpayer and a taxable Canadian corporation to jointly elect under subsection 85(1) where the taxpayer has disposed of eligible property within the meaning of subsection 85(1.1) to the corporation and has received as consideration shares of any class in that corporation.
- File one completed copy of the election and related schedules (if any) as follows:
  - 1 - a) one copy by the transferor, or
    - b) two or more copies if two or more transferors elect regarding the transfer of the same property (co-ownership), or two or more members of the same partnership elect for the transfer of their partnership interests. In these situations, one transferor designated for the purpose should file simultaneously one copy for each transferor, together with a list of all transferors electing. This list should contain the address and Social insurance number or Business Number of each transferor;
  - 2 - on or before the **earlier date** on which any one of the parties to the election is required to file an income tax return for the taxation year in which the transaction occurred, taking into consideration any election under subsection 99(2) (due date);
  - 3 - at the tax centre where the transferor's income tax return is normally filed. Where two or more co-owners or members of a partnership referred to above elect, the elections will be processed in bulk and should be filed at the tax centre of the transferee; and
  - 4 - separate from any tax returns. You may put it in the same envelope with a return, but do not insert it in or attach it to the return.
- Sections and subsections referred to on this form are from the *Income Tax Act*.

Do not use this area

Name of taxpayer (transferor) (print)	Social insurance number or Business Number
Address	Postal code
Taxation year of taxpayer for the period from — Year Month Day — to — Year Month Day	Tax services office

Name of co-owner(s), if any (if more than one, attach schedule giving similar details) (print)	Social insurance number
Address	Postal code — Tax services office

Name of corporation (transferee) (print)	Business Number
Address	Postal code
Taxation year of corporation for the period from — Year Month Day — to — Year Month Day	Tax services office
Name of person to contact for additional information	Area code — Telephone number

Penalty for late-filed and amended elections

An election that is filed after its due date is subject to a late-filing penalty. Form T2057 can be filed within 3 years after its due date if an estimate of the penalty is paid at the time of filing. Form T2057 can also be amended or filed after the 3-year period, but in these situations, a written explanation of the reason for why the election is amended or late-filed must be attached for consideration by the Minister and an estimate of the applicable penalty must be paid at the time of submission.

Calculation of late-filing penalty:

Fair market value of property transferred . . . . _____

Less: agreed amount . . . . _____

Difference . . . . _____ A

Amount A _____ x 1/4 x 1% x N* . . . . = _____ B

$100 x N* . . . . = _____ C

*N represents the sum of each month or each part of a month in the period from the due date to the actual filing date. Amount C cannot exceed $8,000.

Late-filing penalty is the lesser of B and C above . . . . _____

Make cheque or money order payable to the Receiver General. Specify "T2057" on the remittance and, to ensure proper credit, indicate the name and social insurance number of the taxpayer, or Business Number if a corporation.

Unpaid amounts including late-filing penalties are subject to daily compound interest, at a prescribed rate.

Do not use this area

Amount enclosed _____

T2057 (05)   (Français ci-joint)   Page 1 of 3   Canada

FIGURE 3.5 CONTINUED

Information required

On the following page, list, describe, and state the fair market value of transferred properties. The description and fair market value of the consideration received has to be shown opposite the related property transferred. Where the transferred property is a partnership interest, attach a schedule of the calculation of the adjusted cost base. If space on the form is insufficient, attach schedules giving similar details. You have to designate the order of disposition of each depreciable property. With this election you do not have to file the following materials: schedules supporting this designation, documentation relating to the responses to the questions below, and a brief summary of the method of evaluating the fair market value of each property transferred. However you have to keep them as the Canada Revenue Agency may ask to see them at a later date.

1 - Is there a written agreement relating to this transfer? .... ☐ yes ☐ no

2 - Does a price adjustment clause apply to any of the properties? (See the Interpretation Bulletin IT-169 for details.) .... ☐ yes ☐ no

3 - Do any persons other than the taxpayer own or control directly or indirectly any shares of any class of the transferree? .... ☐ yes ☐ no

4 - Does a non-arm's length rollover exist between 2 or more corporations? .... ☐ yes ☐ no

   a) Have all or substantially all (90% or more) of all the properties of the corporation(s) been transferred to the transferee corporation? .... ☐ yes ☐ no

5 - Is the taxpayer a non-resident of Canada? .... ☐ yes ☐ no

6 - Are any of the properties transferred capital properties? .... ☐ yes ☐ no

   If *yes,*

   a) have they been owned continuously since Valuation-Day (V-Day)? .... ☐ yes ☐ no
   b) have they been acquired after V-Day in a transaction considered not to be at arm's length? .... ☐ yes ☐ no

   c) since V-Day, has the taxpayer or any person from whom shares were acquired in a non-arm's length transaction received any subsection 83(1) dividends for transferred shares? (If *yes,* provide details of amounts and dates received and attach a schedule.) .... ☐ yes ☐ no

7 - Is the agreed amount of any of the transferred properties based on an estimate of fair market value on V-Day? .... ☐ yes ☐ no

   a) If *yes,* does a formal documented V-Day value report exist? .... ☐ yes ☐ no

8 - Has an election under subsection 26(7) of the *Income Tax Application Rules* (Form T2076) been filed by or on behalf of the taxpayer? .... ☐ yes ☐ no

Where shares of the capital stock of a private corporation are included in the property disposed of, provide the following:

Name of corporation (print)	Business Number	Paid-up capital of shares transferred

Description of shares received

Number of shares transferor received	Class of shares	Redemption value per share	Paid-up capital	Voting or non-voting	Are shares retractable? *
					☐ yes ☐ no
					☐ yes ☐ no
					☐ yes ☐ no
					☐ yes ☐ no
					☐ yes ☐ no

* Retractable means redeemable at the option of the holder.

Informative notes

- The rules for section 85 elections are complex. Essential information is contained in Information Circular, IC76-19 and Interpretation Bulletins, IT-169, IT-291, and IT-378.

- Complete all the information areas and answer all questions. If this form is incomplete, the Canada Revenue Agency may consider the election invalid, and subsequent submissions may be subject to a late-filing penalty.

- If the agreed amount exceeds the adjusted cost base of the property in the election, you must report the difference as a capital gain, as income or a combination of both, whichever applies.

Page 2

FIGURE 3.5 CONCLUDED

Particulars of Eligible Property Disposed of and Consideration Received

Date of sale or transfer of all properties listed below:	Year	Month	Day	Note: For properties sold or transferred on differnet dates, use separate T2057s.

	Property Disposed of			Agreed Amount	Amount to be reported B - A (If > 0 see Note 4)	Consideration Received		Fair Market Value of Total Consideration
	Description	Elected Amount Limits*				Non-share	Share	
		Fair Market Value	A		B	Description	Number and Class	
Capital Property Excluding Depreciable Property	(Brief legal)	$	(See Note 1) $	$	$			$
Depreciable Property	(Description and prescribed Class)		(See Note 2)					
Eligible Capital Property	(Kind)		(See Note 3)					
Inventory Excluding Real Property	(Kind)		(Cost Amount)					
Resource Property	(Brief legal)		NIL					
			NIL					
Security or Debt Obligation Property	(Description)		(Cost Amount)					
Specified Debt Obligation (For financial institutions only)								
Capital Property That is Real Property Owned by a Non-Resident Person								
NISA Fund No. 2								

Note 1: Adjusted cost base (which is subject to adjustment per section 53).

Note 2: The lesser of undepreciated capital cost of all property of the class and the cost of the property.

Note 3: The lesser of 4/3 x cumulative eligible capital and the cost of the property. (New rules will apply on subsequent dispositions of eligible capital property occurring after December 20, 2002).

Note 4: This amount is to be reported either as a capital gain or as income, whichever applies. Also, in the case of depreciable property or eligible capital property, a portion of the amount may have to be reported as a capital gain while another portion may have to be reported as income.

*Refer to current Interpretation Bulletin IT-291 for more information on eligible property and an explanation of the limits.

Election and Certification

The taxpayer **and** corporation hereby jointly elect under subsection 85(1) in respect of the property specified, and certify that the information given in this election, and in any documents attached, is to the best of their knowledge, correct and complete.

_____ **and** _____ _____
Signature of Transferor, of **Authorized Officer** or Authorized Person*   Signature of **Authorized Officer** of Transferee   Date

* Attach a copy of authorizing agreement

Printed in Canada   Page 3

CHAPTER 4

Purchase and sale of a privately held business

Richard D. Leblanc, Miller Thomson LLP

CHAPTER OVERVIEW

This chapter discusses the legal considerations and steps involved in the purchase and sale of a privately held business. In particular, it describes the role of the lawyer in performing legal due diligence and negotiating the agreement between the parties; explains the distinction between a purchase and sale of shares and a purchase and sale of assets; and reviews the documentation requirements and specific legal issues relevant to each form of transaction. All stages of the transaction are discussed, including the letter of intent, due diligence, the agreement of purchase and sale, closing, post-closing matters, and reporting at the conclusion of the transaction.

CHAPTER OBJECTIVES

After completing this chapter, you should be able to:

1. Identify all the steps involved in a typical purchase and sale of shares or assets.
2. Distinguish between a purchase and sale of shares and a purchase and sale of assets and describe the considerations relevant to each.
3. Describe appropriate legal due diligence procedures relating to the purchase of a business.
4. Discuss the specific legal issues that arise in a purchase and sale transaction.
5. Describe the documentation required in a share or asset deal.
6. Identify closing and reporting procedures.

INTRODUCTION

Commercial lawyers are frequently retained to advise on the purchase or sale of an existing business. While the experienced practitioner may view such transactions as routine in nature, each deal engages a broad range of legal and business considerations that must be carefully reviewed and addressed by the legal adviser. The issues encountered, although often quite similar from one transaction to the next, will vary according to the particularities of the target business and the specific agreement between the parties.

In particular, a client may have a business objective that may not be obvious to you. For example, in purchasing a manufacturing enterprise, it may not be the operating business but rather a specific patent or tax loss that the client wants to obtain. Always determine at the beginning the client's business objective for the purchase or sale.

The legal adviser must properly advise the client in respect of the particular legal and business issues to enable the client to assess the business risk of a proposed transaction, to determine the value of the business conveyed, and, ultimately, to ensure the legal effect of the transaction.

Given the variety of issues confronting the practitioner, proper organization and communication between the members of an acquisition team are of paramount importance. Accordingly, each member of a team must be clear about his or her role in the transaction and should be familiar with the typical chronology of an asset or share purchase transaction. The team members should also be aware of the type of deal — that is, whether it involves a purchase of shares or assets — and the specific requirements arising therefrom. Finally, each team member should have a copy of a closing agenda, listing documents and procedures required to complete the transaction. This document should serve as a kind of road map for the transaction, allowing the legal team to track the progress of document preparation and performance of closing conditions.

OVERVIEW OF THE STEPS IN THE DEAL

This section discusses the chronology and significance of each of the steps in a typical purchase and sale transaction. While the timing and formality of each of the steps outlined below will vary according to the specific attributes of a given deal, the outline generally represents the order of events that the members of the legal team can anticipate in most purchase and sale transactions.

Letter of intent

When the acquisition of a business is contemplated, the owner and a prospective purchaser will make preliminary contact and, sooner or later, will negotiate and agree upon the essential elements of the proposed transaction. Quite often, this verbal or "back of the envelope" sketch of the deal describes the value (that is, the business assets or shares) to be acquired by the purchaser and an estimate of the price to be paid to the vendor. At this stage, the parties may wish to further formalize the status of their negotiations by preparing and executing a **letter of intent** (also known as a memorandum of understanding or term sheet). A letter of intent

letter of intent
non-binding letter or memorandum that sets out in writing the essential elements of a proposed transaction; also known as a memorandum of understanding or term sheet

simply confirms in writing the basic terms agreed upon and asserts the will of the parties to continue their discussions; it is usually not intended to constitute a legally binding contract between the parties. Letters of intent should explicitly state that no binding agreement exists between the parties until the negotiation and execution of a formal purchase and sale agreement.

Involvement of counsel

At some point, the parties will involve their legal advisers in the proposed transaction. The initial contact may occur early in the negotiations, or only after a deal has been struck in principle and a letter of intent has been agreed upon and signed. The early involvement of counsel is useful to assist in structuring the transaction and to ensure that the expectations of the parties are realistic and achievable from a legal perspective. In any event, counsel are usually contacted once the main points of the deal have been settled, when due diligence and the drafting of more detailed documentation can begin.

Due diligence

As discussed in chapter 2, due diligence is the conduct of an extensive review of the target business. It usually precedes the conclusion of a formal agreement of purchase and sale. The purpose of the review is to permit the purchaser to make a reasonably accurate assessment of the value of the business and its existing and potential liabilities. The due diligence process can be lengthy and extremely complex, involving the purchaser's financial, business, and legal advisers, and often requiring the input of specialists in other areas as well, such as taxation, pensions, insurance, and environmental issues. The legal adviser's role in this process is often limited to reviewing the target enterprise's constating documents, assessing the legal effect of key agreements, and assisting the client in determining the potential legal exposure of the target enterprise in matters such as employment obligations, intellectual property, litigation, and environmental issues. The conduct of due diligence in an asset or share purchase transaction will be explored in greater detail below.

Drafting and executing the purchase and sale agreement

When counsel initially become involved, the parties may seek advice about the appropriate method of transferring ownership of the business. A business may be acquired in one of two ways: (1) by a purchase of the majority of the voting shares of a corporation or (2) by a purchase of the assets used to operate the business. A more detailed discussion of the considerations informing this choice is set out below. This decision will determine whether the principal document will be an asset purchase agreement or a share purchase agreement.

On completion of negotiations between the parties, counsel can proceed with preparing the agreement. Essentially, an agreement of purchase and sale sets out the parties to the transaction, the assets or shares to be purchased and sold, the consideration to be given in exchange, the representations and warranties made by each of the parties, the effective date of the transaction, and any other conditions of closing. Once the document has been signed, the parties are legally bound by its terms.

Preparation of documents

Quite often, the effective date, or the closing, of the transaction occurs well after the execution of the purchase and sale agreement. This is often the case where the transaction is conditional upon obtaining consents, licences, regulatory approvals, or financing, or where the purchase agreement has been signed pending the satisfactory conclusion of the due diligence review and the confirmation of certain representations made by the vendor. Whether the effective date is to be the date of execution of the agreement or a later date, counsel are responsible for preparing all the documentation required to properly evidence the transaction and ensure its legal effect. The forms of documentation will be discussed in detail below, but include generally:

- documents that transfer (or convey) the shares or assets sold;
- documents that support the corporate authority of the parties to proceed with the transaction;
- ancillary agreements, such as non-competition and consulting agreements;
- documentation evidencing compliance with statutory and third-party contractual requirements;
- legal opinions.

Closing

Closing is the procedure whereby all actions necessary to give effect to the transaction and the conveyance of shares or assets are performed. As indicated above, the closing, or the effective date, of the transaction may occur upon the execution of the purchase agreement and all other necessary documentation. Alternatively, closing may occur weeks or months after the execution of the purchase agreement by consent of the parties in order to give the parties sufficient time to satisfy all conditions of closing. This period, beginning on the date of entering into a binding purchase and sale agreement and ending on the actual date of closing, may be referred to in the agreement as the **interim period**, during which time the business is operated at the vendor's risk. Legal counsel will often advise the purchaser to obtain written assurances — usually in the form of representations and warranties contained in the purchase agreement — that the vendor will operate the business in a manner that will not erode its value during the interim period. The purchaser often requests that financial statements for this interim period be prepared and provided to the purchaser within two or three months after closing. The purchaser and its advisers will examine these statements to ensure that the financial representations and warranties made by the vendor are accurate to the date of closing. If they are not, an adjustment to the purchase price may result.

interim period
period of time, beginning on the date of execution of a share or asset purchase and sale agreement and expiring on the date of closing, during which a business continues to operate at the vendor's risk until the conditions of closing are fully satisfied and the transfer can occur

Post-closing matters and registration

Upon the signing of all the required documents and the payment of the purchase price, the transaction takes effect and the shares or assets conveyed become the property of the purchaser. Nonetheless, a number of matters often remain to be dealt with by counsel after the closing. Depending on the nature of the transaction, these may include:

- calculation and payment of any purchase price adjustments,
- filing of notification required under corporate statutes,
- filing of tax election forms,
- organization of the acquiring corporation,
- delivery of notices to customers and other third parties.

Several registrations may also need to be performed. In addition to corporate filings relating to changes of corporate names, directors, and officers, or the head office address of an acquired corporation, these may include:

- motor vehicle registrations,
- real property registrations,
- registrations under the relevant personal property security legislation,
- intellectual property registrations.

Reporting to the client

Shortly after closing, legal counsel will be expected to organize the closing documentation and to deliver it to the client for its records. The closing records are usually collected together in three-ring or cerlox binders, and form the closing books. These can range from one to a dozen or more volumes, depending upon the size and complexity of the transaction.

NEGOTIATING THE DEAL AND STRUCTURING THE TRANSACTION

Share versus asset transaction

Early in the negotiation process, the vendor and the purchaser must decide whether the transaction will take the form of an asset or a share transaction. Essentially, in an asset purchase transaction, the purchaser buys the assets of the vendor that are used in operating the target business. The purchaser does not, however, acquire the vendor entity itself. In a share purchase transaction, the purchaser buys the entity operating the business, usually a corporation, from the owners or principals. In acquiring the shares, the purchaser becomes the owner of both the entity and its underlying assets and liabilities.

As this chapter will show, the form of transaction that is chosen has significant ramifications in terms of the complexity of the purchase and sale, the scope of the due diligence to be performed, and, most importantly, the tax consequences to the purchaser and the vendor. The various considerations that will influence the parties' decision are outlined below.

General concerns and preferences

PRACTICAL CONSIDERATIONS

There are several practical distinctions between a purchase of the shares of a corporation from its shareholders and a purchase of some or all of the corporation's operating assets. Notwithstanding the classical preference of the vendor for a share deal (the reasons for which are discussed below), a purchase of assets may be suitable where the target business is a division of the vendor. In such a case, it would not be economic to convey either the shares of the entire corporation or non-divisional assets. Accordingly, the vendor and the purchaser may agree to simply "carve out" specific assets of the target business.

The practical advantages of this approach are manifold and include the following:

- the transaction costs will (at least in principle) be lower;
- redundant assets will not be acquired;
- the purchaser may not be required to retain employees of the target business;
- employee benefit plans may not need to be transferred from the vendor; and,
- most importantly, the purchaser will limit its risk to the liabilities attached to the purchased assets.

The latter advantage does not arise in a share purchase, where the purchaser acquires the corporation and its assets along with all of its attendant and contingent liabilities.

In addition to these practical considerations, the respective preferences of the vendor and the purchaser for a share or an asset sale will be influenced by the tax consequences in each case, as outlined below.[1]

MAIN TAX CONCERNS

Each party will want to keep the tax costs to the least amount possible. Since the vendor is accepting consideration in exchange for its property at the date of closing, it will be concerned with its tax exposure in the year of the divestiture. The purchaser, however, will be acquiring a going concern and will therefore wish to structure the transaction so as to reduce its tax liabilities or those of the acquired corporation in the years following the acquisition. The discussion that follows elaborates the tax considerations that need to be analyzed by the vendor and the purchaser in deciding how to structure the deal.

Vendor

As noted above, the vendor's classical preference is for a sale of shares. Historically, the profit realized by a shareholder on a sale of shares (the capital gain) was not taxable; however, the capital gain provisions in the *Income Tax Act* (Canada) (ITA) have since undergone several amendments. Under the current legislation, 50 percent of any capital gain realized on a share sale must be included in the shareholder's income for tax purposes. Nonetheless, a sale of shares may provide a significant tax benefit to the vendor where an asset sale could result in profits from the sale of inventory or recapture of capital cost allowance on the sale of depreciable property. The ITA requires 100 percent of the latter amounts to be included in the vendor's income for tax purposes.

In addition, capital gains of up to $500,000 from the sale of "qualified small business corporation shares" are exempt from tax (ITA ss. 110.6(1), (2.1)). This exemption is restricted to individuals selling the shares of a Canadian-controlled private corporation of which substantially all of the assets are used to carry on an active business in Canada.[2]

A vendor will also prefer a share sale to avoid double taxation of the proceeds received from an asset sale. In a share transaction, the proceeds are paid to the selling shareholders, who are then taxed on any gain or loss realized, based on the price for which they originally acquired the shares. In an asset deal, at the first level of taxation, the corporation is taxed on the proceeds from the sale of assets; at the second level, the shareholders are taxed when the corporation distributes the proceeds in the form of dividends.

Purchaser

The purchaser is concerned with the income tax treatment of the acquired business in the years following the closing. Specifically, the purchaser will be interested in maximizing available deductions against income from the newly acquired business in each taxation year following the purchase. This motive underlies the purchaser's classical preference for an asset deal.

In addition to the possibility of "cherry picking" — that is, selecting desired assets and excluding unwanted assets and liabilities from the purchased business — the purchaser may enjoy deductions against income of the business in respect of capital cost allowance (that is, depreciation) and cumulative eligible capital amounts. The availability of these deductions will depend upon the original tax cost of the assets acquired and the **allocation** of the purchase price to the various classes of assets conveyed to the purchaser (discussed below).

allocation
assignment of a portion of the purchase price to each of the various classes of assets in an asset purchase transaction; affects the calculation of taxable income under the ITA for the parties to the transaction; allocation is as agreed upon by the parties

ALLOCATION OF PURCHASE PRICE IN AN ASSET SALE

Should the parties choose to proceed with an asset deal, they must decide how the purchase price is to be allocated to each class of assets. The various classes of assets in a typical transaction are discussed in a later section of this chapter. The allocation of the purchase price will affect the calculation of taxable income under the ITA for the respective parties to the transaction. The vendor and the purchaser will usually have different preferences, which must be negotiated before the signing of the purchase and sale agreement.

The vendor will prefer to allocate the greatest portion of the purchase price to goodwill and non-depreciable capital property, such as land. As previously discussed, only 50 percent of any capital gain from these assets will be included in the vendor's income for tax purposes. Conversely, the purchaser will prefer to allocate more of the purchase price to inventory and depreciable capital property. Depreciation and losses can be deducted from higher prices in these assets to reduce any income generated by the acquired business.

OTHER TAX CONSIDERATIONS

There are many additional tax considerations that must be taken into account when structuring a purchase and sale transaction. The following summary lists some of the tax consequences of a share or an asset sale that can reverse the traditional preference of the vendor or the purchaser.

Vendor — Tax advantages of an asset sale

- use of accrued non-capital or net capital losses to offset income or gain from the sale
- reduced capital gain on asset sale versus share sale where the tax cost of the assets is greater than the adjusted cost base of the shares
- preferential taxation of proceeds and gains from the sale of property where the vendor qualifies for the small business rate

Purchaser — Tax advantages of a share sale

- use of non-capital loss carryforwards (subject to certain restrictions in the ITA) to reduce future taxable income of the acquired business (note: unused capital losses expire at the time of acquisition)
- realization of deemed losses on acquisition where the fair market value of certain assets is lower than their undepreciated capital cost
- preservation of current capital cost allowance (depreciation) rates where these are high for certain assets of the business

Ultimately, the relative weight of such tax considerations in influencing the vendor's and the purchaser's preferences will depend on the circumstances of the particular situation. (Note that the aforementioned tax advantages are considered by the author to be the typical advantages that may be anticipated by a vendor and a purchaser in a conventional purchase and sale transaction. A more detailed description of the various ITA sections and the effect of their overlaps is beyond the scope of this chapter.)

STATUTORY OBLIGATIONS ARISING ON THE PURCHASE AND SALE OF A BUSINESS

In addition to compliance with filing requirements under the applicable corporate statutes, various obligations arise under other federal and provincial legislation when a purchase and sale of a business occurs. These will depend on the nature of the transaction and the circumstances of the business. The more common statutory requirements are discussed below.

Goods and services tax

The goods and services tax (GST) is a federal tax imposed, at a current rate of 7 percent, on "taxable supplies" of goods and services sold in the course of a commercial activity. The administration of this tax is provided for in part IX of the *Excise Tax Act* (ETA).

Under the ETA, the vendor of a taxable supply has the obligation to collect GST from the purchaser and remit it to the Canada Revenue Agency (CRA). A purchaser who is a registrant for GST purposes may be entitled to an input tax credit in respect of such payment of tax, which may be claimed against the amount of GST due on filing of the purchaser's return.

Property and services provided on a commercial basis may be categorized as "taxable supplies" or "exempt supplies" for the purposes of the ETA. Equity securities, or shares, constitute financial instruments and are considered exempt supplies for the purposes of the ETA. Consequently, no GST is collectible from a purchaser in a share purchase transaction.

Care must be taken to fully examine the GST implications in an asset purchase transaction. While certain assets, such as accounts receivable and goodwill, may be exempt from GST, most of the other classes of property (inventory, equipment, land, and leases of real property) constitute taxable supplies and are subject to GST. However, for certain asset sale transactions, assuming that both parties are GST registrants, the vendor and the purchaser may jointly elect to be relieved from their GST obligations under s. 167 of the ETA. Section 167 provides generally that where the purchaser is acquiring all or substantially all of the assets of the vendor necessary for it to carry on its business, and the joint election is made, the purchaser is relieved from the payment of GST, and the vendor is relieved from the obligation to collect and remit GST. The election is filed using Form GST44 (available online at http://www.cra-arc.gc.ca). The form must be filed by the purchaser with its return for the GST reporting period in which the transaction occurred.

Retail sales tax

In any asset purchase, the parties must review the applicable retail sales tax legislation of the jurisdiction of the vendor. Retail sales tax is a provincial tax paid by the purchaser (the end user) and collected by the vendor (the supplier) of tangible personal property such as tables, chairs, desks, and personal computers. Exemptions from tax are usually available for inventory and raw materials (which will generally be used in further processing and are not destined for the final consumer). In a typical asset purchase transaction, office equipment, motor vehicles, and office supplies are types of property for which retail sales tax will be payable.

In Ontario, s. 6(1) of the *Retail Sales Tax Act* (Ontario) (RSTA) provides that where there is a sale in bulk of assets to which the *Bulk Sales Act* applies, the vendor must first obtain a clearance certificate from the Retail Sales Tax Branch of the Ontario Ministry of Finance. This certificate confirms that all RST collectible or payable by the vendor has been paid or that the vendor has entered into an arrangement satisfactory to the minister for the payment of such tax. It is the purchaser's obligation under the RSTA to obtain a duplicate copy of this certificate. In the absence of the ministry's confirmation, the purchaser will be liable for any unpaid RST owed by the vendor.

Land transfer tax

Where the property to be conveyed in an asset sale includes land including any buildings, estates, options, leasehold interests, and fixtures, provincial land transfer tax will be payable by the purchaser in proportion to the amount of the purchase price allocated to such land and other property, if any.

Competition Act

The *Competition Act* (in this section, "the CA") is a federal statute that aims to regulate competitive business practices and mergers for the maximum benefit of the Canadian economy and Canadian consumers. Section 91 of the CA defines a merger as follows:

> "[M]erger" means the acquisition or establishment, direct or indirect, by one or more persons, whether by purchase or lease of shares or assets, by amalgamation or by combination or otherwise, of control over or significant interest in the whole or part of a business of a competitor, supplier, customer or other person.

Accordingly, this definition encompasses both share purchase and asset purchase transactions.

A merger, as defined, may be:

1. subject to review by the Competition Tribunal ("the tribunal") upon application by the commissioner of competition ("the commissioner") within three years from the date of substantial completion of the merger (a "reviewable transaction"); or

2. subject to prenotification requirements, whereby notice of the intended purchase must be given to the commissioner prior to the completion of the transaction (a "notifiable transaction").

The requirements under the CA for each type of transaction are described below.

REVIEWABLE TRANSACTIONS

Section 92 in part VIII of the CA provides that, upon application by the commissioner that a merger or proposed merger substantially prevents or lessens, or is likely to substantially prevent or lessen, competition in a trade, industry, or profession, among its sources of supply, or among its distribution outlets, the tribunal may:

1. in the case of a completed merger:
   a. order that the merger be dissolved;
   b. order the disposition of assets or shares designated by the tribunal;
   c. in addition to or in lieu of the above action, take any other action with the consent of the person subject to the order and the commissioner; or

2. in the case of a proposed merger:
   a. order that the merger not proceed;
   b. order that part of the merger not proceed;
   c. in addition to or in lieu of the above, in the event that the merger or part thereof proceeds, impose such prohibitions as necessary to ensure that the merger does not prevent or lessen competition substantially, or with the consent of the person subject to the order and the commissioner, order the person to take any other action.

The tribunal must consider several factors in determining whether the merger prevents or lessens competition. These factors are set out in s. 93 of the CA and include:

1. the extent to which foreign products or competitors provide or are likely to provide effective competition to the merging business;

2. whether the business or part of the business of a party to the merger has failed or is likely to fail;

3. the extent to which acceptable substitutes for products supplied by the parties to the merger are available;

4. any barriers to entry into a market;

5. the extent to which effective competition remains or would remain in a market that is or would be affected by the merger;

6. any likelihood that the merger or proposed merger will or would result in the removal of a vigorous and effective competitor;

7. the nature and extent of change and innovation in a relevant market; and

8. any other factor that is relevant to competition in a market that is or would be affected by the merger or proposed merger.

In deciding whether a merger prevents or lessens competition, the tribunal may not rely solely on evidence of concentration of market share (CA s. 92(2)).

Section 95 of the CA provides that the tribunal shall not make an order under s. 92 in respect of unincorporated joint ventures. A merger or proposed merger is exempt from an order of the tribunal where the merger has brought about or is likely to bring about gains in efficiency that will be greater than and will offset the effects of any prevention or lessening of competition resulting from the merger (CA s. 96).

To avoid the negative ramifications of an order under s. 92, s. 102 of the CA provides that the parties may apply to the commissioner for an **advance ruling certificate** (sometimes referred to as an "ARC"). The commissioner has the obligation to consider the application as expeditiously as possible (CA s. 102(2)). An advance ruling certificate is binding upon the commissioner and alleviates the possibility of an order under s. 92. Provided that the transaction to which the certificate relates is completed within one year from the issuance of the certificate, the commissioner may not apply to the tribunal under s. 92 on the basis of the same information upon which the original certificate was based (CA s. 103). The parties to a purchase and sale will often obtain an advance ruling certificate as a condition of closing where the proposed transaction may be near the review thresholds of the CA or may otherwise be perceived to prevent or lessen competition.

> **advance ruling certificate**
> certificate issued by the commissioner of competition confirming that a proposed purchase of a business does not contravene the provisions of the *Competition Act*

In analyzing a transaction to determine whether a proposed merger would have the effect of preventing or lessening competition, counsel should be familiar with the Merger Enforcement Guidelines of the Director of Investigation and Research. While the guidelines are expressly stated to be non-binding, they represent the enforcement approach taken by the Bureau of Competition Policy.

NOTIFIABLE TRANSACTIONS

Under ss. 108-119 and 123-124 of the CA, prenotification is mandatory for certain proposed mergers that meet specified thresholds relating to the size of the parties and the value of the transaction. The first threshold is met where the parties and their affiliates combined have assets in Canada in excess of $400 million or annual gross sales revenues in excess of $400 million (CA s. 109). Once this test is satisfied, the second test must be considered. It will be met in any of the following instances (CA s. 110):

1. where the value of assets of a target operating business in Canada or the sales revenue generated from or into Canada from such assets exceeds $35 million;

2. where the value of shares of a corporation carrying on an operating business and the corporation's aggregate assets in Canada or the gross sales revenue generated in or from Canada from such assets exceeds $35 million, and:

   a. in the case of shares of a public company, the acquiror and its affiliates would acquire more than 20 percent of the voting shares of the corporation, or more than 50 percent of the voting shares of the corporation where the acquiror and its affiliates previously owned more than 20 percent of the voting shares; or

   b. in the case of shares of a private company, the acquiror and its affiliates would acquire more than 35 percent of the voting shares of the corporation, or more than 50 percent of the voting shares of the corporation where the acquiror and its affiliates previously owned more than 20 percent of the voting shares;

3. where, in the case of a proposed amalgamation of two or more businesses, one of which carries on an operating business, the aggregate value of the assets in Canada of the amalgamated corporation or the gross revenue from sales in or from Canada would exceed $70 million; or

4. where, as a result of a proposed amalgamation, the aggregate value of assets or the gross revenue from sales in Canada of unincorporated entities carrying on business would exceed $35 million.

Section 113 of the CA exempts from the prenotification requirement transactions between affiliates, transactions for which an advance ruling certificate has been issued, and such other classes of transactions as may be prescribed. In addition to these general exemptions, there are a number of specific exemptions (CA s. 111), including:

1. an acquisition of real property or goods in the ordinary course of business;

2. an acquisition of voting shares solely for the purpose of underwriting the shares;

3. an acquisition of voting shares or assets that would result from a gift, intestate succession, or testamentary disposition;

4. an acquisition of collateral or receivables, or an acquisition resulting from a foreclosure or default or forming part of a debt workout made by a creditor; and

5. an acquisition of a Canadian resource property.

Once the prenotification information required under s. 114 of the CA has been delivered to the commissioner, and receipt has been acknowledged, the parties must wait 14 days in the case of short-form information and 42 days in the case of long-form information before completing the transaction (CA s. 123).

Investment Canada Act

The *Investment Canada Act* (in this section, "the ICA") is a federal statute that regulates the scope of foreign investment in Canada. All investments involving the establishment of a new Canadian business or a direct or indirect acquisition of control of an existing Canadian business by a "non-Canadian" (ICA s. 11) fall within the purview of the Act. A non-Canadian includes any entity that is not controlled or beneficially owned by Canadians. The legislation divides such investments into two categories — notifiable investments and reviewable investments — described below.

NOTIFIABLE INVESTMENTS

Essentially, in every case where an investment grants control of a Canadian business to a non-Canadian, notification in the prescribed form must be sent to the Director of Investments (in this section, "the Director") at any time prior to the implementation of the investment or within 30 days thereafter (ICA ss. 11(b), 12). On receipt of proper notification, the Director is required to issue a certificate confirming the date on which the completed notice was received and advising the non-Canadian either that the investment is unequivocally non-reviewable or that the investment is non-reviewable after the expiry of 21 days from the date notice was received (ICA s. 13).

The notification form is available online at http://investcan.ic.gc.ca, or may be obtained by writing to:

Industry Canada
Director of Investments
235 Queen Street, 3rd Floor East, Room 301B
PO Box 2800, Station "D"
Ottawa, Ontario K1P 6A5

REVIEWABLE INVESTMENTS

Only investments that exceed certain threshold tests relating to the size of the entities are subject to review by the Director and constitute reviewable transactions (ICA s. 14). Generally, an investment by a non-Canadian, other than an investor that is resident in a World Trade Organization (WTO) country, will be reviewable:

1. where the investor acquires direct control of an existing Canadian business with assets valued at more than $5 million (ICA s. 14(3)), or

2. where the investor acquires indirect control (that is, acquisition of a foreign parent of a Canadian subsidiary) of a Canadian business and:

    a. the assets of the business are valued at more than $50 million (ICA s. 14(4)), or

    b. the Canadian assets acquired constitute more than 50 percent of the total assets of the entities being acquired and the Canadian entity has assets of $5 million or more.

Where the investor is a WTO member, a direct investment will not be reviewable, subject to exceptions listed below, unless the value of the target entity's assets exceeds the value calculated each year in accordance with s. 14.1 of the ICA and published in the *Canada Gazette*. The threshold value for 2005 is $250 million. An indirect investment by a WTO member will be reviewable only where the Canadian assets constitute more than 50 percent of the value of the transaction (ICA s. 14.1(1)). Notwithstanding the above, s. 14.1(5) of the ICA provides that a WTO investor will be subject to the lower $5 million/$50 million limits where the existing Canadian business:

1. engages in the production of uranium and owns an interest in a producing uranium property in Canada,

2. provides any financial service,

3. provides any transportation service, or

4. is a cultural business.

Section 17 of the ICA requires that, in respect of reviewable investments, the non-Canadian making the investment shall file an application with the Director in the prescribed form. A copy of this form is available at the Investment Canada Web site provided above. The application must be filed prior to the implementation of the investment (ICA s. 17(2)(a)) unless a special exemption has been granted by the Director in writing. Such an exemption may be forthcoming where delay in the implementation of the investment would impose undue hardship on the investor.

The application will be reviewed by the Director to determine whether the investment is likely to be of net benefit to Canada (ICA s. 21). Section 20 of the ICA sets out the following factors to be taken into account in making this assessment:

1. the effect on:

   a. the level of economic activity in Canada,

   b. employment,

   c. resource processing,

   d. the utilization of parts and services produced in Canada, and

   e. exports from Canada;

2. the degree and significance of participation by Canadians in the Canadian business or new Canadian business in any industry or industries in Canada;

3. the effect of the investment on productivity, industrial efficiency, technological development, product innovation, and product variety in Canada;

4. the effect of the investment on competition within any industry in Canada;

5. the compatibility of the investment with national industrial, economic, and cultural policies; and

6. the contribution of the investment to Canada's ability to compete in world markets.

Under s. 21 of the ICA, the Director must review the application within 45 days (subject to possible extension) and send a notice to the applicant either approving or denying the application. In the event that the application is denied, the applicant has the right to make representations in person or by agent and to submit undertakings within 30 days of receiving the notice from the Director. Where an application has been denied, the investor is prohibited from making the contemplated investment; or, if it is implemented, the investor must divest itself of control of the Canadian business so acquired (ICA s. 24).

The review process focuses on the assessment factors set out in s. 20 of the ICA and listed above. To assist the review, the investor is required to provide annual reports or financial statements of its three most recent fiscal years, including both balance sheets and income statements. The investor must describe its business and the business of the target entity. Copies of the three most recent annual reports or financial statements of the target entity must be included, as well as an assessment of the value of its Canadian assets. The most critical element of the application is the requirement to provide the investor's plans for the Canadian business as compared with the target's current operations. The plans must be drafted to address the assessment factors in s. 20 with a view to demonstrating that the investment is likely to result in a net benefit to Canada. The investor should specifically emphasize issues of employment; additional investment; utilization of Canadian resources, parts, services, and suppliers; the extent of Canadian participation in the business; change in productivity in the business; changes and improvements in the nature of the service; and international competitiveness. Industry Canada recommends that applicants provide as much detail as possible and provide three-year projections for the Canadian business for employment, sales, exports, capital expenditures, and (where relevant) research and development expenditures. Industry Canada also recommends that the applicant provide three copies of the information plus one copy for each province in which the Canadian business is carried on, in order to expedite the review process.

Bulk sales legislation

The *Bulk Sales Act* (in this section, "the BSA") is an Ontario statute that protects creditors from the improvident effects of a sale of a debtor's assets. The BSA applies to sales of "stock in bulk" out of the usual course of business (ss. 1, 2), which in practice includes nearly all asset transactions involving the sale of a business. Failure to comply with the BSA could result in the transaction being nullified or could result in the purchaser being liable to unpaid creditors for the vendor's debts.

There are three ways to comply with the statute:

1. The vendor may obtain an **exemption order** from the court upon providing affidavit or other evidence indicating that the sale is advantageous to the vendor and will not impair its ability to pay its creditors in full (BSA s. 3). These orders are hard to obtain, as the court must be satisfied that after the sale, the vendor is still able to pay all of its creditors.

2. The purchaser may obtain from the vendor a statement verified by affidavit setting out the secured and unsecured creditors of the vendor and the amounts due to each of them (BSA s. 4). Prior to receiving such statement, the purchaser may pay a deposit equal to up to 10 percent of the purchase price. The balance of the purchase price is due only when at least one of the following conditions has been satisfied:

    a. the statement of creditors does not disclose claims by either the unsecured or secured trade creditors in excess of $2,500;

    b. the statement indicates that all claims of secured and unsecured creditors have been paid in full; or

exemption order
a court order that may be obtained by a vendor granting an exemption from the requirements of the *Bulk Sales Act* where it is demonstrated that the sale in bulk will not prejudice the creditors of the vendor

c. adequate provision has been made for the payment of all creditors and those creditors are to be paid forthwith upon completion of the sale, unless a creditor has waived its claim in the appropriate form (BSA s. 8(1)).

Within five days of the completion of the sale, the purchaser must file in the court office in each county where the stock in bulk is located, an affidavit setting out particulars of the sale and including copies of the vendor's statement and any creditor waivers (BSA s. 11).

3. The purchaser may pay the purchase price to a trustee. The purchaser will acquire the assets upon delivery by the vendor to the purchaser of consents from 60 percent of the unsecured creditors of the vendor with claims in excess of $50 and upon delivery to all of the vendor's secured and unsecured creditors of notice in the prescribed form (BSA s. 8(2)).

Securities legislation

Securities laws are investor protection statutes that generally require issuers or traders of securities to provide prospectus-level disclosure to certain purchasers of securities. A prospectus is a document that sets out information about an issuer and its securities sufficient to permit an investor to make an informed decision about a prospective investment. In Ontario, the issuance and the trading of securities are governed by the *Securities Act* (in this section, "the SA").

In the context of this discussion, the SA generally will not apply to asset purchase transactions. However, it will apply to:

1. transactions involving the issuance of shares as consideration and
2. transactions involving the purchase and sale of a "control block" of shares.

A control block is a quantity of shares held by a person or group sufficient to materially affect the control of the issuer, and is deemed to be 20 percent of the issued voting shares (SA s. 1(1), definition of "distribution").

Section 53(1) of the SA requires that where a distribution is to be made in a transaction described in (1) or (2) above, the vendor must issue a prospectus in respect of the proposed distribution unless an exemption from this requirement is specifically provided under the SA. The SA provides for two principal exemptions from the prospectus requirement: the "closely held issuer" exemption and the "accredited investor" exemption. These exemptions are set out in Ontario Securities Commission (OCS) rule 45-501. Legal counsel for each of the purchaser and the vendor will need to ensure that any issuance of shares or sale of shares resulting in a change of control falls within one of the enumerated exemptions.

- *Closely held issuer exemption.* A closely held issuer is an issuer of shares whose shares are subject to restrictions on transfer requiring the approval of the shareholders or directors, and whose outstanding securities are beneficially owned, directly or indirectly, by not more than 35 persons or companies (OSC rule 45-501, s. 1.1). Under the exemption, a closely held issuer may raise an aggregate of up to $3 million in any number of financings, and the holder of shares in a closely held issuer may transfer its shares regardless of a purchaser's financial resources or level of sophistication.[3] To qualify for the exemption, the vendor shall not have paid or incurred selling or promotional expenses in connection with the trade, and no promoter of the issuer shall have acted as a promoter of any other issuer that issued a security in reliance upon the exemption within the 12 months preceding the trade (OSC rule 45-501, s. 2.1(1)(c)). An information statement reasonably similar to Form 45-501 F3 must be provided to a purchaser at least four days prior to the date of the trade unless following the trade the issuer will have not more than five beneficial shareholders (OSC rule 45-501, s. 2.1(2)).

- *Accredited investor exemption.* "Accredited investors" are investors who are deemed to have sufficient financial acumen, resources, and sophistication to make a trade without the statutory need for prospectus-level disclosure. Such investors include, generally, banks and other financial institutions; governmental authorities; certain pension funds; registered charities; individuals who exceed certain high net-worth and income thresholds; investors that are related to an officer, director, or promoter of the issuer; promoters of the issuer; certain mutual funds; and companies, limited partnerships, limited liability partnerships, trusts, or estates with net assets of at least $5 million (OSC rule 45-501, s. 1.1).

While these two exemptions constitute a general restatement of the rules applicable in Ontario, legal counsel should always seek specialized securities advice in relation to each jurisdiction in which distributions of securities are made.

THE DUE DILIGENCE PROCESS

As discussed in chapter 2, the purpose of the due diligence process is to ensure that a purchaser takes good title to valuable property with little or no risk of being subjected to a material legal liability or adverse claim that could significantly undermine the value of the purchased business.

In the purchase or sale of a business, legal due diligence is one component of the broader financial and operational assessment of the value of a going concern. The financial due diligence conducted by the purchaser's accountants or other financial advisers will often provide the purchaser with the necessary hard data from which a purchase price will be formulated. The operational review, often conducted by the purchaser itself, involves comprehensive market analysis; physical inspection of the business premises; interviews with key personnel; study of systems and procedures; review of employee matters; review of marketing, distribution, and supply arrangements, and an analysis of the target's administration.[4]

What to look for in reviewing existing contracts

The searches described above will be supplemented by a comprehensive review of the target's commercial contracts. Specific attention must be paid to the following:

1. Is the vendor or target corporation a proper party to the contract?

2. Is the contract in full force and effect, is it in breach, or has it expired?

3. Does the contract contain specific bars to assignment to a purchaser by the vendor, or does change of control of the vendor's shares trigger termination of the contract?

4. Does the contract require notices to be delivered upon assignment?

5. Does the contract bind successors and assigns?

6. Is performance or payment under the contract contingent upon the occurrence of specific events?

7. Do the contracts create specific material liabilities for the subject corporation?

8. In the case of employment contracts, will the purchaser be assuming onerous termination pay obligations?

What to look for in the minute book review

In an asset or share purchase transaction, a full legal audit of the underlying business must be conducted. In the case of a share deal, the minute books of the target company must be carefully reviewed. In addition, a full corporate review must be performed, which will include the vendor, the target company in the case of a share sale, and the assets to be acquired. The searches required in the corporate review are described in chapter 2.

When reviewing the minute books, including the constating documents, resolutions, and registers of the corporation, specific attention must be paid to the following:

1. ensuring that the corporation and its subsidiaries are duly incorporated and organized;

2. confirming authorized, allotted, and issued capital;

3. reviewing the share attributes and any limitations on the shares or respecting the transfer of shares;

4. reviewing any amendments in share capital, other amendments, redemptions, dividends, purchases, or reclassifications;

5. reviewing the existence of stock option or employee purchase plans;

6. reviewing the existence of debentures and warrants;

7. reviewing the proper approval of material contracts;

8. reviewing the existence of shareholder agreements;

9. ensuring that the particulars of the articles, bylaws, and minutes are consistent with the requirements of the governing legislation;

10. ensuring that directors and officers have been validly elected and appointed, that proper notice was delivered to directors and shareholders prior to each meeting, and that quorum was obtained at each meeting at which business was transacted;

11. ensuring that corporate actions, such as amalgamations and continuances, were all validly effected in accordance with the relevant legislation; and

12. discovering the existence of litigation, disputes, or any material fact that may be relevant to the due diligence process.

Types of searches to conduct and the consequences of registration

The legal due diligence process is often initiated with the ordering of searches. By interpreting such searches, legal counsel will be in a position to advise the client on a range of matters, include the following:

1. the corporate existence and status of an opposing party or target corporation (corporate registry searches);

2. any material liens, charges, or encumbrances against the real or personal property of the target business (searches under the *Personal Property Security Act* (Ontario) [PPSA] and the federal *Bank Act*; ships' registry, land titles, rolling stock, intellectual property, Quebec hypothec, and land registry office searches);

3. the existence of any bankruptcy proceedings, executions, or litigation against a vendor of assets or the target corporation (bankruptcy, land registry, and court registry searches);

4. title to real property, intellectual property, and certain personal property (land titles and registry office searches, Canadian Intellectual Property Office searches, and ships' port of registry searches);

5. the existence of outstanding tax liabilities (CRA searches and RST).

These and the multitude of additional searches that may be performed are described in greater detail in chapter 2.

Employee considerations

The due diligence process will involve a detailed human resources audit of the target business. In addition to operational considerations such as the productivity, seniority, and skill level of the workforce, the parties will need to quantify the hard costs of terminating and assuming employees in connection with the purchase or sale. The purchaser will also need to assess any actual or contingent liabilities, such as lawsuits, orders, grievances, or termination pay obligations in connection with a proposed purchase. The depth of this analysis will depend upon the size of the vendor, the number of employees, and the precise nature of the sale. Specialized counsel should always be consulted to advise on employment law concerns, especially where the workforce is unionized and where the vendor sponsors pension or benefit programs on behalf of its employees. The following summary outlines the main concerns of the purchaser in a typical transaction:

1. *Jurisdiction of employees.* While the rights of most employees are governed by the legislation of the province in which they are employed, certain employment relationships are governed by federal employment and labour relations laws. Employment standards, including the statutory rights, of employees of businesses that fall under federal jurisdiction (such as banking, aeronautics, shipping, and interprovincial transportation and communications) are set out in the *Canada Labour Code*.[5] The equivalent legislation in Ontario is the *Employment Standards Act, 2000* (ESA).

2. *Termination and severance obligations.* Where all or part of a business is sold and the purchaser retains an employee of the vendor, the individual's employment is deemed not to have been terminated (ESA s. 9(1)). Accordingly, in an asset sale, a purchaser that prefers to retain the vendor's employees will inherit the employees without interruption in their seniority or length of employment. The direct ramification is that the purchaser and not the vendor will be liable for the costs of any termination of transferred employees

following the closing. Liability for termination pay may arise upon termination in the following circumstances:

a. pursuant to a contract of employment;

b. as damages for wrongful dismissal by operation of the common law; or

c. under the employment standards legislation of the relevant jurisdiction.

Damages for wrongful dismissal under the common law can be quite onerous; they are determined as a function of an employee's position, years of service, age, ability to find equivalent employment, and conduct during service. Under s. 57 of the ESA, employees who have been employed for longer than three months are generally entitled to 1 week of notice or pay in lieu thereof for each complete year of service. Where 50 or more employees are terminated in the same 4-week period, notice periods varying from 8 to 16 weeks are imposed pursuant to the regulations (OR 288/01, s. 3(1)). Section 63(1) of the ESA also imposes an obligation on employers to pay severance pay to employees whose employment is "severed," as defined.

Accordingly, the parties will often apportion the liabilities that are anticipated upon the sale of assets of a business. The vendor may assume the costs of terminating employees prior to closing. The vendor may also agree to indemnify the purchaser for post-closing termination costs relating to the seniority and years of service that the employee accrued prior to closing. Alternatively, the purchaser may agree to assume all employees subject to an initial trial period during which it determines its personnel requirements. Reasonable termination costs arising during this period are often borne by the vendor or as otherwise agreed by the parties.

In order to accurately assess its potential exposure to such liabilities, the purchaser will require detailed employee lists and records indicating, at a minimum, the employee's position, age, length of service, salary, and any bonus, options, or other benefits. In addition, copies of all employment contracts, consulting agreements, management agreements, severance agreements, and stock option, pension, and employee benefit plans must be obtained and reviewed.

3. *Labour relations.* Section 69(2) of the *Labour Relations Act, 1995* (Ontario) provides that the purchaser of an existing business is bound by any collective agreement in force and by any application for union certification or termination that is before the Labour Relations Board. In addition, s. 69(3) provides that the purchase of a business will not result in any change to a union's authority to act as bargaining agent on behalf of existing employees. Accordingly, appropriate due diligence inquiries must be made to ensure that there is no known union organizational activity among the current employees, that there have been no applications for union certification, and that no collective agreement or accreditation orders exist. Where such agreements or orders exist, the purchaser will need to obtain and review them to understand the ramifications of the collective agreement for the purchased business.

In addition, the purchaser will need to ascertain whether the vendor is the subject of any proceedings:

a. under s. 70 of the *Labour Relations Act, 1995* (Ontario) or s. 94 of the *Canada Labour Code*, including complaints for unfair labour practices; and

b. for any labour-related grievances or arbitrations.

4. *Human rights issues.* In addition to disclosure of any employee litigation, complaints, or grievances as discussed above, the purchaser will require disclosure of such action arising from alleged breach of the provisions of the applicable human rights legislation (for employees of businesses under federal jurisdiction, the *Canadian Human Rights Act*; for employees of employers in Ontario, the *Human Rights Code*).

5. *Pension and benefit plans.* As indicated above, the purchaser will need to obtain copies of all pension and employee benefit plans. Generally, a share purchase does not occasion a change to an existing plan; accordingly, a purchaser of shares will focus on the cost of the existing plan to the business going forward. In an asset purchase, the considerations are manifold and complex, including whether the predecessor plan will be transferred in whole or in part to the acquiring entity or whether a new plan will be formulated. This aspect of due diligence and the related negotiation and drafting of pension-related materials are often accomplished with the assistance of pension and benefit advisers.

6. *Other matters.* The purchaser will want to review the vendor's records to verify that there are no outstanding penalties, prosecutions, orders, or claims under:

a. pay and employment equity legislation (in Ontario, the *Pay Equity Act* and the *Employment Equity Act, 1995*);

b. occupational health and safety legislation of the relevant jurisdiction (the *Canada Labour Code* for enterprises subject to federal jurisdiction; in Ontario, the *Occupational Health and Safety Act*); and

c. the ITA, the *Employment Insurance Act*, the *Canada Pension Plan*, and the *Employer Health Tax Act* (Ontario) to ensure that the vendor has complied with its remittance obligations.

The purchaser will also need to review the accounts, claims history, and records of the vendor with respect to workers' safety legislation in the relevant jurisdiction (in Ontario, the *Workplace Safety and Insurance Act, 1997*). This may be of particular relevance in jurisdictions where (unlike Ontario) the workers' safety authority requires the purchaser of a business to assume the vendor's prior record.

DOCUMENTS REQUIRED FOR AN ASSET PURCHASE AND SALE

The following discussion reviews the forms of documentation typically employed in an asset purchase and sale and the considerations relevant to each.

The closing agenda

As discussed in chapter 1, the closing agenda is simply a list of all the documents and conditions required to complete the transaction. The closing agenda will set out the parties to the transaction, the date and place of pre-closing (if applicable)

conditions of tender
conditions relating to the exchange of consideration due on the closing of a purchase and sale transaction

and closing, the **conditions of tender**, the documentation required to effect the transaction, any additional requirements, such as the delivery of minute books and consideration, and post-closing requirements. The closing agenda is in many ways the "recipe" for the transaction and, when well drafted, provides an invaluable communications and organizational tool. Commonly, the closing agenda will also recite the terms and conditions of the closing, including provision for an escrow closing (described in chapter 1).

Elements of a typical agreement of purchase and sale

The agreement of purchase and sale will set out, at a minimum, the identity of the parties, the nature of the assets to be purchased, the consideration to be paid, the parties' mutual promises to purchase and sell, and the effective date of the transaction. In many asset purchase transactions, the agreement provides for the purchase of all of the business undertaking and any property of the vendor used in connection with the business, and includes (without limitation) a description of the assets to be purchased. These and other elements of the agreement are discussed below.

ASSETS TO BE PURCHASED

Often the assets to be purchased are specifically described in schedules to the agreement. As discussed earlier, the purchaser and the vendor will negotiate the allocation of the purchase price among the various categories of assets. These categories are briefly described in the following summary.

1. *Inventory.* This usually includes all raw materials, work in progress, finished goods, and parts used in the production of manufactured goods. It is not uncommon for the parties to agree to a price based on a physical inventory conducted before or after closing and a related adjustment to the purchase price if necessary. The purchaser should exclude all damaged or obsolete inventories.

2. *Machinery and equipment.* This includes the fixed assets of the business used for production and the general equipment of the vendor. Where such assets are leased, the agreement may provide for assignment of the leases along with the requisite third-party consents. The purchaser should obtain representations and warranties regarding the condition of these assets and should attempt in all cases to identify the assets as accurately as possible.

3. *Real property and leases of real property.* This includes the land and building to be conveyed to the purchaser, or, in the case of leased premises, the leases to be assigned to the purchaser in conjunction with the necessary landlord consents.

4. *Accounts receivable.* These include the book debts and should exclude all accounts that are not collectible. The purchaser may decide not to purchase any of the receivables, or may purchase them at a discount to offset the likelihood of non-collection. A joint election is available under s. 22 of the ITA that permits both the vendor and the purchaser to benefit from neutral tax treatment of the purchased accounts. (The election is made by filing the prescribed form, T2022.) There may be a **post-closing adjustment** for purchased receivables that remain uncollected after a set period for closing.

post-closing adjustment
amendment of the purchase price after closing to account for variation from inventory count, equipment valuation, shareholders' equity, or working capital as set out in the agreement of purchase and sale

5. *Intellectual property.* This includes patents, trademarks, trade secrets, copyrights, business and trade names, Web domain names, and other intellectual property. It may also include licences to use intellectual property owned by third parties, such as computer software. The parties will have to ensure that special rules relating to the effective transfer of title to these assets are complied with and that all licences are properly assignable.

6. *Licences and permits.* These include any licences and permits required to operate the purchased business.

7. *Prepaid expenses.* These may include prepaid rent, insurance premiums, and supply costs paid by the vendor beyond the date of closing.

8. *Goodwill.* Goodwill is the intangible value of a business created by a combination of the business's name, location, customer lists, and reputation. The purchaser will often seek to assume the business identity of the purchased business, relying upon this goodwill to generate future revenue.

The parties may agree to specifically exclude certain assets from the purchased business. Cash, intercompany debt owed to the vendor, and aged accounts receivable are examples of commonly excluded assets.

ASSUMED LIABILITIES

In order to effectively balance risk, the purchaser may specify in the agreement which liabilities it will be assuming in connection with the purchased business. These liabilities may relate to specific contracts, debt obligations, accounts payable, warranty claims, licences and permits, and other liabilities necessary for the functioning of the purchased enterprise.

CONSIDERATION

The agreement will state the form of consideration to be paid in exchange for the assets. The most desirable form of consideration is cash. Other forms of consideration include promissory notes, shares of private or public companies, options, consulting agreements, and "earnouts." Earnouts are mechanisms that calculate future payments on the basis of the purchased entity's performance over an established period of time. Consulting agreements and earnouts are useful to defer payments of the purchase price while providing the vendor with a future income stream and deferred tax liability. Earnouts and other financing alternatives are discussed in chapter 5.

REPRESENTATIONS AND WARRANTIES

The agreement will include representations and warranties — declarations by the parties — affirming, as applicable, the party's authority to transact, the title to the assets, the health of the purchased business, the condition of particular assets, and the status of other circumstances that may materially affect the value of property sold. Breach of a representation or warranty may give rise to a right of damages in favour of the party that relied upon such a representation or warranty to that party's detriment.

It is in the interests of the purchaser to secure strong representations and warranties from the vendor, in order to substantiate and formalize the assumptions upon which the purchase price is based and to quantify the risk of operating the purchased business as a going concern. The vendor, on the other hand, will prefer to provide as few representations and warranties as possible. In respect of risks that are not easily verified, such as the existence of environmental problems, threatened legal proceedings, and market conditions relating to the acquired business, the vendor will often attempt to qualify a related representation by making it "to the best of [the vendor's] knowledge." This type of wordsmithing becomes an exercise in risk allocation because the truth of the representation cannot be demonstrated in a cost-effective manner at the date of closing. The purchaser is well advised to resist accepting such qualification where the purchase price is negotiated in heavy reliance upon the truth of the particular representation or warranty.

As discussed earlier, often the effective date of closing is subsequent to the date of the purchase and sale agreement. In these circumstances, the parties are usually asked to provide a **"bring down" certificate** before the agreement is signed. This is a statement by an authorized officer of the vendor or the purchaser (as the case may be) certifying that the representations and warranties made by that party as of the date of execution of the agreement are still current as at the date of closing.

The parties should also discuss and specify in the agreement the effective duration, or "survival," of representations and warranties. This point is relevant to the ability of a party to bring an action for damages in the event that a representation or warranty is breached. In Ontario, the determination of the survival period has become a great deal more complicated as a result of the enactment of a new limitations statute, the *Limitations Act, 2002* (LA 2002), which came into force on January 1, 2004, replacing the prior *Limitations Act*.

Previously, notwithstanding the existence of statutory limitations provisions, it was common for the parties to effectively set their own limits for the actionability of representations and warranties, by specifying the applicable survival periods in the purchase and sale agreement. Different survival periods were often provided for different representations and warranties. For example, the representations and warranties relating to corporate authority and title might continue in perpetuity; those relating to tax would expire at the end of the applicable tax reassessment limitation period; and those relating to product liability or environmental matters might extend several years from the date of closing, in order to address specific risks inherent in the purchased business. These different survival periods created different outcomes from those that would have resulted from the statutory limitation provisions if the agreement between the parties had been silent. (For example, under the predecessor *Limitations Act*, claims in contract were limited to six years after the cause of action arose.) In effect, the parties could choose to contract out of the limitations statute.

The new Act appears to make this approach unlawful by stating that a limitation period set out in the statute applies notwithstanding any attempt to vary or exclude it (LA 2002 s. 22). Generally, the basic 2-year limitation period provided by the LA 2002 would apply to a breach of representation or warranty, no matter what the parties said in the agreement. However, the LA 2002 also incorporates a concept of discoverability, extending the basic limitation period to a maximum of 15 years, depending upon when the injury caused by the breach ought to have been discovered. Accordingly, a breach of a representation or warranty would appear to be

bring down certificate
certified statement by an officer of the vendor or purchaser confirming that the representations and warranties made at the time of the execution of the purchase agreement are also true and correct at the date of closing

actionable for a minimum of 2 and a maximum of 15 years following the date of closing, depending upon what a court says about objective discoverability of the breach in the particular circumstances. At the time of closing, the parties have no way of knowing what the outcome will be if a particular representation or warranty is breached: Will a court determine that the 2-year period should apply, or will it extend the period, perhaps even to 15 years?

Corporate lawyers, who, along with their clients, desire more certainty than "from two to fifteen years, depending," are struggling to devise methods through which the essentials of the old commercial practice of tailored survival periods can somehow be preserved without offending the new legislation. To (in effect) shorten survival, some suggest that it may be lawful to limit not the right to sue, but only the amount of damages that can be recovered, if a representation or warranty is found to have been breached. Thus, the party with the claim would be entitled only to a nominal sum if an action was brought after the expiry of a fixed period — say, one year following the closing date. To (in effect) lengthen survival, it is suggested that providing separate indemnities — in essence, contractual "insurance policies" — might preserve the actionability of damages for an indefinite period following the closing. For example, the indemnity would be triggered by the suffering of losses, whenever they occur, starting the "limitations clock" on that later date, rather than the date upon which the relevant representation or warranty was breached (that is, the closing date).

The legal reasoning behind these suggested techniques is complex, and it is beyond the scope of this chapter to go into the question in more detail. The important point is that, at the time of writing, there has been no court decision to guide lawyers on whether any suggested method of avoiding the problems posed by the LA 2002 will be enforceable. The courts may decide that all such approaches offend the prohibition in the legislation against varying or excluding the statutory limitation periods. Lawyers are thus left to inform their clients that they will do their best with the agreement, but the survival period for representations and warranties may still be anything from 2 to 15 years, depending upon what a court decides at the time an action is brought.

COVENANTS

Covenants are promises by the parties to perform certain acts, or to refrain from acting in a certain manner, either prior to or following closing. The following are examples of typical covenants:

- to operate the purchased business up to closing in a manner that will preserve the value of the assets;
- to maintain confidentiality;
- to provide access to records;
- to perform such further acts after closing as may be required, including the filing of any tax election forms (for example, pursuant to s. 167 of the ETA or s. 22 of the ITA).

The parties may require that a certificate be provided, similar in form to the bring down certificate referred to above, certifying that all covenants required to be performed prior to closing have been fulfilled.

covenant
promise by a party to an agreement to perform certain acts, or to refrain from acting in a certain manner, either prior to or following closing of the transaction

CONDITIONS OF CLOSING

conditions of closing
terms of the agreement of
purchase and sale that
must be satisfied before
any purchase or sale
transaction can be
completed

Conditions of closing are covenants that are performed on or prior to closing in order to consummate the transfer of the business and assets from the vendor to the purchaser. The failure to perform certain essential covenants, such as the payment of the purchase price or the obtaining of a government ruling, may be fatal to the deal. Certain conditions may be waived by the parties at the time of closing, or the closing can be held in escrow pending satisfaction of the relevant condition. Examples of conditions of closing include:

- negotiation of consulting, management, or employment agreements;
- discharges of security registrations;
- consents to assignments of real and personal property leases;
- consents of suppliers to the transfer of accounts;
- expiry of review periods under the *Competition Act* or the *Investment Canada Act*;
- *Bulk Sales Act* compliance;
- obtaining a clearance certificate under s. 6(1) of the RSTA;
- transfer of employee benefit plans;
- phase I or phase II environmental assessment reports;
- confirmation of non-residency status pursuant to s. 116 of the ITA;
- opinions (discussed below).

NON-COMPETITION AND NON-SOLICITATION AGREEMENTS

When a purchaser acquires a business from a vendor, it may seek assurance that the vendor will not operate a business that competes with the purchaser's newly acquired concern. The parties may negotiate a non-competition agreement that prohibits the vendor corporation or any of its shareholders, directors, officers, or employees from operating a competing business or holding a specified ownership interest in shares of a competing business. The prohibition usually applies to a limited time period and a defined geographic area. The courts have expressed reluctance to give positive effect to non-competition agreements on the basis that they restrict a person's ability to earn a livelihood and are therefore contrary to public policy. In this regard, such agreements must be reasonable having regard to the circumstances, and should be reviewed by a practitioner experienced in such matters.

Non-solicitation agreements are often combined with non-competition agreements. Non-solicitation agreements prohibit the vendor corporation or its agents or principals from soliciting personnel or business from the purchaser's newly acquired business.

Although less common, non-disparagement agreements prohibit specified parties — usually, the vendor and its principals — from openly denigrating the purchaser or the sold business in a manner that may be detrimental to the purchaser or the business.

INDEMNITIES AND REMEDIES

Breach of a representation, warranty, or covenant may give rise to a right to damages under simple contract law. In addition to these common law rights, agreements of purchase and sale will contain specific, and often meticulously drafted, indemnity clauses setting out the specific heads of indemnity, limitations on indemnities, and the procedures for enforcing an indemnity claim. Such indemnities may contain a "basket" or deductible clause setting out the minimum aggregate value of indemnity claims that may be made. This deters frivolous or trivial claims below the specified ***de minimis*** threshold.

de minimis
Latin term meaning "of the least amount"; used in a legal context, for example, to refer to the specified threshold at which a claim for compensation may be made

Conveyancing documents

Several classes of assets are transferred in the purchase of an active business, and an effective form of conveyance needs to be executed in each instance. The documents that are usually required are briefly described below.

- *Personal property.* A bill of sale listing the specific assets sold or a general conveyance of the assets is required to effectively transfer title in personal property. Personal property includes both tangible property, such as equipment, inventory, and motor vehicles, and intangibles, such as intellectual property and accounts receivable. It may be necessary to register a bill of sale in certain jurisdictions.[6] In addition, some special assets require additional transfer documents, such as provincial registration for motor vehicles, ships, or rolling stock; manufacturer's warranties, etc.

- *Personal property leases and licences.* The rights accruing to the vendor under these leases may be transferred by general conveyance or they may be assigned to the purchaser. The validity of such assignments will, however, be a matter of contract, and the assignability of the lease must be verified. At a minimum, notification — and possibly also the lessor's consent — may be required.

- *Real property.* A transfer/deed of land must be filed and registered with the appropriate Land Registry or Land Titles Office.

- *Leases of real property.* An assignment of lease in the correct form accompanied by the landlord's consent is required. This may be required to be registered on title.

- *Accounts receivable.* In addition to the general conveyance, the vendor provides its account debtors with a written direction to forward payments to the purchaser subsequent to the closing date of the sale (s. 53(1) of the *Conveyancing and Law of Property Act* (Ontario)). Additionally, since absolute assignments of accounts receivable constitute security interests under the PPSA, a Form 1C financing statement must be registered against the vendor by the purchaser in respect of uncollected assigned accounts.

- *Intellectual property.* Patents, trademarks, and other intellectual property will be conveyed in the bill of sale or general conveyance. Where such property is a significant component of the purchased assets, the parties should prepare and execute a formal assignment of the property. It will be necessary to register the assignments of patents or trademarks with the Canadian Intellectual Property Office in order to record the correct chain of title on the public register. The parties should be sure to verify local laws for analogous registration requirements in foreign jurisdictions.

Corporate authority

As essential to the agreement as the identity of the purchased assets and the consideration to be paid is the identity and authority of the parties. The identity of the purchaser and the vendor cannot be assumed, and appropriate corporate searches must be conducted to verify existence and capacity. In addition, both the vendor and the purchaser must ensure that all appropriate corporate approvals and authorizations have been obtained. The purchaser will normally require the approval of the board of directors of the corporation authorizing the purchase of assets, the form of documentation, and the execution of the required documents. The vendor must obtain similar board approval as well as a special resolution of the shareholders where it is selling all or substantially all of its property other than in the ordinary course of business (*Canada Business Corporations Act* [CBCA] s. 189(3); *Business Corporations Act* (Ontario) [OBCA] s. 184(3)).

Opinions

Legal opinions are written statements made by legal counsel as to certain matters of law or matters of mixed law and fact that are fundamental to the transaction. Counsel will often be required to opine as to the corporate existence of the client and the proper authorization, execution, delivery, and enforceability of the transactional documentation. In order to be in a position to provide such opinions, legal counsel will rely upon corporate searches and official documents such as **certificates of compliance** (for CBCA corporations) or **certificates of status** (for OBCA corporations) verifying corporate existence. In order to provide opinions as to due authorization and execution, counsel will often prepare and rely upon a certificate of an officer of the client, including:

- certified copies of resolutions authorizing the transaction and the execution of documents, and
- an incumbency certificate, listing all of the incumbent officers and directors of the corporation and signed by those officers who are authorized to execute the purchase and sale documentation.

It is very rare for legal counsel to deliver an unqualified opinion in a transaction. Usually, opinions contain qualifications that have the effect of limiting the breadth of the statements made therein. For example, an opinion as to the enforceability of documents is often subject to applicable bankruptcy laws and the availability of equitable remedies.

Price adjustments

The parties often include a price adjustment mechanism in the agreement to accommodate variances in inventory levels, accounts receivable, equipment value, or working capital. Once these variances are quantified following post-closing review or presentation of interim period financial statements, the purchase price may be adjusted upward or downward in the manner agreed upon. Where such adjustments are anticipated, the purchaser will often hold back a portion of the purchase

certificate of compliance
certificate issued by Industry Canada in respect of a CBCA corporation confirming that the corporation is incorporated and in good standing

certificate of status
certificate issued by the Ontario Ministry of Government Services in respect of an OBCA corporation confirming that the corporation is validly existing

price to be paid to the vendor following closing, subject to setoff for any adjustments. Alternatively, where a portion of the purchase price is paid by promissory note, the parties may agree to adjust the notes post-closing to reflect the amended purchase price.

Post-closing registrations and other matters

In an asset purchase, the following post-closing filings and registrations are often required:

- Where the purchaser is assuming the name of the purchased business, the vendor must file articles of amendment changing its corporate name and should provide a consent to the purchaser to use the business name.

- In the above case, the purchaser should either file articles of amendment to adopt the name of the purchased business or should register the name under the business names legislation of the relevant jurisdiction.

- As indicated earlier, the purchaser must file a financing statement under the PPSA in respect of the purchase of accounts receivable.

- The parties must jointly sign and file election Form GST44 pursuant to s. 167 of the ETA and Form T2022 pursuant to s. 22 of the ITA in respect of accounts receivable, as required.

- The purchaser may wish to register on title a notice of assignment of lease where the lease is already registered.

- The vendor should register under the PPSA any security taken for unpaid portions of the purchase price.

- The purchaser should register assignments of intellectual property, as previously discussed.

- The purchaser must register appropriate bulk sales ownership documentation within five days from the closing date in respect of any purchased motor vehicles.

DOCUMENTS REQUIRED FOR A SHARE PURCHASE AND SALE

Generally, a share purchase is a simpler transaction than an asset purchase. The reason is that the only property being conveyed in a share purchase is the share capital of the target company. Since the individual assets owned by the target company do not change hands, counsel need not focus on the unique transfer and registration requirements of the various asset classes.

Share purchase agreement

Notwithstanding the relative simplicity of the transaction, a share purchase requires the same degree of due diligence and care as an asset purchase. In either case, the purchaser is acquiring an active business and will be equally concerned with the title and condition of the underlying assets, the financial viability of the operation, labour relations, encumbrances against the assets, the absence of litigation, and so forth. Accordingly, the representations and warranties in a share purchase agreement are remarkably similar to those found in an asset purchase agreement. The share purchase agreement may, however, focus more closely on corporate liabilities, which will follow the acquired entity notwithstanding the change in control, such as tax and product liability exposure.

The standard share purchase agreement will also contain representations stating the authorized and issued capital of the target corporation, the ownership of the shares to be transferred, the absence of adverse claims or interests in the shares, and the absence of any agreements, warrants, options, or rights requiring the target corporation to issue from treasury any additional shares to any other party.

The parties to the share purchase agreement include the purchasing entity and the shareholders of the target corporation. Where the shareholders are holding companies, it may be desirable from a purchaser's perspective to add the principals of the holding companies to the share purchase agreement to bind them to the representations and warranties.

Purchase price adjustments on the basis of shareholder's equity calculated after the date of closing from the interim period financial statements are also commonplace.

Share transfer documentation

The conveyancing documentation in a share purchase transaction consists of the following:

stock transfer power of attorney
document granting power of attorney to an individual for the specific purpose of transferring shares

- a **stock transfer power of attorney**, assigning all right, title, and interest in the shares to be acquired ("the subject shares") to the purchaser and appointing an officer of the corporation to transfer the subject shares onto the books and records of the corporation;

- the subject share certificates duly endorsed on the reverse for transfer to the purchaser and surrendered to treasury for cancellation;

- new share certificates issued in the name of the purchaser replacing the cancelled certificates;

- an amended shareholders' register in the minute book of the corporation reflecting the new shareholdings; and

- documentation to terminate or amend any existing shareholder agreement, as needed.

Corporate authority

Both the purchaser and the vendor principals are required to pass board resolutions authorizing the share purchase transaction and approving the form and execution of the accompanying documentation.

Most private companies include share transfer restrictions in their articles that must be complied with. A directors' or shareholders' resolution as required by the articles and authorizing the transfer of the purchased shares must be obtained from the target company's board of directors or shareholders as necessary. In addition, careful regard should be had to the provisions of any existing shareholder agreement respecting the target corporation, especially where the purchaser is purchasing less than 100 percent of the target company's shares.

ITA s. 116 considerations

Section 116 of the ITA imposes upon a purchaser the obligation to withhold a portion of the purchase price from the vendor where the vendor is a "non-resident" of Canada as defined in the Act. In the case of a share transaction, this withholding amounts to 25 percent of the purchase price. Where the vendor does not obtain the requisite clearance from the CRA within the time limits prescribed in the ITA, the purchaser becomes liable to pay the withheld amount to the tax authorities. Accordingly, the purchaser should insist upon obtaining a warranty, certificate, or statutory declaration from the vendor confirming that it is not a "non-resident" of Canada within the meaning of the ITA. Alternatively, the purchaser is not obligated to withhold where the vendor provides a s. 116 certificate (issued by the CRA to the vendor) with a certificate limit equal to the purchase price on closing.

Post-closing registrations

The share register of the purchased corporation must be amended to reflect the new owner, and replacement shares must be issued. Thereafter, new directors must be elected by ordinary resolution of the shareholders. The new directors will then appoint by resolution new officers and new auditors if appropriate. The directors may also, by resolution, change the registered office of the corporation. For a company incorporated under the OBCA, a special resolution of the shareholders is required if the office is moved outside the municipality or geographic township of the current address (OBCA s. 14(4)). Form 1, Notice of Change must be filed within 15 days of the relevant change (*Corporations Information Act* s. 4(1)). Form 6, Notice of Change of Directors must be provided to Industry Canada within 15 days after the change is made (CBCA s. 113). In addition, Form 3, Notice of Change of Registered Office must be filed to report the location of a new head office, also within 15 days of the change (CBCA s. 19(4)).

In the event of a change of name of the corporation, articles of amendment must be filed.

Counsel will often assist in attaining new bank signing authority and current account documentation on behalf of a newly acquired corporation or a corporation formed to acquire assets.

REPORTING TO THE CLIENT

After the closing, the legal team must organize the closing documentation and report the transaction to the client. The closing agenda may be used to prepare a record book index, and the laborious task of identifying and organizing each of the closing documents into tabs in preparation for binding must be completed. This should be performed as soon as possible after the transaction. A reporting letter setting out any limitations on the scope of counsel's advice to the client and containing an exhaustive list of followup matters to be completed, along with a strict delegation of responsibilities, should accompany the record books delivered to the client.

KEY TERMS

advance ruling certificate

allocation

"bring down" certificate

certificate of compliance

certificate of status

conditions of closing

conditions of tender

covenant

de minimis

exemption order

interim period

letter of intent

post-closing adjustment

stock transfer power of attorney

REFERENCES

Statutes, regulations, and rules

Business Corporations Act (Ontario), RSO 1990, c. B.16, as amended.

Bulk Sales Act (Ontario), RSO 1990, c. B.14.

Canada Business Corporations Act, RSC 1985, c. C-44, as amended.

Canada Gazette, vol. 139, no. 7.

Canada Labour Code, RSC 1985, c. L-1.

Canada Pension Plan, RSC 1985, c. C-8, as amended.

Canadian Human Rights Act, RSC 1985, c. H-6.

Competition Act, RSC 1985, c. C-34.

Conveyancing and Law of Property Act (Ontario), RSO 1990, c. C.34.

Corporations Information Act (Ontario), RSO 1990, c. C-39.

Employer Health Tax Act (Ontario), RSO 1990, c. E.11, as amended.

Employment Equity Act, SC 1995, c. 44.

Employment Insurance Act, SC 1996, c. 23.

Employment Standards Act, 2000 (Ontario) (ESA), SO 2000, c. 41, and Ontario Regulation (OR) 288/01.

Excise Tax Act (ETA), RSC 1985, c. E-15, as amended.

Human Rights Code (Ontario), RSO 1990, c. H.19.

Income Tax Act (ITA), RSC 1985, c. 1 (5th Supp.), as amended.

Investment Canada Act, RSC 1985, c. 28 (1st Supp.).

Labour Relations Act, 1995 (Ontario), SO 1995, c. 1, sched. A.

Limitations Act, 2002 (Ontario), SO 2002, c. 24, sched. B.

Occupational Health and Safety Act (Ontario), RSO 1990, c. O.1.

Ontario Securities Commission (OSC) Rule 45-501 — Exempt Distributions.

Pay Equity Act (Ontario), RSO 1990, c. P.7.

Personal Property Security Act (Ontario) (PPSA), RSO 1990, c. P.10, as amended.

Retail Sales Tax Act (Ontario) (RSTA), RSO 1990, c. R.31, as amended.

Securities Act (Ontario), RSO 1990, c. S.5.

Workplace Safety and Insurance Act, 1997 (Ontario), SO 1997, c. 16, sched. A.

Other sources

Albo, Wayne P., Adam Bryk, and Andrew Pigott, *Purchase and Sale of Privately Held Businesses*, 3rd ed. (Toronto: Calcap Corporate Finance Limited, 2000).

Albo, Wayne P., and A. Randal Henderson, *Mergers and Acquisitions of Privately Held Businesses* (Toronto: Canadian Institute of Chartered Accountants, 1987).

Babe, Jennifer, *Sale of a Business*, 5th ed. (Toronto: Butterworths, 2004).

Doherty, Barbara, "Update: Ontario Revamps the Exempt Market — Introducing the 'Closely-Held Issuer' Exemption and the 'Accredited Investor Exemption,'" *eSecurities Notes* (Toronto: Miller Thomson LLP, 2001).

Due Diligence Deskbook, Jonathan M. Vogt, ed. (Vancouver: The Continuing Legal Education Society of British Columbia, 2001).

Gillis, Elizabeth, *Advanced Corporate Legal Procedures* (Toronto: Emond Montgomery, 2004).

NOTES

1. A thorough analysis of the tax considerations is beyond the scope of this chapter. For a more detailed discussion of these issues, see Jennifer Babe, *Sale of a Business*, 5th ed. (Toronto: Butterworths Canada, 2004), 9.020-9.028.
2. For further discussion of the exemption, see Babe, ibid., at 9-4.
3. See Barbara Doherty, "Update: Ontario Revamps the Exempt Market — Introducing the 'Closely-Held Issuer' Exemption and the 'Accredited Investor Exemption,'" *eSecurities Notes* (Toronto: Miller Thomson LLP, 2001).
4. For a comprehensive discussion of pre-acquisition analysis, see Wayne P. Albo and A. Randal Henderson, *Mergers and Acquisitions of Privately Held Businesses* (Toronto: Canadian Institute of Chartered Accountants, 1987), 53-80.
5. See Babe, supra note 1, at 9.230.
6. Ibid., at 9.593.

REVIEW QUESTIONS

1. Briefly explain the difference between a purchase of the assets of a business and a purchase of the shares of a business.

2. Identify the classical preferences of the vendor and the purchaser with respect to the type of transaction used to acquire a business, and explain the reasons for those preferences.

3. Identify one reason why a vendor might prefer an asset sale.

4. Identify one reason why a purchaser might prefer a share purchase.

5. Is GST payable in:
    a. a share purchase transaction;
    b. an asset purchase transaction?

    Who has the obligation to pay the GST? Is any relief available?

6. What document must the purchaser obtain to ensure that the vendor has paid Ontario retail sales tax?

7. What is an advance ruling certificate, and when is it obtained?

8. Explain generally when notification is required under the *Investment Canada Act*.

9. When does the *Bulk Sales Act* (Ontario) apply to a transaction, and how does a purchaser ensure compliance with this Act?

10. Identify three matters to check or verify when reviewing contracts.

11. Identify five matters to review or verify when conducting a minute book review.

12. Name three important employee-related concerns of the purchaser of the assets of a business.

13. What is the difference between a representation and a condition of closing?

14. Name three examples of post-closing registrations.

15. What is the significance of s. 116 of the ITA with respect to the purchase and sale of a business?

CHAPTER 5

Financing the purchase of a privately held business

Tom Tower and Elizabeth Hutchison, Miller Thomson LLP

CHAPTER OVERVIEW

It is often said that once the purchase and sale agreement (and, in particular, the purchase price) has been negotiated, the hard work is over in the sale of a privately held business. However, as earlier chapters have shown, when the agreement is signed, the work is far from over. Chapter 4 dealt, in part, with the documentation requirements for the acquisition component of the transaction. This chapter examines the various financing options available to a purchaser who is unable, or unwilling, to pay the full purchase price in cash. It also explains the procedures and the documentation required to complete the financing arrangements. Although both components (acquisition and financing) are usually worked on simultaneously, the financing arrangements must be completed first, to ensure that the purchaser has the necessary funds available to complete the transaction on the closing date.

CHAPTER OBJECTIVES

After completing this chapter, you should be able to:

1. Describe the financing process and requirements from the onset to the closing of the transaction.
2. Identify the various financing options that may be available and explain the advantages and disadvantages of each.
3. List the due diligence requirements for the financing component of a transaction.
4. Identify basic security documents that are commonly used in financing arrangements.

ALTERNATIVE SOURCES OF FINANCING

Four potential sources of financing will be examined in this chapter:

1. internal financing,
2. vendor take-back financing,
3. bank financing, and
4. equity financing.

It should be kept in mind that these options are not mutually exclusive; in some cases, the purchaser will finance the acquisition from two or more sources. With the possible exception of internal financing, there is no "best" source of financing for all situations. The purchaser, in consultation with its financial and legal advisers, must determine which option or combination of options is the most appropriate, given the purchaser's specific interests, needs, and constraints.

Internal financing

Internal financing usually occurs in a situation where a larger corporation is purchasing a smaller business and the purchaser is able to finance the acquisition out of the revenues from the normal operation of its business. The purchaser is able to raise the funds internally and therefore does not need to seek financing from external sources (such as the vendor, a financial institution, or investors).

Vendor take-back financing

vendor take-back financing
a financing arrangement between the vendor and the purchaser whereby the vendor agrees to defer the payment of a portion of the purchase price until a later time; typically have a three- to five-year term; otherwise, terms vary as determined by the two parties

In a **vendor take-back** (VTB) **financing** arrangement, the purchaser becomes indebted to the vendor by agreeing to pay a portion of the purchase price on closing and the balance at a later date. This form of financing is often used in the purchase of a privately held business when immediate payment of the purchase price is not a principal concern of the vendor. In many cases, the advantage to the vendor in deferring payment of a portion of the purchase price is that the vendor can obtain a higher value for the purchased business. Another advantage of VTB financing is that the vendor can defer part of the income tax payable on any capital gains realized on the sale of the business. The *Income Tax Act* (Canada) allows a vendor to exclude from its income the portion of any proceeds from the sale of a business that is not payable during the year in which the transaction occurs. The vendor will eventually have to recognize the entire gain; however, it will be spread out over more than one year.

VTB financing can also be advantageous to the purchaser. Indeed, where the purchaser is relying heavily on commercial lenders to finance the purchase, a VTB financing arrangement is often necessary to enable the purchaser to contemplate the acquisition of the business. This is due to the fact that financial institutions will rarely finance 100 percent of the purchase price. With VTB financing, the purchaser can supplement its bank financing by, in effect, borrowing from the vendor. VTB financing also acts as an informal insurance mechanism. First, it demonstrates to the purchaser that the vendor has sufficient confidence in the business to expect that it will provide the funds needed for repayment of the outstanding purchase price at a later date. Second, the vendor will be particularly cautious in any representations and warranties that it makes in the purchase and sale agreement, because the purchaser could withhold any outstanding payments in the event of misrepresentation or failure of the vendor to perform the covenants of the contract.

VTB financing arrangements typically have a three- to five-year term; however, there is no unique form of VTB financing. The two parties can draft the arrangement in the terms most advantageous to their needs. For example, the purchaser may or may not be required to pay the vendor interest on the debt. Some VTB financing arrangements provide that the vendor will retain some control over the business until the outstanding purchase price is paid. This can be advantageous for the purchaser, as the vendor's continuing involvement can provide for a smooth transition following the change of ownership.

One form of VTB financing, called **earnout financing**, is particularly beneficial to the purchaser. Earnout financing is an arrangement whereby the purchaser agrees to pay the purchase price (or a portion of it) in the future based on the profitability of the business during a specified period of time following the acquisition. This arrangement provides significant protection to the purchaser in the event that the acquired business proves to be unprofitable. Essentially, the vendor is agreeing to assume the risk of operating the business to the extent of the outstanding portion of the purchase price. Generally, earnout financing is used only when the two parties are unable to agree on the purchase price owing to differing assessments of the future performance of the business.

earnout financing
a type of vendor take-back financing whereby the purchaser of a business will pay the outstanding amount of the purchase price based on the profitability of the business following the sale

Bank financing

Financial institutions (primarily banks) are the most common source of financing for the acquisition of a business. One drawback of bank financing is that the lender often imposes onerous security requirements when it agrees to provide funds to the purchaser of a business. The security that a lender obtains in the borrower's business or assets — that is, the collateral — will be discussed later in this chapter.

There are various forms of bank financing for various purposes. The purchaser (borrower) will usually need to obtain financing from its financial institution for both the acquisition and the future operation of the business. Three types of bank financing that a purchaser may consider are:

1. term debt,
2. traditional operating debt, and
3. mezzanine financing.

The general terms and conditions for each type of loan are described below.

TERM DEBT

A term loan is a loan with a specified maturity date, as opposed to a demand loan, which becomes due at the time the lender demands payment. Term loans are the usual form of financing for business acquisitions. The lender will require that there be sufficient value in the assets of the business being acquired to secure the loan in the event of any default in payment. Following the acquisition, the lender will usually monitor the performance of business to ensure that the assets that have been used to secure the loan maintain their security value. In most circumstances, the lender will be quick to act if the value of the assets decline significantly.

TRADITIONAL OPERATING DEBT

Operating loans are the most common form of financing for the purposes of funding the day-to-day operations of the business (as opposed to financing the purchase of a specific asset). Financial institutions are usually willing to provide operating financing if they are confident in the financial situation of the borrower's existing business (and, when obtained in conjunction with an acquisition, the business that the borrower is acquiring). Unlike term debt, operating loans are usually secured by the inventory and the accounts receivable of the business.

MEZZANINE FINANCING

mezzanine financing
a multilayered financing arrangement in which a borrower obtains funds from more than one lender, resulting in senior and subordinated debt and priority ranking of the lenders' respective interests in the collateral

priority agreement
an agreement between all the participating lenders in a mezzanine financing arrangement, clarifying the ranking of the lenders' respective interests in the collateral

A borrower may wish to obtain financing from more than one lender. Where there are different layers of financing, the first loan is referred to as "senior debt" and the subsequent loan or loans are referred to as "subordinated debt," or **mezzanine financing**.

The key characteristic of mezzanine financing is the subordination of interests in the collateral for the loans. The senior lender's interest ranks ahead of the interests of the mezzanine (or subordinate) lenders. For this reason, the most important document for the lender in such an arrangement is the **priority agreement** between all the lenders. This agreement is carefully and aggressively negotiated to set out clearly the priority of the interests of the lenders (as against each other) in the common collateral. As the security interest for mezzanine financing is subordinated to prior interests, it is a high-risk arrangement for the lender; consequently, the interest rates for these loans are usually higher.

Mezzanine financing is often obtained from public venture capital groups. It is readily available in a very competitive market, where there are a number of financiers willing to invest.

Equity financing

equity financing
a means of raising funds by issuing shares in the capital of the corporation and selling them to investors

Equity financing is quite different from the financing options discussed above. In equity financing, the purchaser raises funds by issuing shares in the capital of the corporation and selling them to investors. Generally, equity financing should be considered only if the existing shareholders of the corporation are willing to give up part of their ownership interest to new investors. In addition, the corporation must be able to demonstrate strong and sustainable growth prospects, as investors will otherwise not be interested in buying shares in the corporation.

Some equity investors (in privately held corporations) will demand a controlling interest in the corporation before making an investment, while others will simply demand that protective rights accompany their investment (through a shareholder agreement). Federal and provincial governments are often willing to make equity investments in companies, but this investment is often modest. Most equity financing for the acquisition of a business is obtained from the same sources as mezzanine financing — that is, public venture capital groups.

STEPS IN FINANCING THE DEAL AND THE NECESSARY DOCUMENTATION

Commitment letters and loan agreements

COMMITMENT LETTERS

When the financing for an acquisition is to be obtained from an external lender, it will usually begin with a letter issued by the lender to the borrower setting out the terms and conditions upon which it is willing to make the loan. The letter will usually include a request for the borrower to sign back the letter to confirm its acceptance. In most cases, counsel to the lender and the borrower do not become involved until the letter has been accepted by the borrower, at which time the lender and the borrower will seek assistance from their respective counsel to implement the transaction legally.

This letter agreement may be referred to by a number of different names, including the "commitment letter," "confirmation letter," "term sheet," or "financial arrangement." In some cases, the letter serves as the formal agreement between the parties with respect to the key business terms and conditions of the loan; in other cases, a separate loan agreement must be signed.

A typical commitment letter includes the following information:

1. the legal name of the borrower,
2. the maximum loan amount,
3. the type and purpose of the loan,
4. the term of the loan (unless it is a demand loan),
5. the calculation of interest,
6. any additional fees that may be charged,
7. a loan repayment schedule,
8. a description of the security for the loan,
9. representations and warranties,
10. covenants, and
11. action to be taken in the event of default.

LOAN AGREEMENTS

Frequently the commitment letter becomes the loan agreement. For example, demand loans generally require only a commitment letter, as the lender can demand to be repaid at any time. For more complex financing arrangements, term loans, or loans of a considerable amount, the lender will usually require that the borrower enter into a more detailed loan agreement (which will supersede the commitment letter) expanding upon the terms and conditions set out in the letter and including extensive covenants, reporting requirements, and various remedies in the event of default.

Public searches and other due diligence

One of the first and most important steps in a financing is the due diligence conducted by the lender and its counsel. In connection with the financing of an acquisition of a business, before the lender agrees to provide the loan, it will usually conduct "business or financial" due diligence, investigating the borrower's existing business and the business to be acquired. In addition, the lender's counsel will conduct "legal" due diligence, obtaining legal information about the borrower and its assets or business, the assets or business being acquired, and whether the latter can legally be transferred to the borrower/purchaser.

As the conduct of due diligence is discussed extensively in chapter 2, it will not be reviewed at length here. Rather, this chapter briefly describes the due diligence necessary for financing an acquisition transaction.

Due diligence searches should be conducted against the borrower/purchaser, any guarantors, and the target corporation (and, in a share purchase transaction, the shareholders of the target corporation). To assist with these searches, the borrower/purchaser should provide the lender's counsel with relevant corporate information and documentation, including:

1. confirmation of the corporate, trade, and business names;

2. a list of the jurisdictions and places of business where the corporation conducts business or has assets (including, in particular, the address of the chief executive office or head office of the corporation);

3. legal descriptions for any real property to be charged (mortgaged);

4. corporate documentation, including articles of incorporation, bylaws, and any unanimous shareholder agreements; and

5. any existing commitments or agreements such as:

   a. real property leases and other specific agreements to be charged;

   b. copies of outstanding security agreements in favour of prior secured creditors (including, for example, any equipment lessors or financiers); and

   c. any other potentially conflicting contracts, agreements, or proceedings.

If due diligence is also to be conducted against an individual (as a personal borrower or guarantor), the lender's counsel should obtain a copy of the individual's birth certificate or certificate of Canadian citizenship to verify his or her legal name for search purposes.

With the information referred to above, the lender's counsel can commence the public searches. There are many searches that must be performed as part of the due diligence process, and several must be performed in more than one jurisdiction. Some of the more important searches are discussed below. Although these are not the only searches that may be necessary, they are the ones that will most frequently need to be performed in completing the due diligence for a financing transaction. A more detailed discussion of these and other searches can be found in chapter 2.

CORPORATE PROFILE SEARCH

A corporate profile search is a public search that must be conducted in the jurisdiction where the corporation is incorporated. It will confirm jurisdiction; all current, former, and predecessor names (French and English); the registered office address; and the names of corporate officers and directors. This search can also supply a certificate of status or compliance to confirm that the corporation is in good standing and up to date in its annual filings under the applicable corporate statute.

PERSONAL PROPERTY SECURITY

A search for possible registrations under the *Personal Property Security Act* (Ontario) (PPSA) is extremely important in a financing transaction. It will reveal all current registrations against the personal property of a corporation or individual. This search is obviously crucial in determining whether any of the assets of the borrower or guarantor are already subject to the security interests of other creditors.

BANK ACT (CANADA), S. 427

A search conducted online at the Canadian Securities Registration System will determine whether any banks have taken a security interest in the inventory of a corporation by filing a Notice of Intention with the Bank of Canada, pursuant to s. 427 of the *Bank Act*.

BANKRUPTCY AND INSOLVENCY ACT (CANADA)

A search can be conducted online to determine whether the corporation or individual is or ever has been bankrupt or subject to any of the provisions of the *Bankruptcy and Insolvency Act*.

BULK SALES LEGISLATION

A search for any bulk sales registered against the corporation should be conducted at the Superior Court of Justice in Ontario *and in any other jurisdiction* where the corporation carries on business. The *Bulk Sales Act* (Ontario) (and similar legislation in other provinces) is intended to protect unsecured creditors of a business from the sale (in bulk) of the assets of the business (other than in the ordinary course of business) without satisfying the corporation's debt to the creditors.

EXECUTION LEGISLATION

A search should be conducted under the *Execution Act* (Ontario) and similar legislation in any other jurisdiction where the corporation carries on business. This search reveals whether any writs of execution or extent, or certificates of lien, have been filed in the sheriff's office against the corporation or individual.

Financing documents

CLOSING AGENDA

While all the necessary due diligence and corporate searches are being completed, a closing agenda should be created. As discussed in chapter 1, this is an essential document that identifies the lender's documentation requirements and that functions, in part, as a checklist to ensure that all the necessary steps are being completed in the financing arrangement. The closing agenda is usually prepared as soon as the commitment letter is received, and it evolves as the transaction proceeds, depending on, among other things, the results of the due diligence process. As we have seen, the closing agenda is not a static document, and it may still be amended even after the closing of the transaction.

For the purposes of the financing component, the closing agenda should include:

- the intended time, date, and location of closing;
- the parties to the transaction (vendor, purchaser, borrower, and lender);
- escrow provisions in the event that the transaction is not completed on the closing date;
- a list of pre-closing documents and delivery dates;
- a description of the financing documentation;
- a list of all guarantors;
- a description of all security and security agreements;
- insurance requirements;
- registration and discharge requirements;
- the payment schedule;
- a list of all officer's certificates, resolutions, and legal opinions; and
- a list of any additional matters that must be dealt with at closing or post-closing.

LOAN DOCUMENTATION

The loan agreement between the lender and the borrower (sometimes referred to as "the credit agreement") is the most important document in the financing of many business acquisitions. Whether it takes the form of a commitment letter or a more extensive, formal loan agreement, it is a necessary element of any financing arrangement where the purchaser is borrowing funds. Other instruments that are used in many financing arrangements include promissory notes, grid notes, and installment notes.

A **promissory note** is often required where the purchaser has obtained financing for the acquisition through an external lender. A promissory note is a signed unconditional promise to pay a certain amount of money to a specified person, to the order of a specified person, or to the bearer. This means that a promissory note is a negotiable instrument; that is, the holder of the note (the lender) can freely assign the debt to another person by a simple endorsement. The note must be signed by the borrower and must set out the exact amount of money to be paid. It should also outline the terms of repayment, including whether the note is redeemable (payable in full) on demand or at a specified future date.

promissory note
a negotiable instrument defined as "a signed unconditional promise to pay a certain amount of money to a specified person, to the order of a specified person or to bearer," often given by the borrower in a financing arrangement with an external lender

A **grid note** has most of the characteristics of a negotiable instrument; however, it does not completely satisfy the specifications as it does not set out the exact sum to be repaid. Instead, grid notes usually specify a maximum level of indebtedness or set out a grid (or schedule) of the amounts of advances made to the borrower by the lender from time to time, and any repayments made by the borrower from time to time. Otherwise, grid notes are similar to other negotiable instruments in that they are assignable and unconditional.

In the context of VTB financing, the notion of a freely assignable negotiable instrument defeats one of the primary incentives for choosing this option. Remember that the purchaser will often want to use VTB financing to ensure that the vendor is honest in its representations and that it will satisfy any covenants agreed upon in the purchase agreement. If a vendor can sell or assign an instrument provided by the purchaser immediately following the sale of the business, the security that the purchaser sought to obtain from the VTB arrangement will no longer be present. To overcome this concern, an **installment note** is frequently used in this type of financing. An installment note is much like a promissory note except that it is non-transferable; consequently, the vendor cannot dispose of or assign its interest in the debt.

SECURITY DOCUMENTATION

As security for the loan, a lender will often take a security interest (or lien) over some or all of the assets of the borrower and/or the guarantor of the loan. The security that will be required for the loan should be generally described in the loan agreement or commitment letter. The types of security that may be required and the related documentation are described below. In all cases, the lender must perform due diligence to confirm that the particular assets given as security have not been assigned, pledged, or otherwise encumbered in favour of another party.

General and specific security agreements

The most common form of security agreement is a **general security agreement**, which gives the lender a broad security interest in all of the present and future property of the borrower. For smaller loans, the lender may agree to take a security interest in specific assets only, through a **specific security agreement**. For example, a lender may require a specific security agreement for motor vehicles, equipment and other machinery, or patents, trademarks, or copyrights that are particularly valuable. While specific security agreements are becoming commonplace, general security agreements remain dominant when dealing with large loans.

Bank Act security

The *Bank Act* contains provisions aimed at promoting the lending of money by banks in exchange for security in the "goods, wares or merchandise" of the borrower. This ***Bank Act* security** is taken pursuant to s. 427 (formerly s. 178). It is security that cannot be arbitrarily demanded by the bank as a condition of the loan; rather, it must be given voluntarily by the borrower. The security interest is created only if it is promised at or before the time that the debt is created. A s. 427 interest cannot be taken for past indebtedness, but it can be taken for acquired property. For *Bank Act* security to be granted, the lender must file a notice of intention with the Bank of Canada's agent in the registration jurisdiction in which the borrower's head office is registered. The filing requirements and the effect of the notice are discussed in more detail below, in the section dealing with registration of security interests.

General assignment of book debt

general assignment of book debt
a security interest in the borrower's accounts receivable

Some financial institutions require that a **general assignment of book debt** be granted to give the lender a security interest in the borrower's accounts receivable (even though this interest may be included in the general security agreement). The terms of the assignment will vary according to the particular circumstances, and the lender will determine whether it wants a general assignment (of all present and future acquired goods) or a specific assignment of particular debts. The borrower's counsel should ascertain that the terms of the assignment are not too broadly worded, to ensure that only relevant collateral is assigned. It is usual for the assignment to provide that, in the event of default, the lender has authority to collect on any debts of the borrower included in the assignment. Most lenders also require that the assignment be registered in all jurisdictions where the borrower does business.

Assignment of insurance

assignment of life insurance
security given to a lender by an assignment of a life insurance policy taken out by a corporate borrower (often known as key man life insurance)

assignment of asset insurance
security given to lender by an assignment of insurance against damage to or theft or loss of assets of the borrower included in the collateral for a loan

Another form of security that a lender may require as a covenant in the loan agreement is over insurance. This can include the **assignment of life insurance** as well as **asset insurance**.

Personal life insurance that is taken as security is often referred to as "key man" life insurance. Many lenders require it in order to protect their interest in the event of the death of a key executive of the borrowing corporation (usually someone without whom the business would collapse). The borrower will take out a life insurance policy and then assign it to the lender, using forms specified for this purpose. In Ontario, the assignment of life insurance is regulated by the provincial *Insurance Act*.

The use of asset insurance as security requires the borrower to maintain insurance coverage to protect the lender in the event of damage to or theft or loss of the assets that have been assigned as collateral for the loan. Asset insurance is assigned when the lender gives the insurer notice of the contract, and the insurer acknowledges this assignment in writing. Once this is completed, the insurance policy should be endorsed to the lender and the insurer should keep the lender updated regarding the status of the policy. Some insurance companies may also require that an assignment form be completed.

Charge or mortgage of land

charge or mortgage of land
an interest in land to which a borrower holds title given to a lender as security for a loan

A security interest in real property is not usually included in the general security agreement. This interest is created by filing a **charge or mortgage of land** on title to a specific parcel of property registered in the borrower's name, granting the lender (the mortgagee) a charge or encumbrance on the property. The lender must perform a land registry search to ensure that the borrower holds free and clear title to the property. The borrower (the mortgagor) remains in possession of the property unless it defaults on the loan, and it retains the right to regain clear title to the property on satisfaction (full repayment) of the debt.

REGISTRATION OF A SECURITY INTEREST IN PERSONAL PROPERTY

A security interest in personal property must be registered in order to protect the lender's priority as a creditor in respect of the security. Currently in Ontario, there are two primary mechanisms for registering a security interest in personal property. The first is provided by the federal *Bank Act* and the second by the PPSA (Ontario). The relationship between the two registration systems remains uncertain, and conflicting claims can arise from the operation of the two statutes. In such cases, the priority of the creditors is determined by common law rules that consider the time at which the respective security interests were granted. It is not uncommon for a bank to file a financing statement pursuant to the PPSA to register the fact that it has obtained a security interest pursuant to s. 427 of the *Bank Act*, although this is not required.

As indicated above, with respect to *Bank Act* security, the lender must file a **notice of intention** with the appropriate agent of the Bank of Canada. The form is provided in the *Registration of Bank Special Security Regulations* (Schedule III). The notice of intention is a simple document that sets out the names of both the borrower and the creditor (the bank) and the mailing address of the party giving the security. The notice must be filed not more than three years and not less than 24 hours before the s. 427 security documents are executed. It must be filed in the registration jurisdiction where the borrower has its principal place of business or residence, and the one filing will suffice for a five-year period. If the secured interest is still in effect after five years, the bank must notify the Bank of Canada; otherwise, it will be cancelled. On filing the notice, the bank retains a right of assignment of property in the event of default by the borrower. This means that the bank can sell any or all of the assigned property to recover the borrower's unpaid debt. If the notice is not filed, the bank will not retain a secured interest with priority over the borrower's subsequent creditors.

The PPSA sets out other procedures for perfecting a security interest in the borrower's personal property (in addition to those specified above in connection with *Bank Act* security). The general priority rules for secured creditors are governed by s. 30 of the PPSA. Section 30 provides that priority will be given to the creditor who has registered its priority interest first by filing a financing statement; however, the rules of priority are complex and there are a number of exceptions to this general rule. The most significant exception is the concept of a **purchase money security interest** (PMSI) in s. 33 of the PPSA. A PMSI is created when a creditor has advanced a loan to finance the purchase of specific inventory or equipment; the borrower's use of the loan for this purpose gives the creditor superpriority over other creditors in respect of the purchased property. Thus, if a bank gave a borrower a loan to purchase a particular piece of equipment or inventory and followed the necessary steps contained in the PPSA to obtain a PMSI, the bank would have priority over all other secured creditors in any claim in respect of such equipment or inventory for which it has provided financing. The reasoning behind this superpriority rule is that the financing arrangement clearly adds to the borrower's pool of assets and that any original secured creditors (with priority by registration) would not have contemplated this collateral when they registered their security interests.

notice of intention
noticed required to be filed with the Bank of Canada in order for a bank to take a s. 427 security interest in the borrower's property

purchase money security interest
an interest giving a lender superpriority over other creditors in respect of assets of the borrower purchased with the borrowed funds

DEALING WITH PRIOR REGISTRATIONS

If any prior registrations are revealed in the public searches, the lender may require the borrower to deal with them in some way, to ensure that its expected priority is established. For example, the lender may require:

- that the registration be discharged entirely, or that it be subordinated and postponed (as discussed below);
- that the secured creditor confirm that it only has an interest in specific assets of the debtor and that it will not use its registration for any other assets of the debtor (by delivering a "non-sheltering letter," also discussed below); or
- that the secured creditor enter into a priority agreement with the lender to clarify their respective priorities.

Discharging security interests under the PPSA

When all of a debtor's obligations to the creditor have been satisfied, any person with an interest in the collateral may demand a discharge of the security interest in accordance with s. 56 of the PPSA. This demand for discharge requires a written notice to be delivered to the secured party asking that a financing change statement be registered pursuant to s. 55.

Discharging security interests under the Bank Act

When all of the borrower's obligations relating to a notice of intention have been satisfied, the borrower may demand that the bank execute and deliver a certificate of release to the Bank of Canada (and file this in the same manner as the notice of intention was filed), confirming that all money due or to become due under the notice of intention has been satisfied, that every security to which the notice of intention relates has been released, and that the notice of intention is therefore discharged.

Subordination agreements

subordination agreement
an agreement between two creditors of the same borrower whereby the creditor that holds the senior debt agrees to subordinate its interest in favour of the second creditor

When a corporation has existing debt and seeks financing from another lender, the new lender may require the creditor that originally had priority in the borrower's collateral to subordinate its interest in favour of the other creditor. This occurs with the creation of a **subordination agreement** between the two creditors in question. Typically, this type of arrangement is found in a situation where the original creditor is related to the borrower and the approval of a loan from an unrelated creditor is conditional upon the subordination of the prior interest. The subordination agreement is the key document governing the priority ranking of interests in the secured property between the two creditors.

Section 50 of the PPSA also provides that where a security interest has been subordinated, a financing change statement may be registered under the PPSA at any time during the period that the subordination is effective to record the subordination (although such a registration is not necessary).

Postponement agreements

postponement agreement
an agreement between two creditors of the same borrower whereby one creditor agrees to postpone repayment of its debt until the borrower has fully satisfied its debt to the second creditor

A **postponement agreement** is similar in effect to a subordination agreement in that it alters the relation between creditors of the same borrower. However, in this case one creditor agrees to postpone repayment of its debt until the borrower has fully repaid its debt to the other creditor. Again, postponement agreements are typically used where the first creditor and the borrower are related parties and the second creditor will advance a loan only if repayment of the first debt is deferred.

Priority agreements

In a situation where the creditor with the prior registration against the debtor is not willing to subordinate its security interest in certain collateral of the debtor, a subsequent lender may require that, as a condition to providing the loan to the debtor, the creditor with priority enter into a priority agreement with the lender, clearly setting out the intention of the two parties as to priority (notwithstanding the order of registration). For example, where the lender is financing specific inventory of the debtor, it may require that the prior registered creditor enter into a priority agreement confirming that, notwithstanding the prior registration, the lender's security interest in inventory financed by it shall have priority over the first creditor's security interest in that inventory. While the same objective is achieved by satisfying the PMSI requirements referred to above, a priority agreement will more clearly and comprehensively set out the priorities between the two creditors and will usually provide for other agreements with respect to their dealings with each other.

Non-sheltering letters

In some cases, a creditor with a prior registration may only have an interest in a specific asset or assets of the debtor, and a subsequent lender may be satisfied with receiving a **non-sheltering letter** (or "disclaimer of interest") from that creditor. The non-sheltering letter will confirm that the creditor only has an interest in certain specified assets of the debtor, refer to the prior registration of that interest, and confirm that the creditor will not shelter any other assets of the debtor under the registration.

non-sheltering letter
a letter given by a prior creditor to a subsequent creditor confirming that the prior creditor only has an interest in a specific asset or assets of the borrower and that it will not shelter any other assets of the borrower under the registration of that interest

Personal and corporate guarantees

In addition to obtaining a security interest in the borrower's collateral, a lender may require a guarantee from a third party as a form of assurance that the terms of the agreement with the borrower will be satisfied. A third-party guarantee is a contractual obligation, negotiated by the two parties, and there is no standard form that it must take. A guarantee can be:

- a performance guarantee, whereby the guarantor makes an assurance that a specific non-monetary obligation will be satisfied; or
- a monetary guarantee, whereby the guarantor agrees to pay on demand if the borrower is in default on its loan payments.

PERSONAL GUARANTEES

A personal guarantee is usually (but not always) a guarantee from a principal shareholder of the borrowing corporation. It must be executed in writing and, for certainty and to avoid confusion, should be given in the individual's legal name as shown on his or her birth certificate or certificate of citizenship. This type of guarantee is particularly valuable because it confirms to the lender that the guaranteeing shareholder has enough confidence in the endeavour that he or she is willing to undertake a personal risk. For this reason, guarantees are significantly more common in bank financing than VTB financing.

CORPORATE GUARANTEES

Section 20(1) of the *Business Corporations Act* (Ontario) (OBCA) allows an Ontario corporation to give financial assistance to a person by means of a guarantee. Section 20(2) requires that the shareholders of the guarantor be notified of the financial assistance (unless it falls into one of the exceptions set out in s. 20(3)). With respect to federal corporations, restrictions against federal corporations providing financial assistance have been repealed, and there are no similar shareholder notice requirements under the *Canada Business Corporations Act* (CBCA).

Legal opinions

As part of the transaction, the lender will usually require a legal opinion letter from the borrower's (and any guarantor's) counsel. The opinion is based on law, rather than fact. It confirms that all legal aspects of the transaction are valid and that the parties are entitled to receive what they have contracted for. Although opinions are not used in every type of financing, they have become commonplace and provide a good opportunity for counsel to record the process, any instructions that they received, and all legally binding agreements.

A financial institution may require that the legal opinion be delivered on one of its own forms, and it is necessary to ascertain whether or not this is the case prior to writing the opinion. In 1997, the Personal Property Security Opinion Committee of the Ontario Bar Association drafted an illustrative opinion in an effort to standardize the form of opinions given, and this is a useful guideline for drafting opinions in Ontario. While it pertains particularly to personal property security issues, the approach used in the sample opinion can be easily adapted for use for other forms of security.

Report to client and closing book

As indicated earlier in this chapter, the closing agenda should evolve during the transaction. If properly kept up to date, it will be a useful tool in assisting the lender's counsel with preparing its report to the lender and the closing book of documents. The agenda should also set out any matters that the parties agreed would be dealt with on a post-closing basis.

The report will generally follow the format and content of the opinion letter obtained from the borrower's counsel. It should also outline the searches conducted and how prior registrations were dealt with, and it should describe all registrations made against the borrower in favour of the lender. It is also an opportunity for the lender's counsel to set out any significant instructions it may have received during the course of the transaction that varied from the original instructions provided at the onset of the transaction.

The closing agenda should also form the basis upon which the closing book is prepared. Assuming that the closing agenda has been kept up to date, it should be relatively easy (though time-consuming) to compile the closing book.

Ideally, all post-closing tasks will have been completed before the closing book is delivered; however, this does not always occur. The closing book should include copies or originals (where available) of all relevant documents relating to the transaction. It can serve as an extremely useful reference tool for the client, counsel, and any auditors, as it should contain all necessary information relating to the transaction.

KEY TERMS

assignment of asset insurance

assignment of life insurance

Bank Act security

charge or mortgage of land

earnout financing

equity financing

general assignment of book debt

general security agreement

grid note

installment note

mezzanine financing

non-sheltering letter

notice of intention

postponement agreement

priority agreement

promissory note

purchase money security interest

specific security agreement

subordination agreement

vendor take-back financing

REFERENCES

Bank Act, SC 1991, c. 46.

Bankruptcy and Insolvency Act, RSC 1985, c. B-2.

Bills of Exchange Act, RSC 1985, c. B-4.

Bulk Sales Act (Ontario), RSO 1990, c. B.14.

Business Corporations Act (Ontario) (OBCA), RSO 1990, c. B.16, as amended.

Canada Business Corporations Act (CBCA), RSC 1985, c. C-44, as amended.

Execution Act (Ontario), RSO 1990, c. E.24.

Income Tax Act, RSC 1985, c. 1 (5th Supp.), as amended.

Insurance Act (Ontario), RSO 1990, c. I.8.

Personal Property Security Act (Ontario), (PPSA), RSO 1990, c. P.10, as amended.

REVIEW QUESTIONS

1. List the four sources of financing potentially available for the purchase of a privately held business.

2. Choose the most appropriate answer:

   Internal financing is a form of financing where:

   a. the purchaser becomes indebted to the vendor by the requirement that the purchaser pay the balance of the purchase price at a later date.

   b. The purchaser obtains financing from one or more lenders and the "senior" lender maintains priority position on all the collateral.

   c. A larger corporation is purchasing a smaller business and the purchaser is able to finance the acquisition through its own funds produced from the normal operation of its business.

   d. The purchaser raises funds by issuing shares in the capital of the corporation to investors who pay for them.

3. Choose the most appropriate answer.

   Vendor take-back financing can be advantageous to a purchaser because:

   a. It provides for a smooth transition to new ownership if the parties agree that the vendor will be involved in the business for a period of time.

   b. It enables a purchaser who cannot borrow from other sources to contemplate the acquisition of the business.

   c. It serves as an informal insurance mechanism in that it demonstrates to the purchaser that the vendor has sufficient confidence in the business to trust that it will generate the income needed by the purchaser to repay the outstanding purchase price at a later date.

   d. All of the above.

4. What is earnout financing, and how does it benefit the purchaser?

5. Explain the difference between a term loan and a demand loan.

6. What is a priority agreement, and when is it most commonly used in a transaction?

7. Public searches provide the lender with important information about the borrower and its assets/business, the assets or business being acquired, and when these assets can be legally transferred to the borrower/purchaser. List the six searches that are most frequently conducted by the lender in completing the due diligence for a financing transaction.

8. What is the purpose of searching under bulk sales legislation?

9. What is a promissory note?

10. What is the difference between a promissory note and an installment note?

11. Describe how a lender may take insurance as a form of security.

12. List the two primary mechanisms for registering a security interest in personal property.

13. What is a purchase money security interest?

14. What is the reasoning behind granting a purchase money security interest?

15. What is the difference between a postponement agreement and a subordination agreement, and when may these agreements be used?

16. What is the purpose of a non-sheltering letter?

17. What are the two forms of guarantee that a creditor may require as assurance that the debtor will satisfy its obligations under the contract?

18. A corporation wishes to give financial assistance to its subsidiary corporation by means of a guarantee. Does it make a difference whether the parent corporation (the guarantor) is an OBCA or a CBCA corporation? Explain your answer.

Glossary of terms

advance ruling certificate   certificate issued by the commissioner of competition confirming that a proposed purchase of a business does not contravene the provisions of the *Competition Act*

allocation   assignment of a portion of the purchase price to each of the various classes of assets in an asset purchase transaction; affects the calculation of taxable income under the ITA for the parties to the transaction; allocation is as agreed upon by the parties

assignment of asset insurance   security given to lender by an assignment of insurance against damage to or theft or loss of assets of the borrower included in the collateral for a loan

assignment of life insurance   security given to a lender by an assignment of a life insurance policy taken out by a corporate borrower (often known as key man life insurance)

***Bank Act* security**   security taken in the goods, wares, or merchandise of the borrower pursuant to s. 427 of the *Bank Act*

bring down certificate   certified statement by an officer of the vendor or purchaser confirming that the representations and warranties made at the time of the execution of the purchase agreement are also true and correct at the date of closing

capital gain   in tax law, the portion of the proceeds from the sale of an asset in excess of the initial tax cost of the asset, to be included in the calculation of the recipient's taxable income for the year

capital loss   in tax law, the shortfall that results where the proceeds from the sale of an asset are less than the initial tax cost of the asset, deductible in the calculation of the recipient's taxable income for the year

certificate of compliance   certificate issued by Industry Canada in respect of a CBCA corporation confirming that the corporation is incorporated and in good standing

certificate of status   certificate issued by the Ontario Ministry of Government Services in respect of an OBCA corporation confirming that the corporation is validly existing

charge or mortgage of land   an interest in land to which a borrower holds title given to a lender as security for a loan

closing agenda   a step-by-step plan for closing, which outlines all of the necessary time lines, locations, parties, and signatories to the transaction, documentation requirements, and the escrow terms of the closing; it often functions as a checklist for completion of tasks and documentation relating to the transaction

conditions of closing   terms of the agreement of purchase and sale that must be satisfied before any purchase or sale transaction can be completed

conditions of tender   conditions relating to the exchange of consideration due on the closing of a purchase and sale transaction

consideration   payment; the value that flows from the purchaser to the vendor in a purchase and sale transaction; in an asset or share purchase, usually takes the form of monetary or a combination of monetary and non-monetary payment in exchange for the assets or shares

continuance   a procedure that allows a corporation governed by the laws of one jurisdiction to leave that jurisdiction and to continue and become governed by the laws of another jurisdiction

contributory   a person who is liable to contribute to the property of the corporation in the event of the corporation's being wound up under the OBCA

covenant   promise by a party to an agreement to perform certain acts, or to refrain from acting in a certain manner, either prior to or following closing of the transaction

de minimis   Latin term meaning "of the least amount"; used in a legal context, for example, to refer to the specified threshold at which a claim for compensation may be made

Director   the director appointed under s. 260 of the CBCA or under s. 278 of the OBCA, as the case may be

due diligence   the comprehensive investigation into and review of the business, financial operations, and legal status of a corporation or business

earnout financing   a type of vendor take-back financing whereby the purchaser of a business will pay the outstanding amount of the purchase price based on the profitability of the business following the sale

equity financing   a means of raising funds by issuing shares in the capital of the corporation and selling them to investors

escrow closing   the delivery of the substance of the transaction on a particular date with the understanding that it is to be held by a third party, the escrow agent, until the unfulfilled condition of closing has been met

exemption order   a court order that may be obtained by a vendor granting an exemption from the requirements of the *Bulk Sales Act* where it is demonstrated that the sale in bulk will not prejudice the creditors of the vendor

general assignment of book debt   a security interest in the borrower's accounts receivable

general security agreement   an agreement between a borrower and a lender, giving the lender a broad security interest in the borrower's property; typically limited to personal property; generally used in large loans

grid note   an assignable, but non-negotiable, note that specifies the maximum amount of indebtedness or sets out a grid of repayment based on the amount of money advanced by the lender

horizontal short-form amalgamation   an amalgamation of two or more wholly owned subsidiaries of a corporation, requiring approval by resolution of the directors of each corporation but not the approval of shareholders

installment note   similar to a promissory note but non-transferable; often used in vendor take-back financing

interim period   period of time, beginning on the date of execution of a share or asset purchase and sale agreement and expiring on the date of closing, during which a business continues to operate at the vendor's risk until the conditions of closing are fully satisfied and the transfer can occur

letter of intent   non-binding letter or memorandum that sets out in writing the essential elements of a proposed transaction; also known as a memorandum of understanding or term sheet

liquidator   a person appointed by the court to supervise and carry out the liquidation and dissolution of a corporation, including paying or making adequate provision for claims against the corporation and distributing any remaining property to the shareholders

long-form amalgamation   an amalgamation of two or more corporations, requiring an amalgamation agreement to be approved by special resolution of the shareholders

mezzanine financing   a multilayered financing arrangement in which a borrower obtains funds from more than one lender, resulting in senior and subordinated debt and priority ranking of the lenders' respective interests in the collateral

non-sheltering letter   a letter given by a prior creditor to a subsequent creditor confirming that the prior creditor only has an interest in a specific asset or assets of the borrower and that it will not shelter any other assets of the borrower under the registration of that interest

notice of intention   noticed required to be filed with the Bank of Canada in order for a bank to take a s. 427 security interest in the borrower's property

paid-up capital   a tax law concept; essentially, the amount or sum of amounts received by a corporation as consideration for a particular share, a particular class of shares, or all shares issued by the corporation; may be distributed to shareholders tax-free in certain circumstances

post-closing adjustment   amendment of the purchase price after closing to account for variation from inventory count, equipment valuation, shareholders' equity, or working capital as set out in the agreement of purchase and sale

postponement agreement   an agreement between two creditors of the same borrower whereby one creditor agrees to postpone repayment of its debt until the borrower has fully satisfied its debt to the second creditor

pre-closing   a meeting before the closing of a transaction at which counsel for both parties discuss and attempt to resolve outstanding issues, agreed-upon changes to documents are made, closing documents may be signed, and the closing date is confirmed

priority agreement   an agreement between all the participating lenders in a mezzanine financing arrangement, clarifying the ranking of the lenders' respective interests in the collateral

promissory note   a negotiable instrument defined as "a signed unconditional promise to pay a certain amount of money to a specified person, to the order of a specified person or to bearer," often given by the borrower in a financing arrangement with an external lender

purchase money security interest   an interest giving a lender superpriority over other creditors in respect of assets of the borrower purchased with the borrowed funds

SEDAR   System for Electronic Document Analysis and Retrieval; the electronic filing system for the disclosure documents of public companies and mutual funds across Canada

special resolution   a resolution passed by a majority of not less than two-thirds of the votes cast by the shareholders who voted in respect of the resolution or signed by all the shareholders entitled to vote on the resolution

specific security agreement   an agreement between a borrower and a lender giving the lender an interest in specific assets of the borrower; generally used for smaller loans

stated capital   a corporate law concept; essentially, the sum of all amounts received by a corporation as consideration for a class or series of shares issued by the corporation; subject to restrictions on distribution to shareholders

stock transfer power of attorney   document granting power of attorney to an individual for the specific purpose of transferring shares

subordination agreement   an agreement between two creditors of the same borrower whereby the creditor that holds the senior debt agrees to subordinate its interest in favour of the second creditor

taxable Canadian corporation   a Canadian corporation (that is, a corporation either incorporated in Canada or resident in Canada continuously since June 18, 1971) that is not exempt from tax under the *Income Tax Act* (Canada)

vendor take-back financing   a financing arrangement between the vendor and the purchaser whereby the vendor agrees to defer the payment of a portion of the purchase price until a later time; typically have a three- to five-year term; otherwise, terms vary as determined by the two parties

vertical short-form amalgamation   an amalgamation of a corporation and one or more of its wholly owned subsidiaries, requiring approval by resolution of the directors of each corporation but not the approval of shareholders

Index